FERRIES
of the British Isles
& Northern Europe
1999

Published by

ISBN 1 871947 57 X

Ferry Publications
PO Box 9
Narberth
Pembrokeshire SA68 0YT

Tel: +44 (0) 1834 891460   Fax: +44 (0) 1834 891463

CONTENTS

Introduction	3
A Guide to using this book	4
Foreword	8
The Dart Line Story	9
Round Britain Review	18
The Fast Ferry Year	35
The Rise of the Ro-Pax	41
Scandinavian and Northern Europe Review	49
GB & Ireland Passenger Operations	58
Domestic Services	89
Freight-only Ferries	110
Chain, Cable etc ferries	144
Major Passenger - only Ferries	146
Northern Europe	146
Other Vessels	188
Late News	189
Index	190

© Ferry Publications 1999

Clansman *(Brian Maxted)*

INTRODUCTION

This is the twelfth edition of this book, which first appeared as the 24 page 'home published' *'Car Ferries from Great Britain and Ireland'* in 1983. This year we run to 192 pages and are pleased to be sponsored by *Dart Line*. The book aims to list every passenger/vehicle ferry in Great Britain and Ireland, ro-ro freight vessels which operate regular services between Great Britain and Ireland and to nearby continental destinations and major passenger/vehicle ferries in other parts of Northern Europe. The coverage of Northern Europe is not fully comprehensive (to make it so would probably triple the size of the book) and does not include freight-only operations and vessels. Also, ro-ro vessels engaged in 'deep sea' and Mediterranean trade and those operated solely for the carriage of trade cars or livestock are not included in the book.

Each operator is listed alphabetically within sections - international and Northern Ireland routes, domestic services, freight-only operations, chain, cable and float ferries, passenger only ferries, other North European passenger operators and vehicle/passenger vessels owned by companies not currently engaged in operating services. After details relating to each company's management, address, telephone numbers, email, web site and services, there is a fleet list with technical data and then a potted history of each vessel with previous names and dates.

1999 will be a significant for all ferry operators. At the time of going to press, the prospects for extension seem bleak. However, several Scandinavian operators have already taken steps to ensure that, whatever happens, sales will continue, by diverting services via Norway and Estonia, which are outside the EU, and Åland, which has special tax status. UK operators have no such option (it would be impractical to divert Western Channel services between Britain and France via the Channel Islands) but will try to capitalise on the differences in duty paid prices between the UK, France and Belgium, as will operators between Scandinavian countries and Germany. However, it seems inevitable that some services will cease and, in many cases, frequencies reduced and the industry will become more transport rather than leisure orientated. Whilst ro-paxes and fast ferries will continue to develop, the era of the eighties style cruise ferry is probably over.

What is inevitable is that the ferry industry will continue to change - and continue to be of great interest, both to those involved in the industry and to the outside observer. I hope this book adds to the interest.

Whitstable, Kent
March 1999

Nick Widdows

A GUIDE TO USING THIS BOOK

Sections Listing is in seven sections: *Section 1* - Services from Great Britain and Ireland to the continent and between Great Britain and Ireland (including services to/from the Isle of Man and Channel Islands), *Section 2* - Domestic services within Great Britain and Ireland, *Section 3* - Freight only services from Great Britain and Ireland and domestic routes, *Section 4* - Minor vehicle ferries in Great Britain and Ireland (chain and cable ferries etc), *Section 5* - Major passenger only operators, *Section 6* - Major car ferry operators in Northern Europe, *Section 7* - Companies not operating regular services possessing vehicle ferries which may be chartered or sold to other operators.

Order The company order within each section is alphabetical. Note that the definite article and words meaning 'company' or 'shipping company' (eg 'AG', 'Reederei') do not count. Sorting is by normal English convention eg 'Å' comes at the start, not at the end of the alphabet as is the Scandinavian convention. Where ships are numbered, order is by number whether number is expressed in Arabic or Latin digits or words (eg SUPERSEACAT TWO comes before SUPERSEACAT THREE).

Company information This section gives general information regarding to status of the company ie nationality, whether it is public or private sector and whether it is part of a larger group.

Management The managing director and marketing director or manager of each company are listed. Where these posts do not exist, other equivalent people are listed. Where only initials are given, that person is, as far as is known, male.

Address This is the address of the company's administrative headquarters. In the case of some international companies, a British and overseas address is given.

Telephone and Fax Numbers are expressed as follows: +[*number*] (this is the international dialling code which is dialled in combination with the number dialled for international calls (00 in the UK, Ireland and most other European countries); it is not used for calling within the country), ([*number*]) (this is the number which precedes area codes when making long distance domestic calls - it is not dialled when calling from another country or making local calls (not all countries have this)), (this is the rest of the number including, where appropriate, the area dialling code). In a few cases free or local call rate numbers are used for reservations; note that these are not available from overseas. Telex numbers are also included where applicable; it should be noted that many operators no longer use this service, its role having largely been taken over by fax and Email.

Internet Email addresses and Website URLs are given where these are available; the language(s) used is shown. Note that use of the Internet is increasing quickly and new sites may come into use during the currency of this book. If a web site is not shown for a particular operator, it may be worth trying one or more search engines to see if a new site has opened. In a few cases Email facility is only available through the Website. To avoid confusion, there is no other punctuation on the Internet line. All these addresses can be accessed from: http://homepages.enterprise.net/nickw00000 (note change from last year) and this will be updated at regular intervals as new web sites come on line. It should be noted that some sites are not always up to date and it is disappointing that few operators use this facility for 'real time' data showing day by day service changes.

Routes operated After each route there are, in brackets, details of *1:* normal journey time, *2:* regular vessel(s) used on the route (number as in list of vessels) and *3:* frequencies (where a number per day is given, this relates to return sailings). In the case of freight-only sailings which operate to a regular schedule, departure times are given where they have been supplied. Please note that frequencies can vary over the year and freight operations are often restricted at weekends.

Winter and Summer In this book, **winter** generally means the period between October and Easter while **summer** means, Easter to October. The **peak summer period** is generally June, July and

August. In Scandinavia, the summer peak ends in mid-August whilst in the UK it starts rather later and generally stretches into the first week of September. Dates vary according to operator.

Spelling The 'Cook's European Timetable' convention is used in respect of town and country names - local names for towns (eg Göteborg rather than Gothenburg) and English names for countries (eg Germany rather than Deutschland). Many towns in Finland have both Finnish and Swedish names; we have used the Finnish name except in the case of Åland. In the case of Danish towns, the alternative spelling of 'å' or 'aa' follows local convention. The following towns, islands and territories have alternative English names: Antwerpen = Antwerp, Dunkerque - Dunkirk*, Fyn - Funen, Genova - Genoa, Gent - Ghent, Göteborg - Gothenburg, Helsingør - Elsinore*, Jylland - Jutland, København - Copenhagen, Oostende - Ostend, Sankt-Peterburg - Saint Petersburg, Sevilla = Seville, Sjælland - Sealand, Venezia - Venice, Vlissingen - Flushing*. (* local name now in common usage in UK).

Terms The following words mean *'shipping company'* in various languages: Redereja (Latvian), Rederi (Danish, Norwegian, Swedish), Rederij (Dutch), Reederei (German), Zegluga (Polish). The following words mean *'limited company'*: AB - Aktiebolag (Swedish) (Finnish companies who use both the Finnish and Swedish terms sometimes express it as Ab), AG - Aktiengesellschaft (German), AS - Aksjeselskap (Norwegian), A/S - Aktie Selskabet (Danish), BV - besioten vennootschap (Dutch), GmbH - Gesellschaft mit beschränkter Haftung (German), NV - naamloze vennootschap (Dutch), Oy - (Finnish), Oyj - (Finnish (plc)), SA - Société Anonyme (French).

Ro-pax Ferries Whilst most conventional vehicle ferries convey commercial vehicle, a ro-pax is designed primarily for the carriage of such traffic but also carry a limited number of ordinary passengers. Features generally include a moderate passenger capacity - up to about 500 passengers - and a partly open vehicle deck.

List of vessels

NO	NAME	GROSS TONNAGE (A)	YEAR BUILT	SERVICE SPEED (KNOTS)	NUMBER OF PASSENGERS	VEHICLE DECK CAPACITY	VEHICLE DECK ACCESS (C)	WHERE BUILT (D)	FLAG (D)
1	NAME	26433t	87	22k	290P	650C 100L	BA2	Town, GE	GB

(A) ‡ = not measured in accordance with the 1969 Tonnage Convention; c = approximate.

(B) C = Cars, L = Lorries (15m), T = Trailers (12m), R = Rail wagons, - = No figure quoted,

p = passenger only vessel, • = laid up vessel.

(C) B = Bow, A = Aft, S = Side, Q = Quarterdeck, R = Slewing ramp, 2 = Two decks can be loaded at the same time, C = Cars must be crane loaded aboard, t = turntable ferry.

(D) The following abbreviations are used. Note that where the code relates to place of construction, it relates to the country that the shipyard was in at the time the vessel was built. Thus vessels built in Split (and other Croatian yards) when it was part of Yugoslavia are shown as 'YU' whilst those built since 1991 are shown as 'CR' for Croatia).

AL = Australia	DK = Denmark	IR = Irish Republic	PA = Panama
AN = Antigua & Barbuda	ES = Estonia	JA = Japan	PL = Portugal
	FA = Faroes	KE = Kergulen Islands (FR)	PO = Poland
AU = Austria	FI = Finland		RO = Romania
BA = Bahamas	FR = France	LB = Liberia	RU = Russia
BD = Bermuda	GB = Great Britain	LT = Lithuania	SI = Singapore
BE = Belgium	GE = Germany (DDR)	LX = Luxembourg	SK = South Korea
CA = Canada	GR = Greece	MA = Malaysia	SP = Spain
CH = China	GY = Germany (FedRep)	NA = Nertherlands Antilles	SV = St Vincent
CI = Cayman Islands			SW = Sweden
CR = Croatia	IM = Isle of Man	NL = Netherlands	UY = Uruguay
CY = Cyprus	IT = Italy	NO = Norway	YU = Yugoslavia

In the notes ships are in CAPITAL LETTERS, shipping lines and other institutions are in *italics*.

Capacity In this book, capacities shown are the maxima. Sometimes vessels operate at less than their maximum passenger capacity due to reduced crewing or to operating on a route on which they are not permitted to operate above a certain level. Car and lorry/trailer capacities are the maximum for either type. The two figures are not directly comparable; some parts of a vessel may allow cars on two levels to occupy the space that a trailer or lorry occupies on one level, some may not. Also some parts of a vessel with low headroom many only be accessible to cars. All figures have to be fairly approximate.

Ownership The ownership of many vessels is very complicated. Some are actually owned by finance companies and banks, some by subsidiary companies of the shipping lines, some by subsidiary companies of a holding company of which the shipping company is also a subsidiary and some by companies which are jointly owned by the shipping company and other interests like a bank, set up specifically to own one ship or a group of ships. In all these cases the vessel is technically chartered to the shipping company. However, in this book, only those vessels chartered from one shipping company to another or from a ship owning company unconnected with the shipping line, are recorded as being on charter. Vessels are listed under the current operator rather than the owner. Charter is 'bareboat' (ie without crew) unless otherwise stated.

Gross Tonnage This is a measure of enclosed capacity rather than weight, based on a formula of one gross ton = 100 cubic feet. Even small alterations can alter the gross tonnage. Under old measurement systems, the capacity of enclosed car decks was not included but, under a 1969 convention, all vessels laid down after 1982 have been measured by a new system which includes enclosed vehicle decks as enclosed space, thereby considerably increasing the tonnage of car ferries. Under this convention, from 1st January 1995, all vessels were due to be re-measured under this system; in a few cases, details were not available at the time of going to press. All vessels measured by the old system are indicated with a double dagger '‡'. Note that this generally only applies to larger vessels with enclosed vehicle decks; many open decked vessels have not been re-measured as the changes that the new formula would make are fairly marginal. Tonnages quoted here are, where possible, those given by the shipping companies themselves.

The following people are gratefully thanked for their assistance with this publication: Simon Taylor (*Dart Line*), and many others in ferry companies in the UK and abroad, Anders Ahlerup, Gary Andrews, Cees de Bijl, Dick Clague, Erik B Jonsen, Paul Hynds, Barry Mitchell, Jack Phelan, David Parsons, Matthew Punter, Pekka Ruponen, Michael Speckenbach (Speckus Ferry Information), Henk van der Lugt, Ian Smith (Bézier Design), Foto Flite, Haven Colourprint and Pat Somner (Ferry Publications).

Whilst every effort has been made to ensure that the facts contained here are correct, neither the publishers nor the writer can accept any responsibility for errors contained herein. We would, however, appreciate comments from readers, which we will endeavour to incorporate in the next edition which we plan to publish in spring 2000.

P&OSL Provence (Miles Cowsill)

FOREWORD

I would like to thank the publishers for the opportunity to pen a few words by way of introduction to the latest edition of this excellent guide to our industry. Its publication comes at a time of considerable change and uncertainty, not least of which is the reaction by ferry operators to the impending abolition of duty free sales on intra-European Union ferry services.

Unlike some, for whom duty free sales contribute anything from 20 to 50 per cent of total revenues, Dart Line's operations are not in any way compromised by this threatened loss in revenue. This is due to the fact that we specialise predominantly in the unaccompanied trailer market.

Simon Taylor

The line was formed in January 1996 to operate a twice-daily, freight-only service between Thames Europort and Vlissingen. A second service to Zeebrugge was started in April 1997. Two brand new vessels were placed on the Vlissingen route during 1998, while a third vessel was put on the Zeebrugge run in September last year. In September of this year, the capacity of two of the three vessels on Zeebrugge will be doubled with the introduction of the *Dart 8* and *Dart 9*.

Dart Line now holds more than 10 per cent of the UK-Dutch and UK-Belgian freight markets and we confidently expect these shares to increase substantially as hauliers realise the benefits of using the line's services, especially for non time-sensitive unaccompanied traffic.

At the same time, we have seen an increasing willingness by the haulage industry to reduce the environmental impact of unnecessary road journeys by putting freight on longer sea crossings. We have calculated that by using Dart Line, our customers saved themselves over 10 million road miles last year, compared with sending their traffic via east coast or Channel ports.

Both Dart Line and Thames Europort are subsidiaries of Jacobs Holdings Plc, a publicly-quoted company with interests in shipping, ports, transport and property.

One of the main benefits of using Thames Europort is its ease of access. It is less than a mile from the M25 London orbital and only 16 miles from central London, while our services provide direct links to the extensive Dutch and Belgian motorway networks. As part of our investment programme, trailer storage capacity in Thames Europort is now being increased by 50 per cent to 300,000 units, while camera systems are being installed in all three ports served by the line to provide real-time monitoring and reporting of trailer conditions.

In conclusion, I would like to congratulate Miles Cowsill, Nick Widdows and John Hendy on the publication of an all-encompassing record of this fascinating and ever-changing industry.

Simon Taylor
Managing Director

Dart Line

THE DART LINE STORY

The Dart Line story really starts back in 1986, when a new double linkspan berth called Dartford International Ferry Terminal was opened on the River Thames near Dartford, only 16 miles (25 kilometres) from central London and a few minutes away from the Dartford Tunnel on the then newly opened M25 motorway. The site was owned by the Blue Circle Group, whose main business was the production of cement. Realising the strategic location of the site and its potential as a port and business park, Blue Circle formed a joint venture with Municipal Mutual Insurance to develop the area and appointed DIFT Port Management Ltd, a wholly owned subsidiary of Gray Mackenzie Overseas Ltd, to run the terminal.

Services were established to Zeebrugge in Belgium and Esbjerg in Denmark by Kent Line, a company which later passed into the hands of the Danish Maersk group. Despite the prime location, in the face of strong competition from other ports and the fact that the Dartford Tunnel area was something of a bottle-neck until the new Queen Elizabeth II bridge was opened in 1991, growth was slow. The beneficial effects of the new bridge were somewhat reduced by the early nineties recession and the Kent Line service - by then Dartford - Zeebrugge only - was rather suddenly withdrawn in 1992. The two ships used - the *Maersk Essex* and the *Maersk Kent* - were sold to the DFDS Group and renamed the *Tor Dania* and *Tor Britannia* respectively.

The Dartford Terminal then lay idle for over two years as far as ferry services were concerned. However, in 1994, the closure of Olau Line's Sheerness - Vlissingen service changed the whole Thames/Medway picture. This service had been operated since 1975 with two multi-purpose vessels, supplemented at various times by dedicated freight vessels. For some time before their

Dart 2 *(John Bryant)*

eventual demise, Olau Line had plans to move their operations to Dartford, but this was not to be. The reasons the service closed were complex but the end was somewhat protracted. Although it did not come until May, Sally Line anticipated the event in March by switching the *Sally Sun*, which had until then been providing freight back-up to the passenger ships on the Ramsgate - Dunkerque route, to run from Ramsgate to Vlissingen. Later in the year, a second vessel was provided in the form of the *Sally Eurobridge*, a vessel they had acquired from Schiaffino Line, the Ramsgate - Oostende freight operator they had taken over in 1990. The service was joint with RMT of Belgium, who operated multi-purpose ships from Oostende to Ramsgate in conjunction with Sally Line and already had a sales operation in the Benelux countries, although they played no part in the operation of the service.

Although Ramsgate - Vlissingen is the shortest crossing between the UK and the Netherlands, the route presented a number of problems, not least the crossing time of about five hours, which made for poor utilisation of the ships. Also Ramsgate was rather further away from London and the M25 than Sheerness. However, in September of that year the service was transferred to Dartford - and the port was again in operation. The following year, the *Sally Sun* and *Sally Eurobridge* were replaced by the *Purbeck* and the *Sally Euroway*. Not only could these vessels carry more lorries and trailers but they both had passenger capacities in excess of the normal 12 for a freight ferry - 58 for the *Purbeck* and 92 for the *Sally Euroway*. This enabled a higher level of driver accompanied traffic, the idea being that a driver could enjoy a full rest period on the ferry and be ready to perform a full day's work immediately on leaving it.

But Sally Line's action was not the only response to Olau's demise. There was strong pressure to re-establish a ferry service from Sheerness on the Isle of Sheppey - one of the most deprived areas in South East England. In July 1994 the Mersey Docks and Harbour Company, who were then owners of the port, launched Ferrylink Ferries - a freight-only operation using two Egyptian registered vessels - the *Al Hussein* and the *Nuwayba*. They did not prove totally satisfactory and the standard of accommodation provided for their 12 drivers was below what was expected. However, the freight-only operation was only an interim measure and, in the following year, Eurolink Ferries was launched, using the chartered *Euromantique* and the *Euromagique* - two ro-pax vessels offering a large amount of freight capacity as well as carrying several hundred passengers. The converted freight vessels offered a passenger service and this enabled a large number of freight drivers to be conveyed.

Thus by the end of the summer in 1995 there were four vessels offering a similar driver-accompanied service between Vlissingen and the Thames/Medway area. Unfortunately, there was insufficient traffic around to justify the services provided. Both vessels carried a good load of unaccompanied trailers - but the passenger facilities were wasted on that sort of traffic. As far as Eurolink was concerned, the hoped-for levels of ordinary passengers did not materialise and although this was not an issue for Sally Ferries, the *Purbeck* and *Sally Euroway* - both excellent vessels as anyone who has travelled on them will testify - attracted relatively high charter fees and operating costs and carried relatively little accompanied traffic.

Some of the senior management at Sally Line were convinced that, in the light of the Channel Tunnel and the ending of duty-free sales, the future for cross-Channel ferry operations other than Dover - Calais lay in unaccompanied freight - both for containers and trailers. Accompanied traffic would, it was believed, gravitate towards the Channel Tunnel and the short sea route and Dartford was seen has having higher potential than Ramsgate for unaccompanied traffic - provided the right sort of vessels could be provided.

In September 1994, Jacobs Holdings plc, headed by former Sally Line boss Michael Kingshott, acquired a lease of the Dartford International Ferry Terminal - which they renamed Thames

Dart 5 *(John Bryant)*

Europort - and they purchased the port in 1997. Jacobs Holdings (formerly John I Jacobs) had been involved in shipping for many years, both as ship owners and managers but had never operated a ferry service or, indeed, been much involved in ferries. The new MD was determined to change that. Sally Line's Scandinavian owners (at that time Effjohn International, now renamed Neptun Maritime) remained committed to Ramsgate and were, at the time engaged in a major reorganisation of their operations, including a joint venture with the Holyman Group of Australia, to replace the RMT conventional ferries with fast ferries.

It was logical therefore for the Dartford operation, which was 50 miles away from Ramsgate, to be run by a dedicated management who had a vision as to how the port and its services could be developed. It was agreed that the service should, from the start of 1996, be taken over by a new company called Dart Line, which would be owned by Jacobs Holdings. Simon Taylor, previously MD of Sally Line was to head the new company (as well as all other port and shipping operations of Jacobs) whilst Kevin Miller, who had joined Sally Line from Schiaffino, became his Marketing Director. Helmut Walgraeve, who was Sally's Operations Manager at Dunkerque and Oostende also joined the new team. Most of Sally Line's Dartford-based staff joined the new organisation.

What the new organisation did not want was the ships that Sally had been operating. What were deemed more appropriate for the sort of service envisaged were vessels of the same type as Sally was employing on its Ramsgate - Oostende service, the *Sally Euroroute* and the *Sally Eurolink*. These Romanian-built vessels were part of a class of eight built for the Norwegian Balder group in the 1980s. Following the liquidation of the group, they passed into the ownership of the Romanian state shipping lines Navrom and Romline and were renamed *Bazias 1* to *Bazias 8* and, hence, are normally referred to as 'the Bazias class'. With two large unobstructed vehicle decks with separate loading ramps through the stern of the vessel, they could be turned round quickly despite the absence of a bow door. Simple but comfortable accommodation was provided for twelve passengers in the stern accommodation/navigational block and they were economical to operate. The two

DON'T WORRY IF YOU MISS ONE RO-RO SHIP THERE'LL BE ANOTHER ALONG SHORTLY.

Congested town centres. Overcrowded motorways. Delays everywhere.

The pressure on drivers to meet ships' sailing times, is greater than ever, with no guarantee that vehicles will arrive on time.

That's why it pays to send your roll-on roll-off cargo through the Port of London.

The most direct gateway to the prosperous market of south-east England. The frequency of our services means a ship sails almost every two hours. So before long your accompanied or unaccompanied load will be on its way.

By using London, you won't miss the boat.

 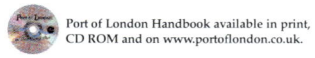 

Port of London Handbook available in print, CD ROM and on www.portoflondon.co.uk.

PORT OF LONDON TRADE DEVELOPMENT
Devon House, 58-60 St. Katharine's Way, London E1 9LB England.
Telephone: +44 (0) 171 265 2656. Fax: +44 (0) 171 265 2699. E-mail address: marketing@portoflondon.co.uk

vessels operated by Sally Line were still required at that time as they conveyed the bulk of the unaccompanied traffic from Ramsgate to Oostende while the driver accompanied traffic used the RMT multi-purpose vessels. So the new team had to find two more of the class for their service.

The first, the *Bazias 2*, was available for charter at fairly short notice. She arrived at Dartford in the late autumn of 1995 and entered service on 12th November - initially sub-chartered to Sally Line as they were still operating the service at that time. She was renamed the *Dart 2*, using the old 'Bazias' numbers - a useful convention in dealing with the Romanian owners. As had been the case with Sally Line, Romanian deck crew and junior officers were complemented by British or Irish Masters, Chief Engineers and catering staff (the catering staff were replaced by Romanians in 1998). The new ship replaced the *Purbeck*.

On 1st January 1996, Dart Line took over the service using the *Dart 2* and the *Sally Euroway*, sub-chartered from Sally Line. The service remained a joint venture with RMT of Belgium, until that operator ceased operations in February 1997. The second vessel did not arrive until February, as she had been on charter to Grimaldi of Italy in the Mediterranean followed by a brief charter to Sudcargos of France and this was the earliest she could be released. Named the *Perseus* during the charter, she had previously been the *Bazias 5* and thus became the *Dart 5*.

Her arrival should have seen the departure of the *Sally Euroway*; however, this plan had to be postponed when the *Dart 2* was 'arrested'. A lawyer boarded the ship at Dartford and affixed a writ to her mast, inhibiting her future use until the dispute was settled. The charge was not against Dart Line but against the ship's owners, Romline, in respect of a previous charter of the vessel. The *Dart 2* was out of commission for 14 weeks and the dispute was only settled when Jacobs purchased the ship from Romline for £3.8 million. As part of the payment, Jacobs settled the outstanding claim and the writ was withdrawn.

Docking at Dartford looking towards the Queen Elizabeth II bridge. *(John Hendy)*

By summer 1996, Dart Line at last had two matching vessels and could bid farewell to the *Sally Euroway*. The decision to opt for more basic vessels was vindicated as the traffic of unaccompanied trailers and containers continued to grow but the small number of drivers continued to be accommodated and it was seldom necessary to deny anyone a berth. Despite the relatively slow speed of the vessels (only 75% of the *Sally Euroway* in top condition) the brave decision was made to offer a twice-daily service which required some rapid handling at the two terminals. Containers were loaded on low trailers, known as Mafis, and with the excellent headroom of the Bazias vessels, it was found possible to 'double stack' - placing two containers on one trailer - which further speeded up loading and unloading. Although there were container cranes alongside the berth at Dartford, and container fixing point on the upper deck of the ship, containers were never loaded that way and the cranes were subsequently removed.

Although they were doing good business between Dartford and Vlissingen, Dart Line began to look for possibilities for expansion. Vlissingen, as a port, faced stiff competition from Rotterdam, Hoek van Holland and Scheveningen, all of which were closer to the economic heartland of The Netherlands. Dart Line felt that re-opening the Dartford - Zeebrugge service, which had been abandoned in 1992, had great potential. Zeebrugge is the largest freight ferry port in Belgium, as well as being a major container port - containers being a type of traffic Dart Line were developing. The Zeebrugge authorities were undertaking a major development of the port and had constructed a new two berth ro-ro terminal on reclaimed land just inside the entrance to the outer harbour. The decision was therefore taken to take a lease on this installation and start a Zeebrugge service in addition to the Vlissingen one in 1997.

The company decided that the ideal ships for the route would be two additional Bazias class vessels and their search was aided by events taking place at Ramsgate. As mentioned, the conventional multi-purpose ferries of RMT were to be replaced by fast ferries, which could not convey freight, in March 1997. The *Sally Euroroute* and *Sally Eurolink* would no longer be suitable for the Oostende service since they would not be able to convey all the drivers previously accommodated. Now having the *Purbeck* (back from a short charter to Irish Ferries) and the *Sally Euroway*, in autumn 1996 Sally Line chartered the *Sally Euroroute* to Belfast Freight Ferries, who renamed her the *Merle*. Both she and her sister were owned by a joint Sally Line/Romline company called Rosal SA. In January 1997, Jacobs Holdings took over Sally Line's share in this company, leading the way clear for the *Sally Eurolink* to move to Dart Line and become the *Dart 4* (having been the *Bazias 4*). It was decided to leave the *Merle* with Belfast Freight Ferries and seek another vessel to launch the Zeebrugge service. The *Merle* is, however, known as the *Dart 3* within the Jacobs organisation, a name she has never actually carried.

Meanwhile, the Vlissingen service had been give a boost by the closure of Eurolink's Sheerness - Vlissingen service in December 1996. Eurolink's freight customers were encouraged to switch to Dart Line and Dart Line had the option to use Eurolink's ro-pax vessels until the end of their charter period. In the event this option was not taken up as they were not deemed suitable.

The Zeebrugge service was announced in February 1997 and launched on 10th April of that year. The service was started by the chartered *Merchant Victor* as the *Dart 4* was not initially available. The *Dart 4* entered service two weeks later, enabling a twice daily service to be operated, and the two ships ran together for four weeks. The *Merchant Victor* was replaced by the *Lyra*, which until 1996, had operated as the *Laxfoss* on Eimskip services between Iceland and the UK. However, it was decided that she was better suited to the Vlissingen route and one of the Bazias class vessels on that route was switched to Zeebrugge. Later in the summer she was replaced by the Greek registered *Thelisis*. This vessel was placed on the Zeebrugge service and the Vlissingen route again became the preserve of two Bazias ships. Although the *Thelisis* was of similar size and layout to the Bazias class, she lacked headroom and was rather slower. However, in November it was possible to acquire yet another Bazias vessel - the former *Bazias 1*. Unlike the others, she was not owned by Romline but by Octogon Shipping (note spelling of 'Octogon'), a private sector company operated by Captain Idu, a former Managing Director of Romline. She had been on a year's charter with Ignazio Messina of Italy under the name *Jolly Arancione*. The *Dart 1*, as she became, differed from the other ships in having a full Romanian crew and all Dart Line provided was pilots for the Thames and the Schelde.

Lembitu *(John Bryant)*

Commercially, the Zeebrugge service was highly successful and traffic levels soon exceeded those on the Vlissingen route. This was despite tough competition from P&O and Cobelfret. As well as direct links to the European motorway system, the new berth has a railhead which now has a twice daily service to Antwerp where containers can make connections to all parts of Europe. The deep sea container services from the port provided a new market in the form of feeder traffic.

It was not long before consideration was being given as to how capacity could be increased on the new route. One option looked at was lengthening two of the ships - a relatively simple exercise given their layout. Indeed, Cobelfret were operating four Chinese-built ships, based on the same basic design but 27.4 metres longer, from their terminal across the river at Purfleet. However, in the end it was decided not to pursue this plan.

During 1998 it also became increasingly apparent that the four Bazias class vessels operating on the two routes no longer provided the ideal solution - but for different reasons. On the Zeebrugge route they were no longer large enough, whilst on the Vlissingen route they were not quite fast enough. Whereas, on the Zeebrugge route, ships can maintain full speed until just before entering the harbour, the Vlissingen route is not only rather longer but requires a slow approach up the Schelde, constant changes of course and then a long reverse into the berth. The 15 knot service speed of these vessels could often be reduced if they had not been dry-docked for some months (with barnacles etc scraped off the hull) and also if the tide was against them (the Thames, Thames Estuary and Southern North Sea having particularly strong tides). Indeed, on some occasions a ship would have the tide against her for both of her daily voyages and this would mean that by the end of the week she would be running several hours late. This time could be regained at weekends and Mondays, when services were reduced, but poor timekeeping was a deterrent to shippers on the route.

The interim answer to these two problems was to charter two faster vessels for the Vlissingen service and operate three of the Bazias vessels on the Zeebrugge service, giving up to three sailings each way per day. The two chartered vessels were the *Varbola* and the *Lembitu*, part of an order for four vessels placed by the Estonian Shipping Company (ESCO) at the Astilleros Huelva shipyard in Spain. ESCO was formerly the state shipping company of Estonia, although it is now largely owned by Norwegian and American interests. The *Varbola* came direct from the shipyard whilst the *Lembitu* came to Dart Line after a period on charter to P&O Ferries (Irish Sea) on the Liverpool - Dublin route, whilst the *European Leader* (formerly the *Buffalo*) was being lengthened. In early 1999 they were renamed the *Dart 6* and the *Dart 7* respectively.

Two knots faster than the 'Bazias' vessels, they find keeping to the schedule much easier, although their capacity is rather lower and their design is rather less efficient in terms of cargo handling. There is a higher proportion of void areas and the upper vehicle deck is reached from a rather narrow ramp from the lower deck, rather than a wide ramp direct from the stern. This makes loading and unloading more difficult and the area above the ramp - covered by a large hatch - cannot be used. Dart Line have had new lashing points fixed to the upper deck in order to squeeze in another lane of trailers. The new ships carry an Estonian crew plus two Dart Line masters - one for day and one for night - who also hold pilotage certificates for the Thames and Schelde.

The 'spare' Bazias class vessel, the *Dart 4*, was chartered to Belfast Freight Ferries. This operator was already running two vessels of this type - the *Merle* on charter and their own River Lune, formerly the *Bazias 7*. The charter enabled their *Saga Moon* to be moved to fellow Cenargo company Merchant Ferries. The charter ended in February 1999 and the ship was made available for further charter.

For the longer term, Dart Line have looked seriously at building new vessels, which would combine the speed and technical efficiency of the new craft with the excellent cargo layout of the Bazias vessels.

However, in March 1999 it was announced that Jacobs Holdings had purchased three Japanese built deep sea ro-ro/container ships from the People's Republic of China. The *Xi Feng Kou, Gu Bie Ku* and *Zhong Jia Kou* (to be renamed the *Dart 8, Dart 9* and *Dart 10* respectively) have almost double the capacity of the Bazias class ships. The three vessels will be substantially modified before entering service during 1999, including the fitting of a stern ramp, to replace the existing quarter ramp. The current plan is that, in late summer 1999, the *Dart 8* and *Dart 9* will be placed on the Zeebrugge service, along with the *Dart 2*. The *Dart 4* and *Dart 5*, will take over the Vlissingen service and the time charter of the *Dart 1, Dart 6* and *Dart 7* ended. The *Dart 4* and *Dart 5* are to be fitted with Azimuth propellers, which will increase service speed by about 1.5 knots and, because they can rotate 360 degrees, will greatly assist manoeuvring and docking.

As the Dart Line ships remain at sea most of the time, there is ample scope for third party companies to use the ample facilities at Thames Europort, especially where they do not compete with Dart Line's own trade. For example, car carrying company UECC use the terminal to take British-made Ford cars to Spain.

The Dart Line story is one of success in a heavily congested market by tailoring a service carefully, providing good quality but without unnecessary frills. As Britain enters the 21st Century, there will be an increasing emphasis on environmentally friendly transport. By taking traffic from the crowed roads of Kent, Dart Line will be making its contribution, and as exhortation is replaced by incentive and compulsion, will be well placed to capitalise on this.

Nick Widdows

ROUND BRITAIN REVIEW

NORTH SEA

There has been much happening in the North Sea sector during 1998 as all companies gear themselves towards the probable ending of duty-free concessions within the EU this coming summer. Of all operators it is DFDS that has made the most obvious change with the closure of the Harwich - Gothenburg route followed by the introduction of a Newcastle - Kristiansand - Gothenburg link in February 1999. The call at the Norwegian port allows duty-free to continue, Norway electing to remain outside the EU's sphere of influence.

In order to bring them up to the latest SOLAS requirements, both the *Princess of Scandinavia* and her sister the *Prince of Scandinavia* were fitted with stability sponsons at Gdansk during early 1998 and thus modified, their future looks safe for at least another five years. The 'Prince' has settled down on the Harwich - Hamburg link while the displaced *Admiral of Scandinavia* (ex *Hamburg*) has carried increased loadings on the Newcastle - IJmuiden service. She was also fitted with sponsons during early 1999 and will be joined in service by the *King of Scandinavia* (ex *Venus*) this coming summer.

A previous DFDS vessel, Color Line's *Color Viking* underwent a £2 million refit early in 1998 during which time she was also fitted with sponsons and had much work completed to improve her public areas. Then came the surprise announcement that as from 1st December the ship and the Color Line UK - Norway operations were being taken over by Fjord Line. The ship has been duly renamed *Jupiter*.

A well-known name to disappear during 1998 was that of Fred. Olsen & Co. Two new super freighters, the *Bayard* and *Brabant* joined the fleet from Fincantieri's Ancona yard in December 1997 and April 1998 but within months it was announced that they had been resold to Trasmediterranea and that the Olsen operations and remaining ships had been sold to DFDS. The *Borecay* had previously been sold to DFDS and renamed *Dana Minerva* and the *Balduin* and *Borac* followed being renamed *Tor Norvegia* and *Tor Humbria*. With this achieved, the DFDS web then spread to involve every country around the North Sea. Three new freighters, the first two being the *Tor Selandia* and *Tor Suecia*, were ordered from Fincantieri at Ancona to work the AngloBridge Immingham - Gothenburg link while two large former American military ro-ro ships *American Condor* and *American Falcon* (renamed *Tor Scandia* and *Tor Flandria*) were acquired to work the EuroBridge link from Ghent to Gothenburg.

A company trading as East Coast Ferries, and backed by Commodore Ferries, began operations between Hull and Dunkerque in September 1998. Initially they used the chartered *Merchant Venture* and *Octogon-3* although the former vessel was soon replaced by the *Loon-Plage*. Two groundings in the Humber estuary and a general lack of traffic saw operations closed on 20th January. Another company to fail was the Estonian concern Esco Euro Lines who attempted to provide a successful link Hull with Kiel using their *Transestonia*.

The long awaited news regarding new vessels for the P&O North Sea Ferries' Hull - Europoort link was announced in January 1999. Twin £90 million cruise ferries have been ordered from Fincantieri's Venice yard. The 60,600 gross tons ships are due to enter service in April and December 2001 thereby replacing all four ships presently employed on the route. Their speed of 22 knots will knock some 2 hours 30 minutes from the crossing time and capacity will be for 1,360 passengers, 136 crew and 3,400 lane metres of freight on three decks. The 250 cars will be side-loaded into their own garage.

At Harwich, the troubled Stena Line BV service linking the Hook of Holland hit rock bottom on 3rd January 1998 when the HSS 1500 craft *Stena Discovery* was badly damaged by strong waves

PLAIN SAILING

From the M20 motorway, the dual carriageway leads directly into the Port of Dover where streamlined check-in systems make boarding quick and easy.

Ferries depart up to four times an hour around the clock on the short sea crossing to Calais - plus there is a freight service to Zeebrugge and fast ferry service to Ostend!

A brief but welcome break from driving, the ferry crossing provides the perfect opportunity to take in some sea air, to stretch your legs, to enjoy a meal, do some shopping, or simply relax whilst, at the same time, keeping on the move towards your continental destination.

It's the high road to Europe and a rewarding experience - from every point of view!

PORT OF DOVER

Port of Dover, Harbour House, Dover, Kent CT17 9BU
Website: www.doverport.co.uk   E-mail: pr@doverport.co.uk

in the North Sea. The vessel was immediately withdrawn from service and the Stranraer-based HSS *Stena Voyager* was transferred to maintain the schedules as from 21st January until replaced by the errant 'Discovery' on 10th April. Further problems occurred at Harwich in August when the HSS-dedicated berth sank at its moorings and the Master of the incoming fast craft had to deal with mutinous behaviour from his 1,350 passengers.

EASTERN CHANNEL

Dart Line continued to make headway during the year with the delivery in August and September of two new Estonian ro-ro vessels for the Dartford - Vlissingen route. This occurred at a time when the Sally service at Ramsgate was about to terminate and the company were hopeful of picking up some of the pieces. During March, Dart acquired three large Chinese ro-ro vessels two of which will be placed on the Zeebrugge service later this year.

The short-lived trading partnership between the Australian company Holyman and Sally Ferries foundered during 1998 with Sally's Finnish owners, Neptun Maritime Oyj blaming their offspring for the group's financial losses. Holyman are believed to have lost BEF 1 billion during their short existence. The joint Ramsgate - Ostend service commenced on 1st March 1997 but lasted barely a year before Hoverspeed at Dover offered Holyman a berth on a 50-50 basis and, using the *Holyman Diamant*, the service was switched as from 5th March. The 81 metre InCat vessels both lost their 'Holyman' name prefixes and as the *Rapide* and *Diamant*, the Hoverspeed service has traded at a profit on the new route.

Meanwhile the Sally Freight operations continued using the chartered *Euroway* and *Eurocruiser* in conjunction with Sally's own *Eurotraveller*. The *Eurocruiser's* charter finished in

Princess of Scandinavia *(John Bryant)*

THE FERRY & RO/RO PORT IN THE NETHERLANDS

TWICE DAILY VLISSINGEN TO DARTFORD

DART Line

DEDICATED CAR SHIPMENTS UK, IRELAND AND SPAIN

FLOTA SUARDIAZ, S.A.

RO/RO LINER SERVICES PORTUGAL, MAROCCO, CANARY ISLANDS

N.V. HAVEN VAN VLISSINGEN

STEVEDORE-WAREHOUSES-BONDED STORAGE-FORWARDING-INTERNATIONAL TRANSPORT

Head-office: Stadhuisplein 20
P.O. Box 398
NL-4380 AJ VLISSINGEN

Phone: +31 (0)118 42 60 00*
Fax: +31 (0)118 41 05 45
E-mail: sales@hvv.nl

May after which she went back to the Harwich - Hook route assuming her previous identity as the *Rosebay*.

The replacement for the *Eurocruiser* was the *Eurovoyager*, the former RMT vessel *Prins Albert*. Since the Belgian Government withdrew from the Ostend - Ramsgate link in February 1997, all three of their conventional vessels had been laid-up in the dock system at Dunkerque. The 'Albert' was sold to the British concern, Denval who transferred her ownership to the Slovenian company TransEuropa Shipping Lines. The same owners later purchased the former *Princesse Marie-Christine* and renamed her *Primrose*. It will be remembered that the first vessel of this class - the *Prinses Maria-Esmeralda* became their *Wisteria*.

The *Eurotraveller* eventually commenced the 'turn up and go' Sally Direct multi-purpose service in April but the Belgian authorities refused to allow passengers to disembark. The problem was finally resolved in July but, apart from at weekends, traffic levels were poor and Silja finally pulled the plug in November. Taking up the service without so much as missing a sailing were Ramsgate New Port in conjunction with TransEuropa Shipping using their *Eurovoyager* which was later joined by the ro-ro ship *Juniper*.

The twin RMT Boeing jetfoils were also sold during the year becoming the *Alder Blizzard* and *Alder Wizzard* for use in the Baltic. They finally left Ostend by lift ship in September.

As for their former RMT flagship *Prins Filip*, she was purchased by Stena Ferries in June, renamed *Stena Royal* and offered for charter. The first such occasion duly occurred in November when the ship was taken on a four month charter by P&O Stena Line for service on their Dover - Zeebrugge freight link vice the *European Pathway* which was out of service after sacrificing a gearbox for the *Pride of Burgundy*.

At Dover, the 10th March 1998 had seen the establishment of the P&O European Ferries /Stena Line joint venture and the start of rationalisation of services on the Dover - Calais link. It was stated that about £75 million will be saved and 1,000 jobs lost by the creation of P&O Stena Line which is 60% owned by the British company. The *Stena Invicta* was summarily withdrawn from service as from 18th February leaving the *Stena Empereur* and *Stena Fantasia* to operate with the *Pride of Dover*, *Pride of Calais*, *Pride of Burgundy* and *Pride of Kent*. The *Pride of Bruges* did not, as was expected, transfer to the Newhaven - Dieppe route but shadowed the 'Kent' for the season while the three 'European' class freighters continued to operate the Zeebrugge traffic. Much effort has been made to 'harmonise' the fleets (ie bring the Stena ships up to P&O standards) although during 1998 there were limits to what could be achieved. However, the former P&O fleet lost their 'Pride of' prefixes and gained the letters 'P&OSL' in their place while the *Pride of Bruges* became the *P&OSL Picardy*. Of the former Stena ships, the *Stena Fantasia* was renamed *P&OSL Canterbury* while the *Stena Empereur* became the *P&OSL Provence*.

Hoverspeed's ever-faithful thirty year old SRN 4 hovercraft were pressed back into winter service during 1997-98 after the sudden withdrawal of the *SuperSeaCat Two* in December 1997. The 74 metre craft *SeaCat Isle of Man* took her place and remained on the Dover - Calais service during the year before returning to the Irish Sea early in 1999. Meanwhile the *Hoverspeed Great Britain* again maintained the Folkestone - Boulogne route which for the first time was also operated throughout the winter period.

French operators SeaFrance continued to carry good loadings on their Calais - Dover service with the elderly *SeaFrance Monet* (ex *Stena Londoner*) again appearing during early year refits in 1998 and 1999. Just how much longer she will be able to do this without SOLAS modifications is not known.

At Folkestone, Falcon Seafreight placed the ro-ro vessel *Purbeck* on the Boulogne link during April allowing the chartered Sea Containers ship *Picasso* to return to Birkenhead for lay-up. Traffic grew to such an extent that the *Picasso* returned to offer a two ship service in January 1999.

SeaFrance Nord Pas-de-Calais *(John Hendy)*

Purbeck *(John Bryant)*

WESTERN CHANNEL & CHANNEL ISLANDS

The Newhaven-Dieppe service suffered another poor season during 1998; the route was down by some 62% on passengers, freight by 33% and with the revenue continuing to drop during the last five years by some £16 million. P&O Stena Line, the newly merged company which took over the route from Stena Line in 1998, decided to re-evaluate its future. With the compounded losses and the technical problems of the *Elite* fast craft which had to be withdrawn in October, the company entered discussions between both British and French unions over the route's future. The Newhaven-Dieppe route has been hampered for many years by the lack of a suitable modern linkspan at Newhaven for any larger tonnage than the *Stena Cambria* and although the facilities at Dieppe are modern, the new berth there was actually only designed for an HSS 900 craft. As if these problems were not bad enough, Newhaven is hindered by poor road communications from London and the south coast, and in Normandy the now-completed N26 means that the drive between Le Havre and Calais has been cut to only two and a half hours between each port.

Discussions with the unions continued until early January when it was announced that P&O Stena Line would close the route as it had lost £27 million since 1995 and passenger numbers had dropped from 1.23 million in 1993 to just 760,950 in 1997. The *Stena Cambria* made her last sailing on the four hour route on 30th January and then sailed to Zeebrugge for layup and sale. The 118 French officers and ratings from the *Stena Cambria* were duly redeployed at Dover.

During the protracted negotiations to close the route with the French unions, Sea Containers announced that they would be interested in continuing the most direct route between London and Paris as from April. Sea Containers plan to take over the route as from 24th April using the *SuperSeaCat Two*. Meanwhile as we went to press, the Dieppe Chamber of Commerce were in negotiations with a number of parties to maintain a freight service to Newhaven.

Possibly one of the most interesting developments in the Western Channel last year was the decision of both the Jersey and Guernsey Transport Authorities to invite tenders to operate the services to the Islands from the UK as from 1999. Their decision instantly saw a number of the leading British ferry companies expressing interest in the tender including the existing operators Condor/Commodore, Hoverspeed, P&O European Ferries at Portsmouth and initially Cenargo. The decision to put these services out to tender came in the light of major disruption to the ferry services to the Channel Islands from the UK during 1997 and 1998.

Hoverspeed's proposals for a service were based on a year-round SuperSeaCat service from Weymouth with a conventional ferry providing an all-weather backup plus additional peak sailings with an option of either a fast or conventional ferry service. P&O European Ferries, who based their operations entirely at Portsmouth, tendered their professional document with a daily round-trip by both conventional ship and fast craft. The conventional vessel would have been re-equipped for the Channel Islands service and refurbished to provide a 100 x 4 berth cabins, 400 reclining seats, a club class lounge and the usual other reception areas onboard. A passenger capacity of 1,000 with a vehicle capacity of 330 would have been provided by, it was believed but never disclosed by P&O, the *Pride of Bruges* or the *Stena Cambria*.

P&O planned that the conventional ship would depart from Portsmouth daily at 22.00, sail outward to Guernsey and then onto Jersey and sail back inward to Portsmouth, calling again at Guernsey. In addition to the conventional operation, a fast craft service would have operated from March to November, initially with one craft, supplemented by a second craft from April to September. The fast craft service would also include an extension of the company's existing French operation to include St. Malo.

The existing operator, Condor, meanwhile presented their tender based on two fast craft operating from both Poole and Weymouth with a capacity for 220 cars and 800 passengers.

Pride of Portsmouth *(Miles Cowsill)*

Normandie *(John Bryant)*

SANTANDER — BILBAO — ST. MALO — CHERBOURG — CAEN — LE HAVRE — CHANNEL ISLANDS

PORTSMOUTH.
BRITAIN'S
BEST CONNECTED
FERRY PORT.

CLOSEST MOTORWAY

MOST 5 STAR FERRIES

MOST DESTINATIONS

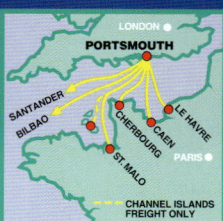

For the majority of travellers in the UK, Portsmouth is clearly the No.1 departure point.

The motorway system leads you virtually to the Port entrance. The ferries are the most luxurious across the Channel. We offer more destinations than any other port. And, you arrive refreshed and ready to continue your journey.

So next time you cross the Channel, set a course for Portsmouth. For further information please call **01705 297391**.

BRITAIN'S BEST CONNECTED FERRY PORT

Additionally, as from January 2000, the company would introduce a new ro-pax vessel which would operate from Portsmouth with their sister company, Commodore Ferries. The new ro-pax vessel would have a passenger capacity for 500 cars with 41 cabins, based on a similar type hull to that of the *Ben-my-Chree* operated by the Isle of Man Steam Packet Company.

On the 1st June the Jersey Authorities announced that they were in favour of Condor continuing the service to the Islands from the UK, meanwhile the Guernsey Authorities announced that they were in favour of P&O European Ferries. On paper the proposals made by P&O European Ferries were the strongest, especially as they were ready to introduce a conventional ship as from 1st January 1999 and also they would operate two fast craft from Portsmouth, which is the key to all the Channel Islands operations with its excellent road communications. Condor's proposals offered nothing different from what the Channel Islands have had in the past, which have been the bone of contention and the reasons for tender proposals. The Sea Containers' document was possibly the weakest of all three and based operations entirely on Weymouth, with its poor road communications.

Some two weeks' later the Guernsey Transport Authority reversed their earlier decision with regard to P&O and indicated total support to Condor's proposals instead. By 1st July, it was formally announced that both State Authorities agreed to give the contract to Condor to operate to the Islands as from 1999. As a result of this announcement, Condor immediately purchased the former BCIF vessel *Havelet* from Channel Island Ferries to give them conventional ferry support pending the arrival of the company's new £30 million ro-pax vessel, which keel was laid at Van der Giessen on 6th November. The new vessel, due to be named *Commodore Clipper*, is due to be launched on 8th May and enter service during September this year.

As described by Geoffrey Ede, the Managing Director of Hoverspeed, at the end of this lengthy

Commodore Goodwill *(Philippe Holthof)*

tender saga for the Channel Islands service, "The whole thing has turned out into an exercise to improve Condor but at what future cost to the Islanders."Meanwhile, there have been more positive signs from the Portsmouth operators over the last 12 months with improved passenger carryings. In the light of these improvements, P&O European Ferries introduced a new fast craft service between Portsmouth and Cherbourg in May using the Austal craft *SuperStar Express*. The 82 metre craft, originally built for Malaysian cruise operations, *SuperStar Express* can operate at 38.5 knots with a capacity for 200 cars and 800 passengers. The fast craft entered service on 16th May, offering three round crossings a day with a crossing time of 2 hours and 45 minutes between both ports. The Managing Director of P&O European Ferries at Portsmouth, Captain James Davenport, said following the announcement, "We are excited about this addition to our fleet. The *SuperStar Express* means we can give customers a choice - a high-speed route to Cherbourg or a more traditional leisurely crossing, with both services offering the very best of the P&O experience." Following the success of the *SuperStar Express* in 1998, P&O European Ferries at Portsmouth announced extension of her charter for the 1999 season.

P&O's other routes to Le Havre, Cherbourg and Bilbao continued to see growth with an additional freight vessel *Seahawk* being brought in on charter to support the *Pride of Portsmouth* and *Pride of Le Havre* last year. At the start of 1999 as part of a new marketing policy, P&O European Ferries at Portsmouth was remarketed as P&O Portsmouth.

Brittany Ferries also attracted good levels of business once again, especially on their St. Malo service. For 1999, the same vessels as in the previous year will be deployed on their complex network of routes to and from France to England and Ireland. It was decided during 1998 that the passenger and freight vessel *Barfleur* would no longer be marketed under the Truckline banner but would be brought under the umbrella of the Brittany Ferries' operations. Truckline will remain an important integral part of the Brittany Ferries group, but purely for freight operations.

Portsmouth Commercial Ferry Port decided in 1998 to build a fifth berth on the northern quay. In the light of the Channel Islands tender saga in 1998, a new fast ferry passenger-only service was started by Channel Hoppers, using the fast ferry *Varangerfjord*. It had been planned that the route would start during April but it was not until the last week of May that the operation commenced, linking the Channel Islands with Portsmouth with calls at Sark and Alderney. Despite early commercial operational problems last year, Channel Hoppers plan to be back on the scene again during 1999.

Ferry services to the Isle of Wight have enjoyed a fairly quiet 1998, the highlight being the introduction of Red Funnel's new high-speed craft *Red Jet 3* in August. Her entry into service saw the demise of the company's last two 'Shearwater' hydrofoils from regular service - the last such vessels operational in British coastal waters.

During the refit of Wightlink's Portsmouth - Ryde catamarans in spring 1998, the company again chartered the excursion vessel *Wight Scene*. Meanwhile the classic vessel *Southsea* spent the fiftieth anniversary of her entry into service marooned in Abel's drydock at Bristol where well-meant but ill-founded plans to return her to service had placed her future in jeopardy.

IRISH SEA

On the Irish Sea Irish Ferries continued their programme of restructuring their operations. Having successfully introduced new tonnage both at Dublin and Rosslare over the last four years, in 1998 the company decided that radical steps had to be made to improve their services from Ireland to France in the light of the *Saint Patrick II* and *Saint Killian II* being unsuitable to operate without major expenditure. In the light of this, the company decided to charter the former Stena Line vessel *Stena Normandy*. The *Normandy*, as she is now known, replaced both the 'Patrick' and

Riverdance and **Merchant Brilliant** *(John Hendy)*

SeaCat Danmark *(Miles Cowsill)*

'Killian' with a capacity for 450 cars and 1,600 passengers last March. With only one vessel earmarked to operate their Continental routes, the company decided their links with France would only be based around three ports - Rosslare, Cherbourg and Roscoff. This would allow them to operate a new schedule which would allow constant departure and arrival times, with early morning arrivals in France and Ireland to better facilitate driving to onward destinations for passengers and freight operators.

The abandonment of Cork and Le Havre came as a blow to both ports, which had recently invested heavily improving the port facilities for the company. Prior to entering service on the Continental services, the *Normandy* was deployed on the Rosslare-Pembroke Dock service in the absence of the *Isle of Innisfree*. During 1998, Irish Ferries made a record profit of IR£17.6 million, an increase of 21% on the previous year. Overall passenger numbers grew by some 3% to a record 1.6 million. There was also a significant growth on the Ireland-France routes of some 23% in passenger traffic. Freight carryings on the Irish Sea routes grew by 27% to 139,000 units on both Dublin and Rosslare services. The Dublin route saw a 19% growth in traffic, while the Rossalare route saw a staggering 52% increase.

Swansea Cork Ferries continued to maintain their operations between Cork and Swansea successfully with the Greek registered *Superferry*. The company is looking to replace the vessel in the near future with larger and more suitable tonnage, however the type of vessel will be very much restricted by the tidal restrictions at Swansea. In early 1999 the company was sold by Strintzis Lines of Greece to a new Anglo/Irish group

The *Koningin Beatrix* was joined in October by the *Stena Lynx III* (ex *Elite*) on the Fishguard-Rosslare service, in place of the *Stena Lynx*. The larger capacity fastcraft will be welcomed at the port in the light of the success of the fast ferry route since 1994. Meanwhile at Rosslare the new double-deck linkspan was completed last summer and by early spring of this year similar facilities will be offered at Pembroke Dock for the *Isle of Innisfree*.

Hebridean Isles *(Brian Maxted)*

Pride of Rathlin *(Miles Cowsill)*

At Holyhead, Irish Ferries ordered a new highspeed passenger/car-carrying vessel from Austal Ship's PTY Limited in Western Australia in the summer for entry into service this May. The new craft will have capacity for 800 passengers and 200 cars. Irish Ferries have chosen the name 'Dublin Swift' to market their new highspeed car ferry service, chosen to emphasise its swiftness of passage, with a sailing time of just 1 hour 49 minutes between Dublin and Holyhead. The name also underlines the connections into Dublin City which the new service will provide. In addition to the 'Dublin Swift' designation, the vessel itself will be registered under the name *Jonathan Swift* after the distinguished Dublin writer Dean Swift, whose literary masterpiece 'Gulliver's Travels' is acclaimed throughout the English-speaking world. The new fast vessel, being built at a cost of £29 million, will operate in tandem with the *Isle of Inishmore* and will operate four round sailings a day.

Merchant Ferries started their new ro-pax service at the start of February 1999 with the *Brave Merchant* and *Dawn Merchant*. The scheduled crossing time between Liverpool and Dublin by Merchant Ferries is 7 hours 30 minutes, the crossing time will reduce once the new Mersey river berths are completed some time in the year 2000. Both the *Brave Merchant* and *Dawn Merchant*, built in Spain, are 180 metres long and have a beam of 25 metres, thus being similar in size to the Norse Irish Ferries vessels. They are able to carry 300 passengers/drivers, of whom up to 114 will be accommodated in two-berth cabins. There will also be seating for 100 passengers in large passenger lounge and Dining Room area. The service will compete directly with P&O European Ferries' established service to Dublin.

Meanwhile Norse Irish Ferries started their daytime sailings between Liverpool and Belfast on 10th March 1998, three times a week. The company plan to expand the daytime sailings in the near future.

The keel to the new ro-pax vessel for the Isle of Man Steam Packet Company, the *Ben-my-Chree*, was laid on 28th October 1997 at the Dutch yard of Van der Giessen. In a controversial move, the new vessel replaced both the conventional multi-purpose ship *King Orry* and freight-only vessel *Peveril* and was launched by Mrs Joan Gelling on 4th April.

The new £24 million vessel arrived at Douglas on 6th July and initially entered service on night freight runs until early August when she took up her twice-daily service from Douglas to Heysham. On entry into service of the *Ben-my-Chree*, the *Peveril* was immediately withdrawn but with capacity fears of the new ro-pax vessel, the *King Orry* remained on station until 28th September. The vessel was the immediately sold to Moby Lines and renamed *Moby Love II* for her new role in the Mediterranean.

The fast ferry service between Liverpool and Douglas was maintained by *SeaCat Danmark*, which also undertook calls to Dublin and Belfast. The 'Danmark' this year will be employed on a new fast ferry service between Heysham and Belfast and 1999 sees the return of *SeaCat Isle of Man* from the Dover Strait back to the Douglas-Liverpool route. This year also sees the *Lady of Mann* being fully employed on the Irish Sea, she has proved a valuable asset for the company during the winter period when it has not been possible to operate either a SeaCat or SuperSeaCat service to and from the Island.

The new fast ferry service between Liverpool and Dublin, operated by Sea Containers using *SuperSeaCat Two*, enjoyed mixed fortunes during 1998. The company hope that the extensive modifications that they done to the Italian-built craft will ensure a more reliable service for 1999, until she is replaced by the newer *SuperSeaCat Three*. The now well-established fast ferry service of Sea Containers between Stranraer and Belfast will see the company during 1999 splitting their Scottish link with Troon, whilst the Troon-Belfast service will have a longer period at sea than Stranraer, the company feel that the road communications from the Scottish port are far better than Stranraer, especially for Scottish travellers.

Meanwhile, P&O European Ferries have indicated their intention to run a ferry service between Port Glasgow and Larne in the near future which will see the demise of Ardrossan as their northerly Scottish port. In mid February 1999, P&O European Ferries announced that they plan to make further improvements to their northern Channel service when they announced the building of a new 21,000 tonne passenger/freight ferry from Japan for delivery in June 2000. The new vessel will operate the Larne-Cairnryan route with a service speed of 23 knots, which will reduce the conventional ferry journey time by a quarter to just 105 minutes, which will complement the one hour *Jetliner* service. With twin decks and drive-through bow and stern loading, the new ship will be able to handle 375 cars or 107 commercial vehicles. She will replace the *Pride of Rathlin*, the last of the 'Free Enterprise' class vessels operating in British waters. It is envisaged that the Irish Sea services of P&O will see further orders in the near future.

Stena Line's operations between Stranraer and Belfast have continued a steady increase in passengers, cars and freight over the last twelve months. The route currently is maintained by HSS craft *Stena Voyager*, and the conventional passenger vessels *Stena Galloway* and *Stena Caledonia*.

As part of an expected consolidation in the European freight trade on the Irish Sea, Cenargo acquired Scruttons, whose main activity in the Irish Sea was Belfast Freight Ferries, for £15.5 million in January. Belfast Freight Ferries have now been amalgamated into the Merchant Ferries' operations.

CLYDE & WESTERN ISLES

In Scotland a bridge and causeway in the Western Isles brought an end to two more small ferry routes. The £7.4 million bridge between Harris and Scalpay finally opened in December 1997 after which the Island class vessel *Rhum* was sent to lay-up. Twelve months later the causeway linking North Uist with Berneray saw the end for the Western Isles Islands Council's vessel *Eilean Bhearnaraigh*.

CAMMELL LAIRD SHIPYARD LOCATIONS

GIBRALTAR
P.O. Box 858 · Gibraltar
Tel: 00 350 59400
Fax: 00 350 44404
E-mail: mail@lairds.gi
3 drydocks: 270m x 38m max.
ISO 9002

MERSEYSIDE
Birkenhead · L41 9BP
Tel: +44 (0) 151 650 4000
Fax: +44 (0) 151 650 4050
E-mail: mail@lairds.co.uk
3 drydocks: 289m x 42.7m max.
ISO 9001 & 9002

SOUTH SHIELDS
P.O. Box 7 · NE33 1RN
Tel: +44 (0) 191 455 5515
Fax: +44 (0) 191 454 4090
4 drydocks: 195m x 24.1m max.
ISO 9002

TEESSIDE
Middlesbrough · TS6 6UH
Tel: +44 (0) 1642 440043
Fax: +44 (0) 1642 440078
3 drydocks: 175m x 22.25m max.
ISO 9001 & 9002

TYNESIDE
Hebburn on Tyne · NE31 1SP
Tel: +44 (0) 191 430 1446
Fax: +44 (0) 191 430 1447
2 drydocks: 259m x 44m max.
ISO 9001 & 9002

WEARSIDE
Sunderland · SR21 2EE
Tel: +44 (0) 191 567 4749
Fax: +44 (0) 191 510 0765
1 drydock: 115m x 16.6m max.
ISO 9002

ENGINEERING FACILITY

WEAR ENGINEERING
Sunderland · SR4 6WE
Tel: +44 (0) 191 510 0917
Fax: +44 (0) 191 564 0447
Extensive engineering & fabrication facilities
ISO 9002

TECHNICAL SERVICES

MERSEYSIDE
Birkenhead · L41 9BP
Tel: +44 (0) 151 650 4000
Fax: +44 (0) 151 650 4155
E-mail: ts@lairds.co.uk
Also in London, Newcastle & Oslo
ISO 9001

D.G. ELECTRICAL
Birkenhead · L41 1LT
Tel: +44 (0) 151 637 0444
Fax: +44 (0) 151 637 0555
Also in Newcastle and Kent
ISO 9002

Cammell Laird is the UK's largest shiprepair and conversion company, operating 13 drydocks in the UK, and a further 3 drydocks in Gibraltar, with substantial wet berth and quayside facilities.

The Group has extensive experience in the drydocking, repair and major conversion of a wide range of vessels including freight and passenger RO-RO's, cruise vessels, and fast aluminium monohull & catamaran ferries.

Projects have included ■ **Lengthenings** ■ **Sponsons for SOLAS compliance** ■ **Additional freight handling** (mezzanine car decks, additional freight decks, fixed and hoistable ramps) ■ **Passenger facilities** (cabins, public spaces, crew accommodation, galleys/serveries).

- Some of the largest fabrication and engineering facilities in the UK.
- Specialist marine electrical division D.G. Electrical, provide full system design, installation and commissioning capabilities.
- Cammell Laird Technical Services provide independent design and consultancy services for shipowners and operators, with particular experience in SOLAS compliance studies and are accredited to ISO 9001.

Quality Solutions in Design, Conversion and Repair

Head Office:
Cammell Laird Holdings PLC, 8 Princes Parade, Liverpool, England L3 1DL
Tel: +44 (0)151 236 5500 · Fax: +44 (0)151 236 9094
E-mail: mail@holdings.lairds.co.uk · Website: lairds.merseyworld.com

The new Outer Isles vessel *Clansman* was launched at Appledore by The Princess Royal in March but was late in entering service. With the *Clansman* entering service on 4th July, the *Lord of the Isles* was switched to the Mallaig station.

As Caledonian MacBrayne were two major units short following the sale of the *Iona* to Orkney buyers and the *Claymore* to Sea Containers, the winter refit period always promised to be difficult. And so it proved to be when in April the *Isle of Lewis* failed and major disruption ensued. The *Isle of Mull* was transferred to the Stornoway - Ullapool link while the elderly *Pioneer* moved to Oban. A quick charter of the *Pentalina B* (ex *Iona*) kept traffic flowing on the Mull link, although her passenger certificate for just 150 was far from ideal, while the small Island class vessel *Eigg* was switched to the Mallaig - Armadale crossing of the Sound of Sleat. Normality returned during when mid-May the *Isle of Lewis* returned to service.

The *Pioneer* is due for replacement by November 2000 and an order has made for a new ship to replace the *Hebridean Isles* at Uig (Skye). She in turn is due to replace the *Lord of the Isles* at Mallaig which will then become the spare vessel in place of the *Pioneer*. Another ferry soon to be replaced is the Small Isles vessel *Lochmor*.

Western Ferries have been evaluating a new service linking Ardyne (Cowal) with Ardmaleish (Bute) using their original vessel *Sound of Scarba*.

The Western Ferries (Argyll) ferry *Sound of Gigha* was duly replaced on the Jura - Islay service in July by the £750,000 Mersey-built *Eilean Dhuira*. The ferry is owned by the Argyll and Bute Council and required a further £21,000 ramp modifications before being deemed completely suitable for the Sound of Islay link.

Miles Cowsill & John Hendy

Eilean Dhuira *(Brian Maxted)*

FAST FERRY YEAR

The year 1998 was an important year for the fast ferry business in Northern Europe. For the industry in general it appeared to be a year of consolidation. Compared with previous years a smaller number of new deliveries to operators signified a continuing appeal for new high speed technology tempered by the economic benefits of scale. The total number of global fast ferry deliveries in 1998 amounted to 64 vessels including 16 with vehicle capacity bring the total number of operationally available fast vehicle ferries to 80. A further 21 high speed vehicle ferries remained under build or on order as the year closed. While the overall number of deliveries and orders in 1998 was lower than the previous year's total, newbuild capacities for both passengers and vehicle increased.

As in 1997 a number of high speed car ferries remained laid up for the peak season. Notably the *Pegasus*, *Cat-Link I*, the Chinese built *Afai 08* that was brought to Northern Europe speculatively, and an unsold InCat 86 metre catamaran at the Tasmanian yard. Two key issues lingered on from the previous year and dominated the North European ferry industry news for the early part of 1998. The merger of P&O European Ferries' and Stena Line's short sea operations affected only one fast ferry, the 81 metre InCat Australia wavepiercer *Stena Lynx III*, then operating the Newhaven - Dieppe route. The craft returned to Stena Line's Dover - Calais route in February for less than two months, operating four return trips each day before being transferred back to Newhaven in March to appear in the new livery of P&O Stena Line as *Elite*. Following a disappointing 1998 season on the route P&O Stena Line announced that that the fast ferry service would be withdrawn as they were dissatisfied with the performance of the vessel on that route. Hoverspeed, incidentally, had voiced strong opposition to any plans the merged P&O Stena Line

SuperSeaCat One *(John Hendy)*

may have had to operate fast ferries on the Dover - Calais route on the grounds of unfair competition with its own Hovercraft and SeaCat services. P&O Stena Line subsequently confirmed that the Newhaven - Dieppe route would close completely in early 1999.

Other routes operated separately by P&O European Ferries and Stena Line remained independent with Stena Line continuing to operate its flagship fleet of three HSS 1500 catamarans. The *Stena Voyager* transferred from the Irish Sea to replace the *Stena Discovery* on the Harwich - Hook of Holland route. The *Stena Discovery* had been damaged in early January during a stormy crossing to Holland. More than 50 cars were reported damaged in the incident but none of the passengers on board were injured which could be a useful testimony to the HSS design. The vessel sustained significant damage to its composite material bow structure which necessitated an early return, prior to a planned refit, to the Finnyards shipyard in Rauma, Finland for extensive repairs and modifications. The company's third HSS 1500 *Stena Explorer* remained on Holyhead - Dun Laoghaire with the smaller fast ferry *Stena Lynx*, an InCat 74 metre wavepiercer, continuing to operate Fishguard - Rosslare. Stena Line's other fast ferry the *Stena Lynx II*, a 78 metre wavepiercer, ended its charter and was returned to its owners before entering service across the Straits of Gibraltar. Orginally this was to be with new Spanish operator EuroFerrys but in fact was introduced by Buquebus Espana on a parallel route.

Stena Line's Scandinavian service between Gothenburg and Frederikshavn continued with the HSS 900 *Stena Carisma* operating in conjunction with conventional tonnage. The HSS 900 was introduced in 1997 and is powered by ABB Stal industrial based gas turbines unlike the GE aviation derivative units powering the larger HSS 1500 vessels. Despite fast ferry competition from SeaCat Sweden's *SuperSeaCat One*, Stena Line reports that following the introduction of the *Stena Carisma* to the Sweden - Denmark route the company's traffic rose by approximately 250,000 passengers, 50,000 cars and 15,000 freight vehicles.

Superstar Express *(Miles Cowsill)*

MGM MARINE GLASS MAINTENANCE INTERNATIONAL LTD

SPECIALISTS IN THE RENOVATION PROTECTION & MAINTENANCE OF MARINE GLASS

Marine Glass Maintenance are the specialists in restoring stained inboard or overside exterior glass. Inaccessible glass can be reached by our specialist abseilers.

Once restored, glass is treated with **Sea-Thru**® polymer making it non-stick and easier to maintain.

Bridge glazing can be treated in house using **Sea-Thru**® commercial grade DIY kits. BP Tankers have been servicing their bridge glazing in this way for 5 years. **Sea-Thru**® treatment gives improved all round visibility in severe weather and poor light conditions and is particularly useful on hi-speed ferries, tugs and pilot boats.

Over 85,000 windows are now treated with **Sea-Thru**®.

Clients include:

P&O European Ferries	Irish Ferries
Disney Cruise Line	North Sea Ferries
Sea France	IOM Steam Packet Co
Cunard Line	Fred Olsen SA
Crystal Cruises	P&O Cruises
Celebrity Cruise Line	Seabourn Cruise Line
Radisson Cruises	Royal Caribbean Cruise Line
Airtours Cruises	Princess Cruises
Holland America Line	Hebridean Island Cruise Line

Tel/Fax +44 (0) 1703 453 724 for further information.

Marine Glass Maintenance International Ltd
PO Box 5, Netley Abbey,
Southampton SO31 5ZT, UK.

British Marine Industries Federation

MEROK MARINE INTERNATIONAL
FOR ALL FERRY SEATING SOLUTIONS

Illustrated is our new all aluminium casting and extrusion lightweight seat. The design gives the passengers the maximum of protection because of its unique ability to absorb impact in the event of a collision.

The new base castings and track fixing systems enables the higher standards of the IMO regulations to be achieved.

Passenger comfort has been maintained to complement our existing range and the total seat suspension guarantees this comfort.

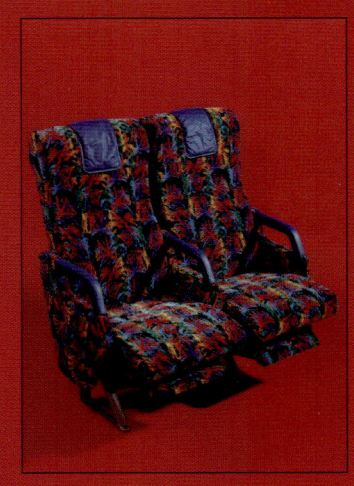

PARK FARM CLOSE PARK FARM IND. EST. FOLKESTONE KENT CT19 5DU
TEL NO: +44 (0) 1303 221616 FAX: NO: +44 (0) 1303 221503
email: merok@btinternet.com

P&O European Ferries meanwhile continued with the Mjellem & Karlsen built monohull *Jetliner* on the Irish Sea route linking Cairnryan to Larne scheduled with a passage time of just one hour. P&O sprang something of a surprise by announcing a summer charter of the Austal Ships 82 metre catamaran *SuperStar Express* for operation on the Western Channel route from Portsmouth to Cherbourg. The craft has capacity for 175 cars and 900 passengers, alternatively 10 coaches can be carried with a reduction in car volume to 70 units. Powered by four MTU 20v 1163 TB73L diesel engines service speed at full deadweight is 38 knots with fuel consumed at the rate of approximately 5 tonnes per hour. The company reports that the introduction of the fast ferry, which has significantly reduced passage time on the route, has stimulated market growth and the charter will continue.

The second main topic occupying the minds of the fast ferry industry in early 1998 was the restructuring of the Holyman Group. Holyman had significant interests in fast ferry operations in Denmark with Cat-Link, the Eastern Channel with Holyman Sally Ferries and the Western Channel with Condor Ferries. All of the group's fast ferry operations were experiencing problems of one sort or another. In Denmark Cat-Link, owned jointly with Scandlines, operating the Arhus - Kalundborg route with a pair of InCat 78 metre wavepiercers and the only Austal Auto Express 79 catamaran came under pressure both commercially and environmentally with concerns being raised locally over fast ferry noise, wash and fuel consumption issues. The Cat-Link operation was eventually absorbed by Scandlines who embarked on a plan to replace the existing three fast ferries with two larger and faster vessels, *Cat-Link IV* and *Cat-Link V* (which claimed the Hales Trophy and the Blue Riband during the Atlantic crossing of its delivery voyage from the builder in Tasmania), both InCat 91 metre catamarans. Each of these has capacity for approximately 220 cars and both craft feature a vehicle exit door on the upper deck tiers, starboard side, to facilitate a faster discharge. By employing this new tonnage Scandlines is able to improve operational and economic efficiency and, to some extent, placate the environmental lobby by reducing the total number of sailings.

On the western Channel Condor Ferries deployed a second 86 metre InCat Australia wavepiercer *Condor Vitesse* to run a second route from the mainland to the Channel Islands. Now operating from both Poole and Weymouth Condor Ferries hoped to redress some of the criticism received the previous year when operating the single craft service with the *Condor Express*. This vessel had experienced continual technical problems during 1997 which seriously impaired reliability and lost market confidence. Determined efforts to resolve the engineering issues and the introduction of the second craft was an attempt to win the route franchise which had now been opened up to tender.

P&O European Ferries and Hoverspeed made apparently serious applications to win the route with both pledging to back up a fast ferry service with conventional ferries. In the end Condor Ferries retained the franchise with a mixed package involving the two 86 metre catamarans supported by the catamaran *Condor 10* and the conventional ferry *Havelet*. Holyman however withdrew from the operation by disposing of its interests to Commodore Shipping.

More serious problems faced Holyman Sally Ferries where continuing losses on the Ramsgate Oostende and Ramsgate - Dunkerque route during 1997 carried over into 1998 and compounded the Holyman Group's problems. Part of the problem was unreliability of the Oostende craft but also the fact that reliance on three fast ferries, a single conventional mixed traffic ship and two dedicated freight vessels in place of four ships and two Jetfoils serving Oostende and two ship plying the Dunkerque route, effectively closed the door to a significant volume of freight and coach traffic previously enjoyed by the Ramsgate based routes. Following the closure of the Dunkerque service in 1997, Holyman Sally Ferries was dissolved in early 1998 and Holyman entered into a new arrangement with Hoverspeed to operate the two catamarans *Rapide* and *Diamant* from Dover Hoverport's fast ferry linkspan to Belgium.

FERRIES OF THE BRITISH ISLES & NORTHERN EUROPE

Rapide *(Hoverspeed)*

Jonathan Swift *(Irish Ferries)*

As a point of interest the two Boeing Marine Systems Jetfoil type 929-115 hydrofoils, *Princess Stephanie* and *Prinses Clementine*, formerly operated by Belgian state owned Oostende Lines have been disposed of. The two craft had been laid up in Oostende since the introduction of the Holyman Sally Ferries catamaran service in 1997. Now renamed *Adler Blizzard* and *Adler Wizard* respectively, the craft have been purchased by a German company. The *Adler Blizzard* for operation on a Baltic route.

Hoverspeed retained the two remaining SRN 4 amphibious hovercraft on the Dover - Calais route as first choice vessels but the supporting *SuperSeaCat Two* monohull was transferred to Irish Sea duties on the Liverpool - Dublin route. With a passage time scheduled at four hours the previous journey time by ship was reduced by two and a half hours, allowing departures from Liverpool to be timetabled at 08.15 and 18.00 with returns from Dublin at 13.00 and 23.00 hours. The monohull was replaced on the English Channel by the 74 metre catamaran *SeaCat Isle of Man*. SeaCat Scotland's Stranraer - Belfast route was maintained by *SeaCat Danmark* following the charter of *SeaCat Scotland* to Argentine operator Ferrylineas. For 1999 Hoverspeed has announced that it was taking up the Newhaven - Dieppe route, recently vacated by P&O Stena Line, with a SuperSeaCat monohull made available by the imminent delivery of two newbuildings from the Fincantieri yard in Italy. This new capacity together with the return to the United Kingdom of catamaran *Atlantic II* from Argentina will also allow expansion of Irish Sea services while parent company revealed that it was interested in acquiring a ferry operation in Turkey, a venture that subsequently seems to have been put on hold.

One interesting fast ferry development in Northern Europe in 1998 was the introduction of an high speed passenger service from Portsmouth to the Channel Islands. Operating under the name of Channel Hoppers the company scheduled a single Kvaerner Fjellstrand 38.8 metre Advanced Slender Catamaran *Varangerfjord* which entered service in June. One return trip per day was planned from Jersey to Portsmouth with calls at Guernsey and Sark. This ambitious timetable was later modified and the company experienced operating restrictions imposed by the United Kingdom Maritime and Coastguard Agency. Initial wave height limitations of 1.0 metre were later increased but remained well below the 3.5 metre limitation imposed on Condor Ferries much larger high speed craft. Although Channel Hoppers had a mixed season the company is sufficiently encouraged to return for the 1999 summer season and has indicated that it will operate a second craft, possibly from Torquay, a route reprising an earlier Condor service operated by a hydrofoil and latterly the passenger catamaran *Condor 9* for a single season.

Outstanding orders for fast ferries include the Alstom Leroux Naval Corsaire 11500 monohull car ferry *Gotland* due to be delivered to Rederi AB Gotland for the spring of 1999. The company operates a route from Oskarshamn and Nynashamn in southern Sweden to Visby on the island of Gotland. The Corsaire 11500 will have capacity for 700 passengers and 140 cars or 108 cars and 8 coaches, with a service speed of 35 knots. Powered by four Ruston diesel engines the steel hulled vessel is the first fast ferry to receive a limited ice capable notation.

Another important feature is the attention to environmental issues. A statement by the shipyard emphasised that the vessel will comply with the vigorous anti-pollution requirements of the Swedish authorities. The main engines are adapted to incorporate Siemans Selective Catalytic reduction Units designed to reduce Nox emissions.

Irish Ferries announced an order for an Austal 86 metre Auto Express high speed car ferry to be delivered in time for the 1999 season. The craft is valued at US$40 million and has capacity for up to 800 passengers and 200 cars. Operating between Dublin and Holyhead the fast ferry will scheduled up to four return services per day with the service speed of 39 knots allowing a passage time of two hours.

Paul Hynds

THE RISE OF RO-PAX

Over the last few years, an armada of new ferries have arrived on European shores bearing a new title: the 'Ro-Pax' ferry. The term has seen increasing currency recently; being used to describe vessels as diverse as Finncarrier's 112 passenger *Finnhansa* series ferries through to the massive 2200 passenger *Isle of Inishmore*. With more and more companies introducing either ferries designated as 'ro-pax' or announcing the inauguration of 'ro-pax' services, operators, travellers and enthusiasts alike may well be feeling a little bewildered by this new turn of phrase that has entered the shipping world. This article attempts to chart the rise of the ro-pax ferry during the 1990s and point to ways in which the terminology can best be applied to the increasingly diverse ferry industry in the forthcoming decade.

The word 'ro-pax' is a hybrid of 'ro-ro', traditionally denoting freight-only ferries (although all drive on vessels are technically roll-on, roll-off) and 'pax' or passenger. Ro-Pax ferries have a mixture of high freight capacity and a significant amount of passenger accommodation. However, a look at the accompanying table shows the diverse nature of vessels currently basking in the title. Not only are there a large number of freight ferries that have been converted to carry several hundred passengers, but also many purpose built vessels with passenger capacities the equal of the superferries of the 1980s. It sometimes seems that any operator with freight tonnage currently under construction is classifying it as a ro-pax vessel and a recent but growing trend is seeing routes that have traditionally operated as freight only beginning to advertise for passengers. However, it is also true that the ferries now being introduced to replace the classic cruiseferries of the 1980s are also being given the tag 'ro-

Stena Challenger *(Miles Cowsill)*

pax'; there is no more obvious example of this than the recent order by P&O for the world's largest ferries.

History

A history of the ro-pax is of course a history of the ferry: from the very beginning of modern car ferry services in the 1950s, the trend was to see vessels designed with an increasing amount of freight space. Freight ferry services have increased in importance dramatically since the entry of the UK into what is now the European Union and this sector has gradually experienced more choice and diversity than the passenger market.

In the 1970s, Sealink realised that a number of their 1960s-built passenger and car ferries, including the *Dover* and *Holyhead Ferry 1*, were in dire need of some ability to convey this increasingly lucrative freight traffic and sent them to shipyards to be enlarged to full 'multi-purpose' mode. Prior to this, the Atlantic Steam Navigation Co. were ahead of their time, giving their large series of freight vessels a modest passenger capacity. However, it was in 1977 when Brittany Ferries unveiled their new *Cornouailles* that arguably the first true ro-pax ferry was seen. The *Cornouailles* had the ability to carry a large amount of freight for her owners' Plymouth-Roscoff service and additionally boasted a respectable, although not particularly high, passenger capacity. Brittany Ferries' original service was inaugurated in 1973 as a freight only route and whilst passengers were carried from the following year with the introduction of the multi-purpose *Penn-ar-Bed*, the *Cornouailles* married these two principles in a way that had never before been seen. It is a testament to this idea that the ship has appeared in every edition of this book, now running to the Channel Islands as Condor's *Havelet* providing a freight and limited passenger back up to the services' fast catamarans.

During the early 1980s, the conversion of a number of freight-only vessels into those with the capability of carrying several hundred passengers became quite a common occurrence. As the short sea operators began to modernise their fleets from the first generation car ferries, a relatively simple operation could see an existing freight ship return to passenger service after only a few months. Notable vessels from this era included the Stena designed *Darnia* which Sealink had operated in a freight only mode for a number of years, to which accommodation was added for 412 passengers and Townsend Thoresen's home grown *European Gateway* which underwent a similar conversion. As with the *Cornouailles*, these were pressed into service on mainstream passenger routes. The reasons for this were quite clear: freight was becoming the backbone of many ferry services and operators had to ensure they had sufficient capacity for this whilst maintaining the ability to carry passengers as well. A hybrid vessel allowing both possibilities was the answer and conversions proved to be far cheaper than newly built tonnage. As the decade progressed, this practice became more common with further conversions being undertaken, notably by Townsend Thoresen on their *Baltic Ferry* and *Nordic Ferry* and DSB on the Mercandia freighters *Kraka*, *Lodbrog* and *Heimdal*.

By their very nature, the ro-pax ferries at this time lacked large amounts of cabin accommodation and did not offer anywhere near the facilities of the large cruiseferries, which were pioneered by North Sea Ferries and DFDS in the 1970s and developed into a new generation by Silja, Viking Line and TT-Line in the 1980s. The trend was to place the 'new' ships on the short-sea services and notably away from the heart of ferry operations such as Dover - Calais. At this stage, these routes were still featuring true multi-purpose ships of the *St Anselm* and Spirit of Free Enterprise classes where the emphasis on passenger accommodation was placed.

Ben-my-Chree *(Philippe Holthof)*

The birth of the modern ro-pax came in 1988 when TT-Line introduced their *Nils Dacke* and *Robin Hood*, to carry a full freight complement in addition to several hundred tourist cars and their passengers. These were dubbed 'Combi-Carriers' at the time but it is clear that they became the standard from which a whole flotilla of similar vessels was commissioned. The pair was placed into service opposite the very well appointed *Peter Pan* and *Nils Holgersson* acting as the principle carriers of cargo (thus freeing up space on the true passenger vessels) but also to provide valuable support to the mainstream service. Eventually, these ships were upgraded in 1993 with the installation of the full complement of passenger facilities and replaced their cruiseferry consorts. However, 1996 saw their initial role revived with the building of two new ferries carrying the same names.

Development

Originally, it could be argued that the new types of ferries were freight-only at heart, although operators were including sizeable passenger facilities. This was firstly to meet the increasing standards of lorry drivers as more traffic became accompanied, and secondly to enable companies to gain increasing returns through the carriage of passengers on existing services. Operators would sometimes advertise services in their passenger brochures but with a rider that these were a 'No Frills' facility. This was aptly demonstrated by Brittany Ferries' later use of the *Cornouailles* on the Truckline Poole - Cherbourg service between 1986 and 1988. The Nordo-Link service between Malmo and Travemunde also began carrying passengers in 1990 on their *Lubeck Link* and *Malmo Link* challenging the established services of TT Line. Recent years have seen the establishment of budget services by Finnlines rivalling

Stena Jutlandica *(Miles Cowsill)*

the luxurious services of Baltic giants Silja and Viking Lines. The Irish Sea, for many years offering a far wider choice of services for freight drivers than passengers, has seen a sudden increase as Norse Irish Ferries, Merchant Ferries and P&O all open up their freighters to carry passengers. In the case of the first two operators, this has been achieved through the construction of large and well appointed ro-pax vessels with facilities of the same standard as their conventional cousins at Dublin and Rosslare.

However, the term ro-pax has also diverged: in addition to referring to vessels constructed largely for freight services (that incidentally allow a few passengers) it has now been used to describe vessels that, to all intents and purposes, are mainstream multi-purpose vessels engaged primarily on passenger routes.

The early 1990s saw the advent of two ships that were to take this concept further. Brittany Ferries replaced the *Cornouailles* with the *Barfleur*, offering capacity for nearly 1200 passengers in accommodation that rivalled 'cruiseferry' fleetmates *Bretagne* and *Normandie* on a supposedly 'no frills' service. Indeed, the *Barfleur* deviated from this philosophy to such an extent that by 1999, the 'Truckline' tag was dropped in favour of the parent company brand. The following year saw the arrival of the *Pride of Burgundy*, converted from a 200 passenger freight ship whilst still under construction, for P&O's flagship passenger route between Dover and Calais. Again, she partnered the large passenger carriers *Pride of Calais* and *Pride of Dover* and was briefly the largest ferry on the English Channel.

The shipbuilders Van der Giessen de Noord in Rotterdam have been pioneers in the development of 'ro-pax' ferries, being responsible for, amongst others, two large vessels for Irish Ferries. The lead ship *Isle of Innisfree*, offered the standard provision for a large freight ship such as the *European Seaway* and the *Norbank*, but in addition had the ability to carry

Creative and innovative thinking

the capability to understand and analyse

Our reputation

Our reputation in shipbuilding is based on straightforward principles. Readiness to listen to the customer. Capability to understand and analyse his requirements. Expertise in technology, planning and organization.

PO Box 1
2920 AA Krimpen aan den IJssel
The Netherlands
telephone +31 (0)180 591200
telefax +31 (0)180 518180

van der Giessen-de Noord
shipbuilding division

1700 passengers. Whilst this ship has the profile of other more standard ro-pax ships, her 1997 fleetmate *Isle of Inishmore* (along with near sister *Stena Jutlandica*) was to offer accommodation for 2200 passengers with four passenger decks stretching nearly the full length of her hull. The late 1990s saw the yard develop a more sober ro-pax design in the form of the *Ben-my-Chree* for Sea Containers and the *Commodore Clipper* for Commodore.

The term ro-pax has also been used to describe the series of large vessels that have been constructed in for Mediterranean operators Minoan and Superfast. Since 1995, fifteen ships have been built or ordered by the two companies with a range of passenger facilities in excess of the *Isle of Inishmore* but with the addition of a large number of cabins. Finally, January 1999 saw P&O place an order for the world's largest ferries, designed to specifically replace the 31,000 grt passenger ships *Norsea* and *Norsun* in addition to the large freighters *Norbank* and *Norbay*. These latest giants have taken the term ro-pax to new and dizzying heights.

Such ships, could perhaps be better described as 'Pax-Ro' as their primary purpose is the carriage of passengers (with facilities to match) and the large freight capacity is simply a bonus, albeit a necessary one. The equivalent vessels of the last decade were the Sealink *St Anselm* series or the Thoresen 'Super Viking' ships.

The Contemporary Situation

Regular readers of 'Ferries of the British Isles and Northern Europe' and 'European Ferry Scene' will be familiar with the growing usage of the term 'ro-pax'. The recent crop over the last few years has demonstrated the difficulties in placing too much importance on these names. The *Isle of Inishmore* is a classic example of this: on paper her credentials are similar to those of *Pride of Dover* or *Stena Danica*, classic superferries of the 1980s. What is different about recent arrivals however, is their profile: modern ferries are moving increasingly towards an open after deck format allowing the potential to carry hazardous cargo, should the need arise, and operators in the Mediterranean have utilised these as camping decks. It is clear that there are a number of interesting trends taking place in ferry construction and operation and that the term 'ro-pax' is covering a variety of these.

Firstly, there is the utilisation of vessels combining a high freight capacity with a full passenger complement. This mix has been present since the very genesis of ferry operation although it has been particularly prominent in the last two decades. North Sea Ferries have always been at the forefront of this with the four generations of *Norwind*, *Norland*, *Norsea* and the 2001 newbuildings. Most of the Mediterranean newbuildings are following in NSF's wake, as are the Irish 'Isles', *Stena Jutlandica* and *Barfleur*.

Secondly, there is the new generation of ships that primarily provide a freight carrying function, but also allow passenger facilities to supplement their main sphere of operation. Stena seem to be the main proponents of this with their *Stena Challenger* Holyhead-Dublin service supporting the HSS. The Stena Seapacer twins now under construction are likely to add this function to the Harwich -Hook of Holland service at the end of 1999. Use of ro-pax ferries to provide support to fast craft is increasingly common with *Ben-my-Chree* and *Commodore Clipper* both fulfilling this role to the Isle of Man and the Channel Islands respectively. On the Irish Sea, Norse Irish Ferries replaced their traditional Liverpool - Belfast freighters in 1997 with the purpose built ro-paxes *Lagan Viking* and *Mersey Viking* and Merchant Ferries launched a rival route in 1999 between Liverpool and Dublin.

The third element of 'ro-pax' describes the use of accommodation on traditional freight ships, often with extremely basic accommodation, to allow limited passengers to be carried. Seeking to exploit the improving facilities on board their ships for truckers, operators are

NORTHERN EUROPE'S RO-PAX FERRIES

Name of Vessel(s)	Operator	YrBlt*	GRT	Pax	Freight
Cornouailles (*Havelet*)	Brittany Ferries	1977	6918t	500P	37L
European Gateway (*Rostock Link*)	Townsend Thoresen	1981*	4263t	330P	92T
Saga Wind (*Sea Wind*)	TT-Line	1984*	15879t	260P	600R
Darnia (*Nord Neptunus*)	Sealink	1982*	8547t	412P	62T
Baltic Ferry/Nordic Ferry + (*Pride of Suffolk/Pride of Flanders*)	Townsend Thoresen	1986*	16776t	612P	81L
Kraka/Lodbrog/Heimdal	DSB	1988-9*	9986t	540P	74T
Nils Dacke/Robin Hood $	TT-Line	1989	24745t	290P	100L
Graip (*Chong Ming Dao*)	Nordstrom & Thulin	1988*	19779t	1600P	88T
Hansa Link (*Moby Rider*)	Nordo-Link	1989*	22508t	200P	140T
Lubeck Link/Malmo Link	Nordo-Link	1990*	33163t	240P	250T
Translubeca	Poseidon	1990	24724t	84P	175T
Stena Challenger/Stena Traveller (*TT Traveller*)	Stena Line	1991	18523t	500P	100L
Urd/Ask	DSB	1991*	11160t	610P	76T
Barfleur	Brittany Ferries	1992	20133t	1173P	125T
Gotaland	Sweferry	1992*	18060t	400P	811R
Rostock	DR	1992*	13788t	110P	598R
Pride of Burgundy (*P&OSL Burgundy*)	P&O	1993*	28138t	1420P	148T
Bergen	Fjord Line	1993	16000t	900P	40L
Isle of Innisfree	Irish Ferries	1995	22365	1700P	142T
Finnhansa series	Finncarriers	1995-6	32531t	112P	250T
Nils Dacke/Robin Hood	TT-Line	1996	26500t	308P	200T
Stena Jutlandica	Stena Line	1996	29691t	1500P	166T
Maren Mols/Mette Mols	Mols Linien	1996	14221t	600P	100T
Finnsailor	Finnlink	1996*	20783t	119P	146T
Mecklenburg-Vorpommern	DFO	1997	35000t	1000P	2150R
Isle of Inishmore	Irish Ferries	1997	34000t	2200P	122T
Gotland (*Finnarrow*)	Gotland	1997	25996t	200P	160T
Mersey Viking/Lagan Viking	Norse Irish Ferries	1997	17000t	340P	160T
Stena Seapacer series	Stena Line	1998-9	30500t	440P	140L
Brave Merchant series	Cenargo	1998	22046t	210P	166T
Ben-my-Chree/Commodore Clipper	IOMSP/Commodore	1998-9	12500t	500P	90T
New P&O design	P&O	2001	60600t	1360P	400T

* Ro-Pax conversion from ro-ro vessel. Date given is that of conversion.
+ Reconverted back to full freight-only specification in 1995.
$ Converted to full passenger configuration in 1993 becoming *Nils Holgersson* and *Peter Pan*
Name and operator given is that of time of construction/conversion. Where the current name is different to that of the original, it is shown in parentheses.

opening their sailings to a limited number of passengers. These services are seldom advertised to the travel trade to any great extent but provide a valuable alternative to conventional crossings. Early editions of this book mention the use by Norfolk Line of their then *Duchess of Holland, Duke of Holland II* and *Duke of Norfolk* and Townsend Thoresen's Dover-Zeebrugge 'European' trio in this manner. This facility has been longstanding on DFDS's freighters to Scandinavia but in a more recent move, P&O have begun to advertise their Irish Sea freight services as 'Value' Routes to motorists. Stena have also utilised spare capacity on the Harwich - Hook service's freight ships *Stena Seatrader* and *Rosebay* to provide 'ro-pax' back-up to the HSS.

Within this book, a wide range of ferries can be found; it is clear that there is also a wide range of 'ro-pax' ferries. The term is diverse, encompassing the finest of cruiseferries and the humblest of freighters. Each provide a unique role whether it is on the flagship services such as Gothenburg - Frederikshavn, operating between the economic margins of the European ferry industry, such as the Channel Islands or faithfully plodding alongside the more glamorous fast ferries. Whether the years to come will continue to see 'ro-pax' ferries grow in number or whether builders and operators will dream up new phrases to describe the vessels of the future, only time and the next generations of superferries and superfreighters will tell.

Matthew Punter

Isle of Innisfree (*Miles Cowsill*)

SCANDINAVIA AND NORTHERN EUROPE REVIEW

This review takes the form of a voyage along the coast of The Netherlands and Germany, round the southern tip of Norway, down the Kattegat, through the Great Belt and into the Baltic (with a diversion to the Oresund) then up to the Gulf of Finland ending in the Gulf of Bothnia

In a surprise move, the car transport company E H Harms announced that they were to launch a new ferry service across the mouth of the River Elbe between Cuxhaven and Brunsbüttel with the former Scandlines ferries *Prinsesse Anne-Marie* and *Prinsesse Elisabeth*. These two popular vessels had operated on both the Århus - Kalundborg and Helsingør - Helsingborg routes and were thought likely to go to scrap until their future for a third career was secured. Later it was announced that a third Scandlines ferry - the former train ferry *Najaden* - was to be acquired but hopes that the service would start in 1998 were dashed by problems in securing a satisfactory site on the eastern bank for a terminal (at Cuxhaven an existing ro-ro berth will be used). The service is now planned to start in June 1999.

The elderly *Esbjerg* and *Nordby*, on Scandlines' service from Esbjerg to the island of Fanø, were replaced by two larger vessels giving almost double the vehicle capacity - the Fenja and Menja. New terminals with increased vehicle handling areas were built on both sides. The two former vessels were sold to Nigerian interests later in the year. The port of Esbjerg lost the weekly visit by the Smyril Line *Norröna* from Tórshavn in the Faroes, with the summer only service being switched back to the more northerly port of Hanstholm. The time saved by the shorter voyage enabled the call at Lerwick in Shetland to be re-instated. For the first time, the service was continued through the winter, although only between Tórshavn and Hanstholm.

Services in the Skagerrak operated much as in 1997, but poorer summer weather meant that Color Line's fast monohull ferry *Pegasus Two* had a less successful season, with a 14% cancellation rate between Larvik and Skagen. The larger *Silvia Ana L* on the Kristiansand - Hirtshals route was better able to cope with the summer gales and, whilst she will return to Color Line in the spring, the *Pegasus Two* will not and her service will not operate.

In the more sheltered Kattegat, services were also similar to 1997, the main difference being that services from Grenaa to Halmstad and Varberg were marketed as Stena Line rather than Lion Ferry, under the control of Stena in Göteborg rather than local management at Varberg. The Varberg vessel - the elderly *Lion Prince* - was renamed the *Stena Prince*. The Halmstad vessel *Lion King* had been replaced by the *Stena Nautica* shortly before the start of the year; this vessel had operated the service in 1995, at that time also called the *Lion King*. Towards the end of the year, Stena Line announced that the future of the Halmstad service was to be reviewed in the light of declining traffic and the prospect of the ending of duty-free. In the event, the service ceased at the end of January 1999 and the *Stena Nautica* replaced the *Stena Prince* on the Varberg service.

1998 also saw the first full year of competition between Stena Line's HSS *Stena Carisma* and Sea Containers' *SuperSeaCat One* between Göteborg and Frederikshavn. Both operators seem to have maintained a reliable service, although it is difficult to determine which has proved the most popular as Stena Line do not publish separate fast ferry figures.

As part of their general retrenchment from European operations, Holyman sold their 50% share of the Århus - Kalundborg Cat-Link fast ferry operation to fellow Australian company InCat. As a builder of high speed craft, InCat's role was very much to provide the hardware and, operationally, the company fell under the control of Scandlines - and began trading as Scandlines Cat-Link. The three existing ships - the two 78 metre InCat *Cat-Link I* and *Cat Link II* and a 79 metre Austal Ships *Cat Link III* - were replaced by two 91 metre InCat craft named *Cat-Link IV* and *Cat-Link V*. Their larger capacity and higher speed enabled the service to be operated by one less craft but with increased capacity. The two smaller "InCats" were disposed of and the *Cat-Link III* became a reserve vessel.

Later in the year it was announced that Scandlines and Mols-Linien would combine their Kattegat ferry operations, with the *Cat-Link IV* and *Cat-Link V* moving to Mols-Linien, who would then operate from Sjællands Odde to both Ebeltoft and Århus. The Scandlines Århus - Kalundborg ro-pax service with the former Sealink operated *Ask* and *Urd* would cease. At the same time Scandlines bought out the InCat share of Cat-Link and took a 40% share in Mols-Linien.

These happenings were largely the result of events further south, with the final opening of the fixed link between the Danish islands of Funen and Sjælland. Whilst the rail link, using a combination of multi-span bridge and tunnel opened in 1997, the road link, crossing the navigable part of the Great Belt on a giant suspension bridge, had to wait until 14th June 1998. The 38 billion DKR scheme means that over 90% of journeys within Denmark can now be accomplished without water transport - although for many this is fairly circuitous and a ferry journey is quicker. It did, however, mean the immediate end of both Scandlines' Knudshoved - Halsskov service and also the privately owned Vognmandsruten's route between Nyborg and Korsør. There could scarcely have been a dry eye when, amid much hooting, the *Arveprins Knud* operated the final Scandlines service at 22.15 from Knudshoved to Halsskov. She was joined on her passage by the remainder of the fleet (except the laid up *Sprogø*). The ships then proceeded in convoy, across the Great Belt, diverting so as to pass under the new bridge, the last vessel arriving around midnight. The three older ships - the *Arveprins Knud, Sprogø* and *Romsø* were immediately laid up and are unlikely to operate for Scandlines again. The modern converted freight ferries *Kraka* and *Lodbrog* were also laid up, although the *Kraka* was soon in action again as a replacement for the *Urd* on the Århus - Kalundborg route, whilst she was being re-engined. Sister vessel *Heimdal*, not owned by Scandlines, returned to her owners Mercandia.

The four Sunderland built Superflex vessels of Vognmandsruten were also laid up, the *Difko Fyn* at Helsingborg in Sweden in the care of HH-Ferries, who are able to use her whenever one of their own vessels is not available.

The ending of their principal domestic route was not the only major event for Danish Scandlines. In July they merged with DFO of Germany to form Scandlines AG, a German registered company, jointly owned by Deutsche Bahn (German Railways) and the Danish Government. In a unique joint venture between two EU countries, the former operations of Scandlines A/S and DFO are now run as a single international company with offices in both Rostock and København. Remaining Danish domestic services are operated by subsidiary company SFDS. Scandlines AB of Sweden remains a separate entity, albeit operating in conjunction with the Danish/German company, but may be merged at a later date.

On a major crossing not threatened by a fixed link, that between Rødby and Puttgarden, the four new train ferries operated their first full year on the intensive service. Some of the older vessels found new careers - the 1974 built *Deutschland* sold to El Salam of Egypt and renamed the *Al Salam 97* and the *Dronning Margrethe II* re-introduced with a German crew running freight-only services on both that and the Gedser - Rostock route. A plan for the *Danmark* to have her engines removed and to be permanently berthed at Puttgarden as a duty-paid supermarket at, selling goods to Danish visitors at lower German prices has not yet come to fruition.

Competition on this busy route was threatened all year but did not materialise. In 1997, Norwegian owned Easy Line initially hoped to run the former Moss - Horten ferries *Ostfold* and *Vestfold* but that fell through. They then hoped to charter two of the Scandlines operated but Mercandia owned *Heimdal*, *Kraka* and *Lodbrog* but were frustrated when Scandlines purchased the latter two. In 1998 they tried to purchase two Superflex vessels *Antonio Machado* and *Miguel Hernandez* from their Spanish owners but were again frustrated. Finally they did manage to acquire a vessel in the form of the *Anja #11* (registered name

How to profit from passenger pleasure

Even as competition amongst operators toughens, there is still one great opportunity for increasing profits and building customer loyalty. The potential that results from extra creativity and efficiency in the provision of onboard hotel services.

Which is why a **free audit service,** from the people who know most about managing successful onboard services, could provide your first step to steering a **more profitable course** in the future.

With fresh ideas from Granada Retail Catering's own specialist marine division, you really can **increase customer uptake** and enhance revenues. And, through introducing more effective purchasing and management controls, we can certainly **improve your margins.**

At Granada Retail Catering, we understand the challenges of on board services for both short and long haul operations – whether for private passengers or commercial freight. Our free audit service is not just a valuable review of your existing facilities, it could be your introduction to the many **exciting options and opportunities** that lie ahead.

GRANADA RETAIL CATERING

Granada Retail Catering, Mulliner House, Flanders Road, London W4 1XQ
Tel: 0181 995 8200 Fax: 0181 995 7594

Anja 11), formerly the *Mercandia I* on Mercandia's Kattegatbroen Juelsminde - Kalundborg service which ceased in 1996. However, they placed her on the Gedser - Rostock route, where the Scandlines service of one fast ferry and one conventional vessel was much less intensive. A second vessel (the *Gitte 3*) will start at Easter 1999.

During the autumn, Easy Line agreed to link up with Difko, owners of the former Vognmandsruten operation, to utilise their vessels on the Rødby - Puttgarden route although services did not start in 1998.

Scandlines also made changes on the Gedser - Rostock route by replacing the *Rostock Link* with the former Great Belt train ferry *Kronprins Frederik*, running as a vehicle ferry. The former vessel, built as the Townsend Thoresen freight ferry *European Gateway*, had been acquired when they took over the service in 1996. She subsequently moved to subsidiary company Amber Line to operate in freight-only mode between Århus and Liepaja (Latvia).

On the Oresund, the three modern ferries *Aurora af Helsingborg*, *Hamlet* and *Tycho Brahe* continued to provide a twenty minute service (as against the 'customer-unfriendly' 22 minute frequency when the *Hamlet* replaced the two 'Prinsesses' in 1997) and HH-Ferries continued their half hourly service (with some forty minute gaps to provide recovery time). As mentioned, HH-Ferries now have the use of the *Difko Fyn* should one of their own vessels be unavailable and a number of terminal changes have been made to enable the carriage of foot passengers.

The future of this route is, of course, threatened by the new Oresund tunnel, due to open in 2000. Running from near København Airport to the South of the city, to near Malmö, the fixed link will be several miles away from this route and a København - Helsingborg trip would take much longer, so some form of ferry service looks likely to continue, although perhaps at reduced frequency. However, the København - Helsingborg rail freight service and the Swedish operated Limhamn - Dragør car and passenger service will cease. Indeed, the latter route looks likely to end in the autumn as Scandlines see no point in operating unprofitably over winter 1999/2000 on a route which has no long term future.

The Rostock - Trelleborg service was, by the autumn, in the situation which its operators had hoped it would be in rather earlier - operated by two large, modern custom built train and vehicle ferries. Whilst the German *Mecklenburg-Vorpommern* was introduced in late 1996, her performance in 1997 was hampered by failures in her novel combined bulbous bow/bow rudder system and she was unable to put to sea in high winds. In 1998, after much head scratching and argument with her builders, modifications were completed and it was possible for her to operate in all sea conditions. Scandlines AB's new vessel, the Spanish built *Skåne*, eventually arrived in August - nearly a year late. She replaced the *Götaland*, which was placed on a freight-only service between Trelleborg and Travemünde and also enabled reserve vessel the *Rostock* to be retired (and subsequently sold).

On the other Sweden - Germany route - that between Trelleborg and Sassnitz - there was no change in hardware but there was a change of terminal. At the beginning of the year, the old installation at Sassnitz was replaced by a new one at nearby Mukran - which was rather confusingly renamed "Fährhafen Sassnitz" (Sassnitz Ferry Port). DFO extended their Mukran - Rønne (Bornholm) summer service to Ystad in Southern Sweden. The service is worked by the elderly *Rügen*.

For the first time since she was introduced in 1977, Silja Line's Gas Turbine Ship *Finnjet* did not operate between Travemünde and Helsinki during winter 1997/98. Instead she was placed on the booming Helsinki - Tallinn route. In response, Finnlines (who once operated the *Finnjet* themselves) introduced their own twice weekly Helsinki - Travemünde service using the *Finnarrow*. This 200 passenger ro-pax vessel was built in Indonesia as the *Gotland* for Rederi AB Gotland and was on charter to Silja Line owned SeaWind Line at the time she was purchased. The service continued until the *Finnjet* resumed her cross Baltic service in June and the *Finnarrow* was then switched to the freight-only Finnlink Kapellskär - Naantali

Silvia Ann L *(Miles Cowsill)*

ONBOARD LEISURE

Onboard Leisure is a company specialising in the supply of Gaming and Coin Operated leisure equipment to the ferry and cruise line industry.

As a company operating exclusively on sea going vessels, Onboard Leisure is able to offer its customers a wide range of Gaming and Leisure options designed to enhance both the passenger sailing experience and the on board leisure spend.

We supply all forms of coin operated gaming and amusement machines, together with a comprehensive Casino package including all equipment, fully trained croupiers and control systems. We are also able to offer our services in the management of passenger facilities.

As part of Kunick Leisure Limited, the experience and dedication of our staff is supported by our ability to offer machine management and security services developed by the largest independent amusement machine operator in the United Kingdom and recognised as being in the forefront of technological advances.

Why not call us in the Isle of Man and let us demonstrate how we can enhance your profits? We look forward to hearing from you.

**Onboard Leisure Limited, 1 Brewery Court, Bridge Street, Castletown, Isle of Man IM9 1ET.
Telephone +44 (1624) 825032. Fax +44 (1624) 825033.**

Stena Germanica *(Philippe Holthof)*

service. She was replaced by the 96 passenger *Translubeca* of German subsidiary Poseidon Schiffahrt, a company which previously operated a joint service with Finnlines but which Finnlines had taken over at the start of the year. The *Finnarrow* did not resume the cross-Baltic service in the autumn, remaining with Finnlink.

Finnlines' Helsinki - Travemünde service was due to receive a fillip during the year with the introduction of the *Finnclipper* and the *Finneagle*, two 440 passenger ro-pax ships which had been ordered from Spain by Stena RoRo and purchased 'on the stocks' by Finnlines in the early part of the year. However, due to production delays, they did not enter service in 1998.

It was all change for the service from the Swedish mainland to the holiday island of Gotland from the start of the year. The concession granted to the Nordström and Thulin owned Gotlandslinjen, which had been awarded ten years previously, came to an end and Rederi AB Gotland, the traditional operator of these services, jointly with Silja Line, started 'Destination Gotland'. Having not operated a service on their own for ten years, Rederi AB Gotland had, nevertheless, continued as a ship owning and management company and had acquired additional vessels. Thus on 1st January the *Nord Gotlandia* and the *Gute* were replaced by the *Visby* (which had operated the service when Rederi AB Gotland ran the service ten years previously and briefly under charter to the newcomer) and the *Thjelvar*. Both vessels had been operating in the UK in 1997 - the Visby as the *Stena Felicity* between Fishguard and Rosslare and the *Thjelvar* as the *Sally Star* between Ramsgate and Dunkerque. Backup freight services in the summer period were to be provided by the *Gute* (which had served with Sally Ferries as the *Sally Sun* and sister company SeaWind Line as the *Sea Wind II*), replacing the *Nord Neptunus* (formerly Sealink's *Darnia* on the Stranraer - Larne route). Only the summer fast ferry was the same as Gotlandslinjen had run - the chartered 74m InCat *Patricia Olivia*. However 1998 was her last season on the route as, when the franchise was awarded, an order was placed for a monohull ferry to be delivered in time for the 1999 summer season. Unlike previously operated aluminium hulled craft, the new vessel will be built of steel and it is hoped to operate her all year round. In December it was announced that Silja Line were to sell their 40% share in the company to Rederi AB Gotland.

The new service was not without teething troubles, as for a time the *Thjelvar* was prohibited from sailing due to deficiencies in her safety equipment and, for a time afterwards, had to operate in a freight-only role. It was also found that she was unable to take some of the highest modern lorries. Meanwhile, Gotlandslinjen's owners Nordström and Thulin were quick to dispose of their fleet - with the *Nord Gotlandia* going to Eckerö Line as the *Nordlandia*, the *Graip* being sold to the Chinese Government and becoming the *Chong Ming Dao*, and the *Nord Neptunus* going to ESCO as the *Neptunia*. Nordström and Thulin were quick to cease all involvement with ferries and sold their 50% share in EstLine to ESCO. They did not re-bid for the Gotland franchise and their experience with passenger shipping had been greatly soured by the tragic loss of EstLine's *Estonia* in 1994.

The vibrant Finland - Estonia market continued to grow. Eckerö Line (as Eestin Linjat was renamed) replaced the *Apollo* (formerly the *Corbiere*) with the larger *Nordlandia* (see above), whilst, as also mentioned, Silja Line placed the gas turbine *Finnjet* on this traffic for the winter. Tallink also introduced a new ship - the *Fantaasia*, formerly Lion Ferry's *Lion King*. At the same time, the *Vana Tallinn* returned to Tallink control following a year operating with TH Ferries, meaning that Tallink were now running no fewer than four ships.

If this were not enough, a new fast ferry service was started by Nordic Jet line, a joint German/Norwegian company. They put into service the *Nordic Jet*, a Kværner Fjellstrand JumboCat 60m, sister vessel of Emeraude Line's *Solidor 3*. Smaller than many current fast ferries, the new service - the first car-carrying fast ferry since Viking Line chartered the *Condor 10* in 1995 - proved so successful that a second vessel was ordered for 1999. Less successful was Tallink's attempt to start a similar service. A firm called Jetson Coast Link were planning to launch a fast ferry service between Sweden and Finland to start in 1998. However, when they learnt that the fast ferry ordered - from Marinteknik in Singapore - was going to be late, the order was cancelled. Tallink announced that they would charter her but in fact construction was so delayed that she was still undergoing sea trials in August, when the Scandinavian summer season was rapidly coming to an end. Plans were shelved until 1999 and, instead, Tallink are to operate the former *Cat-Link III*, an Austal Ships Auto Express 79 craft, to be called the *Tallink Autoexpress*.

In the spring, EstLine at last managed to start a full daily service between Tallinn and Stockholm through the introduction of the *Baltic Kristina*, formerly ScanSov Line's *Illich*, working opposite the *Regina Baltica*. Before that, alternate day's services were provided by the *Neptunia* (formerly the *Nord Neptunus*) with limited passenger capacity. At the time of the *Estonia* disaster in 1994, her near sister, the *Mare Balticum* (ex *Diana II* of Viking Line) had recently been acquired in order to operate a daily service, but when the *Regina Baltica* was acquired in 1996, she was almost immediately chartered to Tallink, where she still serves as the *Meloodia*.

Sweden - Finland services were almost unchanged from 1997 - although big changes are planned for 1999 to cope with the abolition of duty-free. The elderly *Fennia* moved north to the Pietarsaari - Skellefteå route and the summer replacement on her usual route - that between Vaasa and Umeå - was the *Stena Invicta*, rendered surplus following the formation of P&O Stena Line in March. She bore the marketing title 'Wasa Jubilee' but was not officially renamed.

Nick Widdows

DECK EQUIPMENT

DURASTIC
Decks for all Reasons

Durastic Ltd is one of the world's leading suppliers and installers of marine deck covering systems offering a wide range of specifications. From primary underlays; including Durastic's lightweight underlay, to weatherdecks, sound reduction and A60 Solas rated materials; all with associated finishes such as carpets, vinyls and epoxy resins.

A full specification service and experienced, supervised contract teams ensure the best deck coverings are installed to the highest standards. Durastic's products are covered by International Certifications and produced at its ISO 9002 Quality Assured manufacturing facility.

The company's 76 years of technical expertise is reflected in the fact that Durastic is frequently nominated as a supplier and sub-contractor by leading ship owners and is regularly called upon to supervise contracts overseas. For further information on products, specifications or contract services, contact:

Mr J Gallagher
Durastic Ltd
Howdon Yard
Willington Quay
Wallsend
Tyne & Wear NE28 6UL
United Kingdom..

Tel: +44 (0) 191 295 3333
Fax: +44 (0) 191 263 2173

Branch offices: Glasgow, Liverpool, Southampton, Jarrow and representation in 20 countries worldwide.

DURASTIC LTD
FLOORING AND DECKING
A Member of the Rigblast Group

Decks for all reasons

As one of the world's leading suppliers of marine deck covering systems... we can provide a complete service package. From design and specification support through materials supply to installation.

From decorative deck finishes to functional underlays all manufactured to ISO9002

DURASTIC LTD
FLOORING AND DECKING

Howdon Yard, Willington Quay, Wallsend, Tyne & Wear NE28 6UL, United Kingdom..
Tel: +44 (0) 191 295 3333   Fax: +44 (0) 191 2173

A Member of the Rigblast Group

> # SECTION 1 - GB & IRELAND PASSENGER OPERATIONS
> ## BRITTANY FERRIES

THE COMPANY *Brittany Ferries* is the trading name of *BAI SA*, a French private sector company and the operating arm of the *Brittany Ferries Group*. The UK operations are run by *BAI (UK) Ltd*, a UK private sector company, wholly owned by the *Brittany Ferries Group*. Passenger services from Poole, previously marked as *Truckline*, are now marked as *Brittany Ferries*.

MANAGEMENT Group Managing Director: Jean-Michel Masson, **Managing Director UK & Ireland:** Ian Carruthers, **Marketing Director:** David Longden.

ADDRESS Millbay Docks, PLYMOUTH, Devon PL1 3EW.

TELEPHONE Administration: +44 (0)1752 227941, **Reservations:** *All Services:* 0990 360360 (UK only), *Portsmouth:* +44 (0)1705 892200, *Plymouth:* +44 (0)1752 252200, **Fax:** +44 (0)1752 600698, **Telex:** 86878.

INTERNET Website: http://www.brittany-ferries.com *(English, French)*

ROUTES OPERATED *All year:* Roscoff - Plymouth (6 hrs (day), 6 hrs - 7 hrs 30 mins (night); *(5,6)*; up to 3 per day (summer), 1 per week (winter)), St Malo - Portsmouth (8 hrs 45 mins (day), 10 hrs 30 mins - 11 hrs 30 mins (night); *(2 (summer), 2,4 (winter))*; 1 per day), Caen (Ouistreham) - Portsmouth (6 hrs (day), 6 hrs 15 mins - 8 hrs (night); *(3,4)*; 3 per day), Plymouth - Santander (Spain) (24 hrs; *(6)*; 2 per week (summer), *(1)*; irregular (winter)), Roscoff - Cork (14 hrs; *(6)*; 1 per week), Cherbourg - Poole (4 hrs 15 mins; *(1)*; up to 2 per day). *Winter only:* St Malo - Plymouth (8 hrs; *(2,5)*; 1 per week.

CONVENTIONAL FERRIES

1	BARFLEUR	20133t	92	19k	1173P	550C	125T	BA	Helsinki, FI	FR
2	BRETAGNE	24534t	89	21k	2030P	580C	40L	BA	St Nazaire, FR	FR
3	DUC DE NORMANDIE	13505t	78	21k	1500P	350C	44T	BA	Heusden, NL	FR
4	NORMANDIE	27541t	92	20k	2263P	630C	66T	BA	Turku, FI	FR
5	QUIBERON	11813t	75	20k	1302P	300C	35L	BA2	Rendsburg, GY	FR
6	VAL DE LOIRE	31395t	87	21k	1800P	550C	114T	BA	Bremerhaven, GY	FR

BARFLEUR Built for the *Truckline* Cherbourg - Poole service to replace two passenger vessels - the CORBIERE (see the APOLLO, *Langeland-Kiel Linjen*) and the TREGASTEL (see the ST CLAIR, *P&O Scottish Ferries*) - and to inaugurate a year round passenger service. In 1999 the *Truckline* service was marketed as *Brittany Ferries* and she was repainted into full *Brittany Ferries* livery.

BRETAGNE Built for the Santander - Plymouth and Roscoff - Cork services (with two trips per week between Roscoff and Plymouth). In 1993 she was transferred to the St Malo - Portsmouth service. She operates on the Santander - Portsmouth route during the winter.

DUC DE NORMANDIE Built as the PRINSES BEATRIX for *Stoomvaart Maatschappij Zeeland (Zeeland Steamship Company)* of The Netherlands for their Hoek van Holland - Harwich service. In September 1985 sold to *Brittany Ferries* and chartered back to *SMZ*, continuing to operate for them until the introduction of the KONINGIN BEATRIX in May 1986. In June 1986 delivered to *Brittany Ferries* and inaugurated the Caen - Portsmouth service.

NORMANDIE Built for the Caen - Portsmouth route.

QUIBERON Ordered by *Lion Ferry AB* of Sweden. The contract was sold to *Svenska Lastbils AB (Svelast)* of Sweden (a subsidiary of *Statens Järnvägar (SJ), Swedish State Railways*) before delivery

DISCOVER THE ROUTE TO A PERFECT HOLIDAY

SECTION 1

AWARD WINNING CRUISE-FERRIES

TO BRITTANY, NORMANDY & SPAIN

SAVE MILES OF DRIVING

SAIL BY DAY OR OVERNIGHT

GREAT CHOICE OF HOLIDAYS

Sailing with your car to Holiday France or Spain?

Our modern cruise-ferries, with their award-winning service and value, land you closer to where you'd like to be, saving you wasted fuel and effort.

Brochures: Ferry Guide • Gite Holidays • Holiday Homes in France & Spain
Golf Breaks • Hotel Breaks

Brittany Ferries
The Holiday Fleet

BROCHURES **0990 143 537** RESERVATIONS **0990 360 360**
OR SEE YOUR TRAVEL AGENT

Visit us at: www.brittany-ferries.com

and she was delivered to them as the NILS DACKE. She was initially chartered to *Svenska Rederi AB Öresund* (another *SJ* subsidiary) for their service between Malmö (Sweden) and Travemünde (Germany). Sister vessel the GUSTAV VASA (now NORRÖNA of *Smyril Line*) was owned by *Lion Ferry AB* of Sweden and was also chartered to *SRÖ*. In 1976, *Svelast* took over the marketing of the service and it was operated under the name *Malmö-Travemünde Linjen*, with *Lion Ferry AB* operating it as agents. Later in 1976, *Svelast* and *Linjebuss International* (a subsidiary of *Stockholms Rederi AB Svea*) formed a jointly owned subsidiary called *Saga-Linjen* and *Lion Ferry AB* continued as administrative operator. In 1981 a joint marketing agreement was reached with the rival German owned *TT-Linie*, (running between Travemünde and Trelleborg (Sweden)) and the two services were marketed as *TT-Saga-Line*. In April 1982 the NILS DACKE was chartered to *Brittany Ferries* with an option to purchase. She was renamed the QUIBERON and placed on the Santander - Plymouth and Roscoff - Cork services; she also operated between Roscoff and Plymouth. The GUSTAV VASA continued as sole vessel on the Malmö - Travemünde route for a further year until the service was withdrawn. The QUIBERON was purchased by *Brittany Ferries* in 1984 and re-registered in France. Following the delivery of the BRETAGNE in July 1989, she was transferred to the Roscoff - Plymouth service.

VAL DE LOIRE Built as the NILS HOLGERSSON for *TT-Line* of Sweden and Germany (jointly owned with *Wallenius Rederi AB* of Sweden) for their service between Travemünde and Trelleborg. In 1991 purchased by *Brittany Ferries* for entry into service in spring 1993. After a major rebuild, she was renamed the VAL DE LOIRE and introduced onto the Plymouth - Santander and Roscoff - Plymouth/Cork service.

CONDOR FERRIES

THE COMPANY *Condor Ferries Ltd* is a Channel Islands private sector company owned by *Commodore Shipping*, Guernsey.

MANAGEMENT Managing Director: Robert Provan, **General Manager, Sales & Marketing:** Nicholas Dobbs.

ADDRESS Condor House, New Harbour Road South, Hamworthy, POOLE, Dorset BH15 4AJ.

TELEPHONE Administration: +44 (0)1202 207207, **Reservations:** +44 (0)1305 761551, **Fax: Admin:** +44 (0)1202 685184, **Reservations:** +44 (0)1305 760776.

INTERNET Website: http://www.condorferries.co.uk *(English)*

ROUTES OPERATED Fast Car Ferries: *Winter Only:* Weymouth - St Peter Port (Guernsey) (2 hrs 15 mins) - St Helier (Jersey via Guernsey) (3 hrs 35 mins) (Mon, Wed, Fri, Sat, Sun); *(4)*; 1 per day. *Spring and Autumn:* Weymouth - St Peter Port (Guernsey) (2 hrs) - St Helier (Jersey via Guernsey) (3 hrs 25 mins); *(4)*; 1 per day, Poole - St Peter Port (Guernsey) (2 hrs 30 mins) - St Helier (Jersey via Guernsey) (3 hrs 50 mins); *(3)*; 1 per day. *Summer:* Weymouth - St Peter Port (Guernsey) (2 hrs) - St Helier (Jersey via Guernsey) (3 hrs 15 mins) - St Malo (via Guernsey and Jersey) (5 hrs); *(4)*; 1 per day; Poole - St Peter Port (Guernsey) (2 hrs 30 mins) - St Helier (Jersey via Guernsey) (3 hrs 45 mins) - St Malo (via Jersey and Guernsey) (5 hrs 25 mins); *(3)*; 1 per day, Poole - St Peter Port (Guernsey) (2 hrs 30 mins) - St Helier (Jersey via Guernsey) (3 hrs 45); *(3)*; 1 per day. Vessels are likely to be moved between routes.

Fast Passenger Ferries: *Spring and Autumn:*. St Malo - St Helier (Jersey) (1 hr 10 mins) - St Peter Port (Guernsey via Jersey) (2 hrs) (Mon, Wed, Fri); *(5)*, 1 per day. *Summer only:* St Malo - St Helier (Jersey) (1 hr 10 mins) - St Peter Port (Guernsey via Jersey) (2 hrs 10 mins); *(5)*; 1 per day.

Conventional Ferry: No scheduled service at present. Service operates as required when the fast ferries are unable to sail.

Quiberon *(Miles Cowsill)*

Solidor 3 *(Miles Cowsill)*

CONVENTIONAL FERRY

| 1 | HAVELET | 6918t | 77 | 19k | 500P | 200C | 37L | BA2 | Bergen, NO | BA |

HAVELET Built as the CORNOUAILLES for *Brittany Ferries* and used mainly on their Roscoff - Plymouth service. In 1984 she was chartered to *SNCF* for use on their Dieppe - Newhaven service. This charter terminated at the end of 1985 and she was transferred to *Truckline Ferries*. From January 1986 she operated on their Cherbourg - Poole freight-only service and then, in April, she inaugurated the Caen - Portsmouth service for *Brittany Ferries* on a freight-only basis. In June she returned to *Truckline Ferries* and inaugurated a car and passenger service between Cherbourg and Poole. Until 1989 she operated between Cherbourg and Poole all year round, conveying passengers between April and October only. In 1989 she was renamed the HAVELET and sold to *Channel Island Ferries*, holding company of *British Channel Island Ferries*, operating between Poole and the Channel Islands. It was intended that, in 1993, she would be used in a freight-only role; however, due to the level of demand it was decided to allow her to carry passengers and she was crewed accordingly. In 1994, *British Channel Island Ferries* ceased operations and she was chartered to *Condor Ferries* to operate between Weymouth and the Channel Islands. She was withdrawn in autumn 1996 and laid up. In 1998 purchased by *Condor Ferries* for use as a back-up vessel in time of bad weather for the fast ferries between the Channel Islands and the UK. She will be withdrawn in 1999 when the new *Commodore Ferries* ro-pax vessel is delivered.

FAST CAR FERRIES

2•	CONDOR 10	3241t	93	37k	580P	80C	-	BA	Hobart, AL	SI
3	CONDOR EXPRESS	5005t	96	39k	774P	185C	-	A2	Hobart, AL	SI
4	CONDOR VITESSE	5005t	97	39k	774P	185C	-	A2	Hobart, AL	BA

CONDOR 10 InCat 74m catamaran. Built for the Holyman Group for use by *Condor Ferries*. In summer 1995 she was chartered to *Viking Line* to operate between Helsinki and Tallinn under the name 'VIKING EXPRESS II' (although not officially renamed). In summer 1996 she was chartered to *Stena Line* to operate between Fishguard and Rosslare. During recent northern hemisphere winters she has served for *TranzRail* of New Zealand for the service between Wellington (North Island) and Picton (South Island). In May 1997 she was transferred to *Holyman Sally Ferries* and inaugurated a new Ramsgate - Dunkerque (Est) service, replacing the Ramsgate - Dunkerque (Ouest) service of *Sally Ferries*. After further service in New Zealand during winter 1997/98, in summer 1998 she was due to operate between Weymouth, Guernsey and St Malo, but, in the event, the CONDOR VITESSE was chartered for that route and she was laid up.

CONDOR EXPRESS InCat 86m catamaran. She was delivered December 1996 and entered service in 1997. Mainly used on the Poole - Guernsey - Jersey service.

CONDOR VITESSE InCat 86m catamaran. Built speculatively and launched as the INCAT 044. Moved to Europe in summer 1997 and spent time in the both the UK and Denmark but was not used. In 1998, she was chartered to *Condor Ferries* and renamed the CONDOR VITESSE. Mainly used on the Weymouth - Guernsey - St Malo service.

FAST PASSENGER FERRY

| 5p | CONDOR 9 | 752t | 90 | 30k | 450P | 0C | 0L | - | Fareham, GB | GB |

CONDOR 9 FBM Marinteknik catamaran built for *Condor Ferries* and initially mainly used between the Channel Islands and Weymouth. In spring 1994, she was chartered to *Viking Line* and operated between Helsinki and Tallinn as the 'VIKING EXPRESS' (although not officially renamed). During winter 1994/95 she went on charter to the Caribbean. On return in mid 1995 she was laid up for a period before starting a new service between the Channel Islands and Torquay. She operated on this route during summer 1996. In 1997 she operated between Jersey and Poole and Jersey and St Malo and in 1998 operated between St Malo, Jersey, Guernsey and Sark. In 1999 she will operate between

St Malo, Jersey and Guernsey.

A new ro-pax vessel, the COMMODORE CLIPPER, is under construction for sister company *Commodore Ferries*. She will convey passengers and cars and operate in conjunction with *Condor Ferries* fast ferries, providing back-up when the fast ferries are unable to sail as well as an alternate route to the Channel Island. She is shown under *Commodore Ferries* in Section 3.

DFDS SEAWAYS

THE COMPANY *DFDS Seaways Ltd* is the passenger division of the *DFDS Group*, a Danish private sector company which operates in the UK through its subsidiary company *DFDS plc*. In 1981 *Tor Line* of Sweden and *Prinzen Linie* of Germany were taken over.

MANAGEMENT Managing Director *(DFDS plc):* Ebbe Pedersen, **Managing Director *(Scandinavian Seaways Ltd):*** John Crummie.

ADDRESS Scandinavia House, Parkeston Quay, HARWICH, Essex CO12 4QG.

TELEPHONE Administration: +44 (0)1255 243456, **Reservations: *Harwich:*** +44 (0)1255 240240, ***Newcastle:*** +44 (0)191-293 6262, **Fax:** +44 (0)1255 244370, **Telex:** 987542.

INTERNET Website: http://www.scansea.com *(English)*

ROUTES OPERATED *All year:* Harwich - IJmuiden - Esbjerg (call at IJmuiden northbound only) (23 hrs northbound, 19 hrs southbound; *(2)*; 3 per week or alternate days) (call at IJmuiden is for freight only), Newcastle - Kristiansand - Göteborg (25 hrs; *(5)*; 2 per week), Kristiansand - Göteborg (7 hrs (day), 13 hrs 30 min (night); *(5)* 1 per week), Harwich - Hamburg (20 hrs 30 mins; *(4)*; 3 per week (winter), every 2/4 days (summer), Newcastle (North Shields) - IJmuiden (near Amsterdam) (15 hrs; *(1,3)*; 3 per week (winter), 6 per week (summer)). **Summer only:** Newcastle (North Shields) -

The most relaxing route to Scandinavia, Germany & Holland.

Sail away on a sleek white *TravelLiner* from as little as £52 return or take your car and up to four people from £189. There's plenty for everybody to do on board. And a night in a comfortable cabin leaves you refreshed and ready for your onward journey. For a brochure call **0990 333 666** (ref 8B253).

SCANDINAVIAN SEAWAYS
A BETTER WAY OF TRAVELLING

Hamburg (23 hrs 30 mins *(1)*, 21 hrs *(4)*; *(1,4)*; see note). Note: during summer 1999, every third sailing from Newcastle by the ADMIRAL OF SCANDINAVIA goes to Hamburg and every third sailing by the PRINCE OF SCANDINAVIA from Hamburg goes to Newcastle. This results in a service every 3 days from Hamburg to Newcastle and a service from Newcastle to Hamburg at alternate 1 and 5 day intervals.

CONVENTIONAL FERRIES

1	ADMIRAL OF SCANDINAVIA	18888t	76	21k	1132P	400C	45L	BA	Rendsburg, GY	BA
2	DANA ANGLIA	19321t	78	21k	1372P	470C	45L	BA	Aalborg, DK	DK
3	KING OF SCANDINAVIA	13336t	74	22.5k	1100P	300C	38L	BA	Turku, FI	DK
4	PRINCE OF SCANDINAVIA	21545t	75	23k	1692P	385C	70T	AS	Lübeck, GY	DK
5	PRINCESS OF SCANDINAVIA	21545t	76	23k	1704P	385C	70T	AS	Lübeck, GY	DK

ADMIRAL OF SCANDINAVIA Built as the KRONPRINS HARALD for *Jahre Line* of Norway and used on their service between Oslo and Kiel (Germany). Acquired by *DFDS* in 1987, renamed the HAMBURG, re-registered in the Bahamas and replaced the PRINS HAMLET (see the NIEBOROW, *Polferries*) on the Harwich - Hamburg service. In March 1997 she was transferred to the Newcastle - IJmuiden and Newcastle - Hamburg services and renamed the ADMIRAL OF SCANDINAVIA. During winter 1997/98 she was temporarily transferred to the Harwich - Hamburg service.

DANA ANGLIA Built for the Harwich - Esbjerg service and has seldom operated elsewhere.

KING OF SCANDINAVIA Built as the PRINSESSAN BIRGITTA for *Göteborg-Frederikshavn-Linjen* (trading as *Sessan Line*) and *Ragne Rederi AB* of Sweden for their alternate day Göteborg - Travemünde service. The company was taken over by rival *Stena Line AB* in 1981 and later that year she was transferred to their Göteborg - Kiel route, the Travemünde route becoming freight-only. In 1982 a new PRINSESSAN BIRGITTA was delivered and she was renamed the STENA SCANDINAVICA. She remained on the Göteborg - Kiel route until 1987 when she was replaced by the new STENA GERMANICA. During summer 1987 she was chartered to *CoTuNav*, the Tunisian state shipping concern, and used on their service between Tunis and Marseilles (France) and Genova (Italy). In early 1988 a new STENA SCANDINAVICA was delivered and she was further renamed the SCANDINAVICA. In June 1988 she was taken on four months charter by *Sealink British Ferries* and used on additional sailings between Dover (Eastern Docks) and Calais (passenger and freight services) and Zeebrugge (freight-only services). In 1989, after further charter to *CoTuNav*, being renamed the TARAK L, she was sold to *Norway Line*. In 1990 she was renamed the VENUS, re-registered in Norway and took over the Bergen/Stavanger - Newcastle service from the JUPITER (9499t, 1966). In 1994 she was sold to *DFDS*, renamed the KING OF SCANDINAVIA and, in 1995, replaced the WINSTON CHURCHILL (8658t, 1967) on the Newcastle - Esbjerg/Hamburg services. In 1996 she operated alternate sailings from Newcastle to Hamburg and IJmuiden. In March 1997 she was replaced by the ADMIRAL OF SCANDINAVIA. During winter 1997/98 she returned to service, operating on the Newcastle - IJmuiden service. During summer 1998 she was again chartered to *CoTuNav* of Tunisia. During summer 1999 she will sail between Newcastle and IJmuiden.

PRINCE OF SCANDINAVIA Built as the TOR BRITANNIA for *Tor Line* of Sweden for their Amsterdam - Göteborg and Felixstowe - Göteborg services. She was acquired by *DFDS* in 1981 and subsequently re-registered in Denmark. Since winter 1983/4 she also operated on the Harwich - Esbjerg service with the DANA ANGLIA. She has also operated Newcastle - Esbjerg and Amsterdam - Göteborg. During winter 1989/90 she was used as an accommodation ship for refugees in Malmö. In 1991 renamed the PRINCE OF SCANDINAVIA following a major refurbishment. In summer 1994 and 1995 she operated on the IJmuiden (Netherlands) - Göteborg (Sweden) and IJmuiden - Kristiansand (Norway) service and did not serve the UK. In 1996 she was chartered to *CoTuNav* of Tunisia for service between Tunisia and Italy. In March 1997 she was transferred to the Harwich - Hamburg route. During winter 1997/98 she covered for other ferries which were being refitted, including the København - Oslo vessels, and had major modifications made at Gdansk. In summer 1998 she operated every third trip from Hamburg to

Newcastle instead of Harwich; this will be repeated in 1999.

PRINCESS OF SCANDINAVIA Built as the TOR SCANDINAVIA for *Tor Line* of Sweden for their Amsterdam - Göteborg and Felixstowe - Göteborg services. In 1979 she was used on a world trade cruise and was temporarily renamed the HOLLAND EXPO. Similar exercises were undertaken in 1980, 1982 and 1984, but on these occasions her temporary name was the WORLD WIDE EXPO. She was acquired by *DFDS* in 1981 and subsequently re-registered in Denmark. She has also operated on the Harwich - Esbjerg service. Between 1989 and 1993 she also operated Newcastle - Esbjerg and Amsterdam - Göteborg services. In 1991, following a major refurbishment, she was renamed the PRINCESS OF SCANDINAVIA. Since 1994, she generally operated on the Harwich - Göteborg and Newcastle - Göteborg routes. During winter 1998 she had major modifications made at Gdansk. In 1999 she will operate between Newcastle and Göteborg via Kristiansand.

EMERAUDE LINES

THE COMPANY *Emeraude Lines* is a French private sector company.

MANAGEMENT Commercial Manager (St Malo): Jean-Luc Griffon, **Managing Director (Jersey):** Gordon Forrest.

ADDRESS Terminal Ferry du Naye, PO Box 16, 35401, ST MALO Cedex, France.

TELEPHONE Administration & Reservations: *St Malo:* +33 (0)2 23 180 180, *Jersey:* +44 (0)1534 66566, **Fax:** *St Malo:* +33 (0) 2 23 181 500, *Jersey:* +44 (0)1534 68741.

INTERNET Email: sales@emeraude.co.uk **Website:** http://www.emeraudelines.com *(English)*

ROUTES OPERATED Fast Car Ferries: St Malo (France) - St Helier (Jersey) (1 hr 10 mins;*(1,2)*; up to 4 per day), St Malo - St Peter Port (Guernsey) (1 hr 50 mins;*(1,2)*; up to 3 per day).

Fast Passenger Ferries: St Helier - St Peter Port (1 hr; *(1,2)*; 1 per day), St Helier - Sark (1 hr; *3,4)*; 1 per day), Granville (France) - St Helier (1 hr 10 mins; *(3,4)*; 1 per day), Carteret (France) - St Helier (55 mins; *(3,4)*; see note), Diélette (France) - St Helier (1 hr 30 min; *(3,4)*; see note), Diélette - St Peter Port (1 hr 15 mins; *(3,4)*; see note). Note: on most days through the summer there is either a Carteret - Jersey, Diélette - Jersey or Diélette - Guernsey service. Timetable varies according to the Channel islands tidal conditions

FAST CAR FERRIES

1	SOLIDOR 3	2068t	96	33k	430P	51C	-	A	Omastrand, NO	FR
2	SOLIDOR 4	1064t	87	30k	325P	40C	-	A	Mandal, NO	FR

SOLIDOR 3 Kværner Fjellstrand JumboCat 60m catamaran. Built for *Emeraude Lines* to re-establish fast car ferry services.

SOLIDOR 4 Westamarin W5000CF catamaran. Built as the ANNE LISE. In 1992 renamed the MADIKERA and operated in the Caribbean. In 1995 she was sold to *Elba Ferry* and renamed the ELBA EXPRESS; she operated a summer service between Piombino (Italy) and Portoferráio (Elba). In 1999 sold to *Emeraude Lines* and renamed the SOLIDOR 4. After refurbishment, she is due to enter service in spring 1999. Specification above liable to change following refurbishment.

FAST PASSENGER FERRIES

3p	TRIDENT 5	211t	74	28k	200P	0C	0L	-	Mandal, NO	FR

TRIDENT 5 Westamarin W95 catamaran. Built as the VINGTOR for *Det Stavangereske Dampskibsselskab* of Norway and operated between Stavanger and Bergen. In 1990 sold to *Emeraude Lines* and renamed the TRIDENT 5. In 1998 undertook a charter in the West Indies. In 1999 she is expected operate from Carteret and Diélette to the Channel Islands and from Jersey to

the island of Sark. *A second fast passenger craft (4 above) called the Normandy Express will be used in summer 1998. No further information is available at time of going to press.*

FJORD LINE

THE COMPANY *Fjord Line* is 100% owned by *Bergen-Nordhordland Rutelag AS (BNR)*, a Norwegian company. It took over the Newcastle - Norway service from *Color Line* in December 1998.

MANAGEMENT Managing Director (UK): Dag Romslo, **Sales Director (UK):** Mike Wood.

ADDRESS Royal Quays, NORTH SHIELDS NE29 6EG.

TELEPHONE Administration: +44 (0)191-296 1313, **Reservations:** +44 (0)191-296 1313, **Fax:** +44 (0)191-296 1540, **Telex:** 537275.

INTERNET Website: http://www.hanstholmhavn.dk/fjordline/indexuk.htm *(Danish, Norwegian, English)*

ROUTES OPERATED Bergen - Haugesund - Stavanger - Newcastle - Bergen (triangular route), Bergen - Haugesund - Stavanger - Newcastle (Bergen - Stavanger (via 6 hrs), Stavanger - Newcastle (direct: 18 hrs 30 mins, via Bergen: 29 hrs 30 mins), Bergen - Newcastle (21 hrs 15 mins); *(1)*; 3 sailings Norway - Newcastle per week).

Fjord Line also operates between Norway and Denmark; see Section 6.

CONVENTIONAL FERRY

| 1 | JUPITER | 20581t | 75 | 19k | 1250P | 285C | 42T | BA | Nantes, FR | NO |

JUPITER Built as the WELLAMO for *EFFOA* of Finland for *Silja Line* services between Helsinki and Stockholm. In 1981 sold to *DFDS*, renamed the DANA GLORIA and placed onto the Göteborg - Newcastle and Esbjerg - Newcastle services. In 1983 she was moved to the København - Oslo service. In 1984 she was chartered to *Johnson Line* of Sweden for *Silja Line* service between Stockholm and Turku and renamed the SVEA CORONA - the name previously born by a sister vessel, which had been sold. This charter ended in 1985 and she returned to the København - Oslo service and resumed the name DANA GLORIA. During winter 1988/89 she was lengthened in Papenburg, Germany and in early 1989 she was renamed the KING OF SCANDINAVIA. She returned to the København - Oslo route; in 1990 a Helsingborg call was introduced. In 1994 she was sold to *Color Line* (as part of a deal which involved *DFDS* buying the VENUS from *Color Line*) and renamed the COLOR VIKING. In 1998 she was sold to *Fjord Line* and renamed the JUPITER.

IRISH FERRIES

THE COMPANY *Irish Ferries* is an Irish Republic private sector company, part of the *Irish Continental Group*. It was originally mainly owned by the state owned *Irish Shipping* and partly by *Lion Ferry AB* of Sweden. *Lion Ferry* participation ceased in 1977 and the company was sold into the private sector in 1987. Formerly state owned *B&I Line* was taken over in 1991 and from 1995 all operations were marketed as a single entity.

MANAGEMENT Group Managing Director: Eamon Rothwell, **Group Marketing Director:** Tony Kelly.

ADDRESS 2 Merrion Row, DUBLIN 2, Republic of Ireland.

TELEPHONE Administration: +353 (0)1 855 2222, **Reservations: *Dublin:*** +353 (0)1 638 3333, ***Cork:*** +353 (0)21 551995, ***Rosslare Harbour:*** +353 (0)53 33158, ***Holyhead:*** 0990 329129 (from UK only), ***Pembroke Dock:*** 0990 329543 (from UK only), ***National:*** 0990 171717 (from UK only), **Fax: *Dublin:*** +353 (0)1 661 0743, ***Cork:*** +353 (0)21 504651. ***24 hour information:*** +353 (0)1 661 0715.

Isle of Inishmore *(Miles Cowsill)*

INTERNET Email: info@irishferries.ie **Website:** http://www.irishferries.ie *(English)*

ROUTES OPERATED Conventional Ferries Dublin - Holyhead (3 hrs 30 mins; *(1)*; 2 per day), Rosslare - Pembroke Dock (4 hrs 15 mins; *(2)*; 2 per day), Rosslare - Cherbourg (17 hrs 30 mins; *(3)*; 1 or 2 per week), Rosslare - Roscoff (16 hrs; *(3)*; 1 or 2 per week) Note: the Rosslare - Cherbourg/Roscoff service operates on an irregular basis. **Fast Ferry:** Dublin - Holyhead (2 hrs; *(4)*; up to 4 per day).

CONVENTIONAL FERRIES

1	ISLE OF INISHMORE	34031t	97	21.3k	2200P	800C	122L	BA2	Krimpen, NL	IR
2	ISLE OF INNISFREE	22365t	95	21.5k	1700P	600C	142T	BA	Krimpen, NL	IR
3	NORMANDY	24872t	82	20.4k	2100P	480C	52L	BA2	Göteborg, SW	IR

ISLE OF INISHMORE Built for *Irish Ferries* to operate on the Holyhead - Dublin service.

ISLE OF INNISFREE Built for *Irish Ferries* to operate on the Holyhead - Dublin. In 1997 transferred to the Rosslare - Pembroke Dock service; for a short period, before modifications at Pembroke Dock were completed, she operated between Rosslare and Fishguard.

NORMANDY One of two vessels ordered by *Göteborg-Frederikshavn-Linjen* of Sweden (trading as *Sessan Linjen*) before the take over of their operations by *Stena Line AB* in 1981. Both were designed for the Göteborg - Frederikshavn route (a journey of about three hours). However, *Stena Line* decided in 1982 to switch the first vessel, the KRONPRINSESSAN VICTORIA (now the STENA EUROPE of *Stena Line AB*), to their Göteborg - Kiel (Germany) route since their own new tonnage for this route, being built in Poland, had been substantially delayed. She was modified to make her more suitable for this overnight route. Work on the second vessel - provisionally called the DROTTNING SILVIA - was suspended for a time but she was eventually delivered, as designed, in late

1982 and introduced onto the Göteborg - Frederikshavn route on a temporary basis pending delivery of new *Stena Line* ordered vessels. She was named the PRINSESSAN BIRGITTA, the existing ex *Sessan Linjen* vessel of the same name being renamed the STENA SCANDINAVICA (see the KING OF SCANDINAVIA, *DFDS Seaways*). In early 1983 she was substantially modified in a similar way to her sister. In June 1983 she was renamed the ST NICHOLAS, re-registered in Great Britain and entered service on five year charter to *Sealink UK* on the Harwich - Hoek van Holland route. In 1988 she was purchased and re-registered in The Bahamas. In 1989 she was sold to *Rederi AB Gotland* of Sweden and then chartered back. In 1991 she was renamed the STENA NORMANDY and inaugurated a new service between Southampton and Cherbourg. She was withdrawn in December 1996, returned to *Rederi AB Gotland* and renamed the NORMANDY. In 1997 she was chartered to *Tallink* and operated between Helsinki and Tallinn; this charter ended at the end of the year. In 1998 she was chartered to *Irish Ferries*. She briefly operated between Rosslare and Pembroke Dock before switching to the their French services.

FAST FERRY

4	JONATHAN SWIFT	5992t	99	39.5k	800P	200C	-	BA	Fremantle, AL	IR

JONATHAN SWIFT Austal Auto-Express 86 catamaran built for *Irish Ferries* for the Dublin - Holyhead route. Enters service in June 1999.

MERCHANT FERRIES

THE COMPANY *Merchant Ferries* is a British private sector company, owned by *Cenargo*. A 50% share owned by *The Mersey Docks and Harbour Co* was sold to *Cenargo* in 1997.

MANAGEMENT General Manager: Richard Harrison.

ADDRESS North Quay, Heysham Harbour, MORCAMBE, Lancs LA3 2UL.

TELEPHONE Administration: +44 (0)1524 855018, **Reservations:** +44 (0)1524 855018, **Fax:** +44 (0)1524 852527.

INTERNET Email: Merchant.Ferries@btinternet.com

ROUTE OPERATED Liverpool - Dublin (7 hrs; *(1,2)*; 2 per day). *Merchant Ferries* also operate a freight-only service between Heysham and Dublin; see Section 3.

VESSELS

1	BRAVE MERCHANT	22152t	98	22.5k	250P	-	175T	BA	Sevilla, SP	GB
2	DAWN MERCHANT	22152t	98	22.5k	250P	-	175T	BA	Sevilla, SP	GB

BRAVE MERCHANT Built for parent company *Cenargo* and chartered to *Merchant Ferries*. In February 1999 she inaugurated a new service between Liverpool and Dublin.

DAWN MERCHANT Built for parent company *Cenargo* and chartered to *Merchant Ferries*. On delivery in autumn 1998, chartered to *UND RoRo Isletmeri* of Turkey to operate between Istanbul and Trieste. Returned to *Merchant Ferries* in late 1998 and in February 1999, inaugurated a new service between Liverpool and Dublin.

Under Construction

3	NEWBUILDING 1	22152t	00	22.5k	250P	-	175T	-	Sevilla, SP	GB
4	NEWBUILDING 2	22152t	00	22.5k	250P	-	175T	-	Sevilla, SP	GB

NEWBUILDING 1, NEWBUILDING 2 Under construction for *Cenargo*. Likely to be used by *Merchant Ferries* on a new service between Liverpool and Belfast.

> **"If you take care of the means then the end will take care of itself."**

....THE SMART WAY TO CROSS THE IRISH SEA

North Quay, Heysham Harbour,
Morcambe, Lancashire LA3 2UL
Tel: 01524 855018
Fax: 01524 852527

LIVERPOOL ⟷ BELFAST

Sail Away Night and Day

- **Freight Capacity – 2,600 Lane Metres**
- **Easy Motorway Access**
- **Dedicated Car Deck**
- **Driver's Club**
- **Accompanied Articulated Vehicles**
- **Unaccompanied Trailers**
- **Road Trains**
- **Car Transporters**
- **Double Deck Trailers**
- **Rigid Vehicles**
- **Abnormal Loads**
- **Heavy Plant & Machinery**
- **Trade Cars**
- **Dangerous Goods Options**

BELFAST OFFICE
TEL: 01232 779090
FAX: 01232 775520

LIVERPOOL OFFICE
TEL: 0151 944 1010
FAX: 0151 922 0344

NORSE IRISH FERRIES

www.Norse-Irish-Ferries.co.uk

CHOOSE THE DIRECT ROUTE ... EVERYTIME

NORSE IRISH FERRIES

THE COMPANY *Norse Irish Ferries* is a British private sector company. It started as a freight-only operation but passenger facilities were established in 1992.

MANAGEMENT Managing Director: Phillip Shepherd, **General Manager, Liverpool:** Diane Parry, **Director/General Manager, Belfast:** Allister Mulligan.

ADDRESS *Belfast:* Victoria Terminal 2, West Bank Road, BELFAST BT3 9JN, *Liverpool:* North Brocklebank Dock, BOOTLE, Merseyside L20 1BY.

TELEPHONE Administration: *Belfast:* +44 (0)1232 779090, *Liverpool:* +44 (0)151-944 1010, **Reservations:** *Belfast:* +44 (0)1232 779090, *Liverpool:* +44 (0)151-944 1010, **Fax:** Belfast: +44 (0)1232 775520, *Liverpool:* +44 (0)151-922 0344.

INTERNET Website: http://www.Norse-Irish-Ferries.co.uk *(English)*

ROUTE OPERATED Liverpool - Belfast (8 hrs 30 mins; *(1,2)*; 1 per day (Mon, Wed, Fri, Sun), 2 per day (Tue, Thu, Sat). It is intended to operate twice daily services five days per week when a new riverside berth in Liverpool in constructed.

CONVENTIONAL FERRIES

1	LAGAN VIKING	21500t	97	22k	340P	100C	164T	A	Donanda, IT		IT
2	MERSEY VIKING	21500t	97	22k	340P	100C	164T	A	Donanda, IT		IT

LAGAN VIKING, MERSEY VIKING Built for *Leventina Transport* of Italy and chartered to *Norse Irish Ferries*.

P&O EUROPEAN FERRIES (IRISH SEA)

THE COMPANY *P&O European Ferries (Irish Sea) Limited,* is a British private sector company, a subsidiary of the *Peninsular and Oriental Steam Navigation Company*. It was formed in 1998 by the merger of the shipping activities *Pandoro Ltd* and the Cairnryan - Larne services of *P&O European Ferries (Felixstowe) Ltd*.

MANAGEMENT Chairman: Graeme Dunlop, **Managing Director:** J H Kearsley, **Sales Manager:** Philip Simpson.

ADDRESS Compass House, Dock Street, FLEETWOOD, Lancashire FY7 6HP.

TELEPHONE Administration: +44 (0)1253 615700, **Reservations:** 0990 980666 (from UK only), **Fax:** +44 (0)1253 615740.

Website: http://www.poef.com *(English)*

ROUTES OPERATED Conventional Ferry: Cairnryan - Larne (2 hrs 15 mins; *(1)*; 3 per day). **Fast Ferry:** Cairnryan - Larne (1 hr; *(2)*; 6 per day).

CONVENTIONAL FERRY

1	PRIDE OF RATHLIN	12503t	73	17k	1041P	340C	52L	BA2	Schiedam, NL		BD

PRIDE OF RATHLIN Built for *Townsend Thoresen* as the FREE ENTERPRISE VII for Dover - Calais and Dover - Zeebrugge services. After the delivery of new vessels in 1980 she was generally used on the Dover - Zeebrugge service. Extensively rebuilt in Bremerhaven in 1986, through the placing of the existing superstructure and rear part of hull on a new front part of hull. She was renamed the PRIDE OF WALMER in 1988. In summer 1992 she was transferred to the Cairnryan - Larne route and renamed the PRIDE OF RATHLIN.

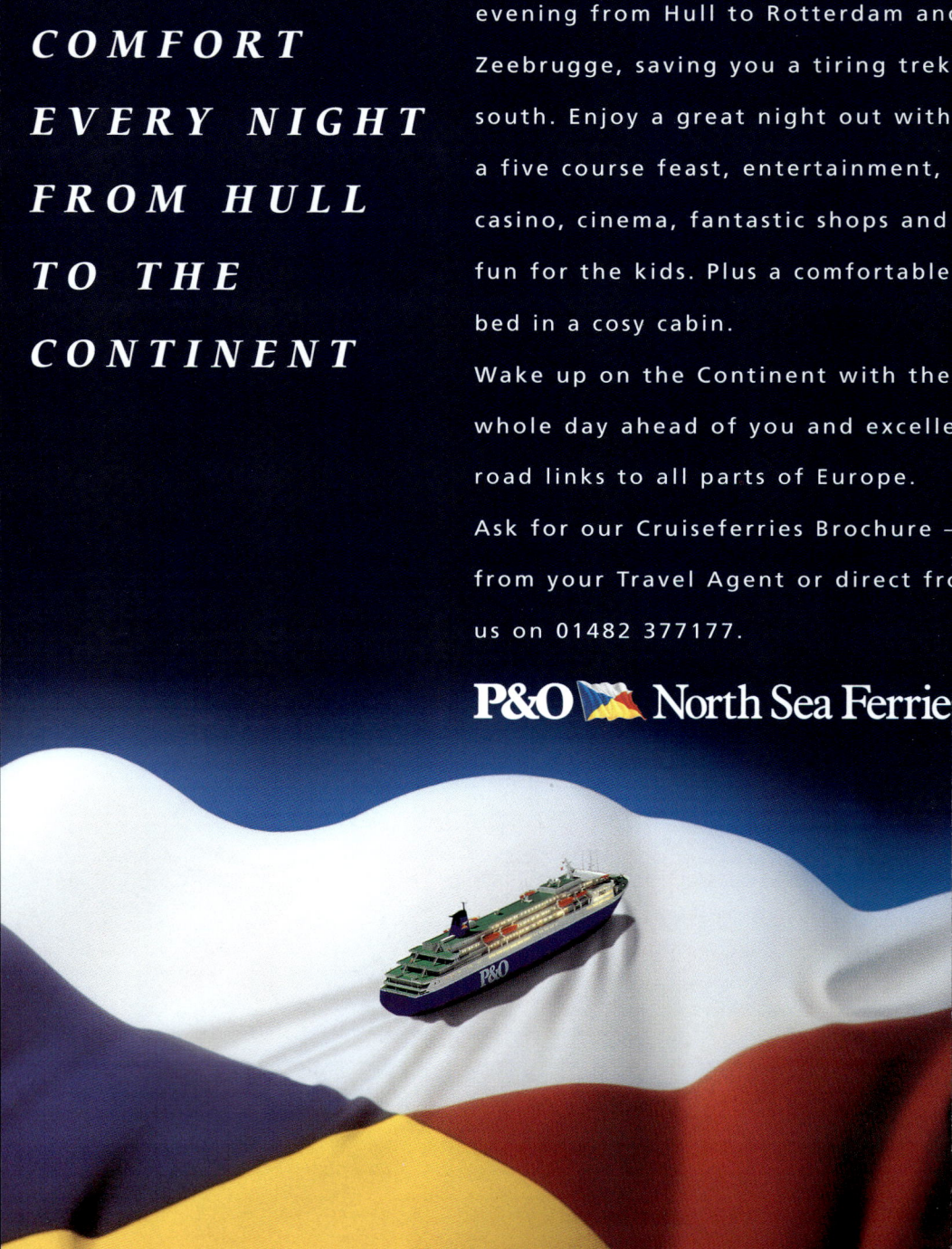

CRUISE IN COMFORT EVERY NIGHT FROM HULL TO THE CONTINENT

P&O North Sea Ferries sail every evening from Hull to Rotterdam and Zeebrugge, saving you a tiring trek south. Enjoy a great night out with a five course feast, entertainment, casino, cinema, fantastic shops and fun for the kids. Plus a comfortable bed in a cosy cabin.

Wake up on the Continent with the whole day ahead of you and excelle road links to all parts of Europe.

Ask for our Cruiseferries Brochure – from your Travel Agent or direct fr us on 01482 377177.

P&O North Sea Ferries

FAST FERRY

2	JETLINER		4563t	96	31k	600P	160C	12T	BA	Bergen, NO	BA

JETLINER Mjellam & Karlsen Jet Ship monohull vessel. Ordered for *Driftsselskabet Grenaa - Hundested* of Denmark and due to be called the DJURSLAND. However, before delivery the company went into liquidation and she was, instead, chartered to *P&O European Ferries*, renamed the JETLINER and inaugurated a fast ferry service between Cairnryan and Larne.

Under construction

3	NEWBUILDING	20800t	00	23k	410P	375C	140T	BA	Shimonoeki, JA	-

NEWBUILDING Under construction for *P&O European Ferries (Irish Sea)* for the Cairnryan - Larne service.

P&O NORTH SEA FERRIES

THE COMPANY *P&O North Sea Ferries Ltd* is a private sector company, a subsidiary of the *Peninsular and Oriental Steam Navigation Company* of Great Britain. Joint ownership with *The Royal Nedlloyd Group* of The Netherlands ceased in 1996 and the name was changed from *North Sea Ferries* to *P&O North Sea Ferries*. The Felixstowe freight-only operations of *P&O European Ferries* were incorporated into this new company.

MANAGEMENT Managing Director: Peter van den Brandhof, **Passenger Managers:** *UK:* Tony Farrell, *Netherlands:* Peter Goomans, *Belgium:* Christian Berkein, *Germany:* Peter Blomberg.

ADDRESS *UK:* King George Dock, Hedon Road, HULL HU9 5QA, *Netherlands:* Beneluxhaven, Rotterdam (Europoort), Postbus 1123, 3180 ROZENBURG ZH, Netherlands, *Belgium:* Leopold II Dam 13, Havendam, B-8380 ZEEBRUGGE, Belgium.

TELEPHONE Administration: *UK:* +44 (0)1482 795141, *Netherlands:* +31 (0)181 255500, *Belgium:* +32 (0)50 54 34 11, **Reservations:** *UK:* +44 (0)1482 377177, *Netherlands:* +31 (0)181 255555, *Belgium:* +32 (0)50 54 34 30, **Fax:** *UK:* +44 (0)1482 706438, *Netherlands:* +31 (0)181 355215, *Belgium:* +32 (0)50 54 71 12.

INTERNET Website: http://www.ponsf.com *(English)*

ROUTES OPERATED Hull - Rotterdam (Europoort) (14 hrs; *(2,4)*; 1 per day), Hull - Zeebrugge (14 hrs; *(1,3)*; 1 per day).

CONVENTIONAL FERRIES

1	NORLAND	26290t	74	18.5k	881P	500C	134T	A	Bremerhaven, GY	GB
2	NORSEA	31785t	87	18.5k	1250P	850C	180T	A	Glasgow, GB	GB
3	NORSTAR	26919t	74	18.5k	881P	500C	134T	A	Bremerhaven, GY	NL
4	NORSUN	31598t	87	18.5k	1250P	850C	180T	A	Tsurumi, JA	NL

NORLAND Built for the Hull - Rotterdam service. In April 1982 she was requisitioned for the Falkland Islands Task Force by the Ministry of Defence. She took part in the invasion of the Islands, disembarking troops and equipment at San Carlos. After the cessation of hostilities, she made trips to Argentina and Uruguay and was then employed on a shuttle service between Port Stanley and Ascension. She returned to Hull on 1st February 1983 and re-entered service on the Rotterdam service on 19th April. In 1987 she was lengthened and refurbished to a similar standard to the NORSEA. She replaced the NORWAVE (3450t, 1965) on the Hull - Zeebrugge service.

NORSEA, NORSUN Built for the Hull - Rotterdam service. The NORSUN was owned by *Nedlloyd* and was sold to *P&O* in 1996 but retains Dutch crew and registry.

NORSTAR Built for *North Sea Ferries* for the Hull - Rotterdam service. In 1987 she was lengthened

FERRIES OF THE BRITISH ISLES & NORTHERN EUROPE

FLY OR CRUISE FROM PORTSMOUTH.

The choice is yours with P&O Portsmouth. Let the superfast SuperStar Express whisk you in style and comfort to Cherbourg in just 2 hours 45 minutes. Alternatively, cruise at your leisure to Cherbourg or Le Havre on the Channel's best-appointed Cruiseferries. With time to appreciate the immaculate service and top-class amenities onboard; from casinos, top cabaret and great discount shopping to Les Routiers accredited restaurants, Club Class lounges and children's entertainers during the holidays. Either way, you'll arrive relaxed and perfectly placed to continue your journey, or to encounter the delights of Normandy and Brittany.

FOR FURTHER DETAILS AND TO BOOK, CALL 0870 2424 999, OR SEE YOUR TRAVEL AGENT.
FOR A FULL BROCHURE CALL 0870 9000 212, QUOTING FERP.
Ships and facilities may vary between routes.

Altogether more civilised.

P&O PORTSMOUTH

PORTSMOUTH TO BILBAO, CHERBOURG & LE HAVRE

and replaced the NORWIND (3692t, 1966) on the Hull - Zeebrugge service. She was owned by *Nedlloyd* and was sold to *P&O* in 1996 but retains Dutch crew and registry.

Under construction

5	NEWBUILDING 1	60600t	01	22k	1360P	250C	285T	AS	Venezia, IT	-
6	NEWBUILDING 2	60600t	01	22k	1360P	250C	285T	AS	Venezia, IT	-

NEWBUILDING 1, NEWBUILDING 2 On order for *P&O North Sea Ferries* to replace the NORSEA and NORSUN plus the freight vessels NORBAY and NORBANK on the Hull - Rotterdam service. Vessels will also accommodate 125 x 12 metre double stacked containers.

P&O PORTSMOUTH

THE COMPANY *P&O Portsmouth* is the trading name of *P&O European Ferries (Portsmouth) Ltd*, (until start of 1999 trading as *P&O European Ferries*) a British private sector company, a subsidiary of the *Peninsular and Oriental Steam Navigation Company*.

MANAGEMENT Chairman: Graeme Dunlop, **Managing Director:** Capt James Davenport, **Head of Passenger Marketing & Sales:** Richard Kirkman, **Freight Director:** Lawrence Strover.

ADDRESS Peninsular House, Wharf Road, PORTSMOUTH PO2 8TA.

TELEPHONE Administration: +44 (0)1705 301000, **Reservations:** 0870 2424999 (from UK only), **Fax:** +44 (0)1705 301134.

INTERNET Website: http://www.poportsmouth.com *(English)*

ROUTES OPERATED Conventional Ferries: Portsmouth - Cherbourg (5 hrs (day), 7 hrs - 8 hrs 15 mins (night); *(1,2,3 (1 once weekly))*; 2 day crossings, one night crossing per day), Portsmouth - Le Havre (5 hrs 30 mins (day), 7 hrs 30 mins - 8 hrs (night); *(4,5)*; 2 day crossings, one night crossing per day), Portsmouth - Bilbao (Santurzi) (35 hrs (UK - Spain), 30 hrs (Spain - UK); *(1)*; 2 per week). **Fast Ferry:** Portsmouth - Cherbourg (2 hrs 45 mins; *(6)*; 3 per day).

CONVENTIONAL FERRIES

1	PRIDE OF BILBAO	37583t	86	22k	2553P	600C	90T	BA	Turku, FI	GB
2	PRIDE OF CHERBOURG	14760t	75	18k	1200P	380C	53L	BA2	Aalborg, DK	GB
3	PRIDE OF HAMPSHIRE	14760t	75	18k	1200P	380C	53L	BA2	Aalborg, DK	GB
4	PRIDE OF LE HAVRE	33336t	89	21k	1600P	575C	118T	BA	Bremerhaven, GY	GB
5	PRIDE OF PORTSMOUTH	33336t	89	21k	1600P	575C	118T	BA	Bremerhaven, GY	GB

PRIDE OF BILBAO Built as the OLYMPIA for *Rederi AB Slite* of Sweden for *Viking Line* service between Stockholm and Helsinki. In 1993 she was chartered to *P&O European Ferries* to inaugurate a new service between Portsmouth and Bilbao. During the summer period she also operates, at weekends, a round trip between Portsmouth and Cherbourg. In 1994 she was purchased by the *Irish Continental Group* and re-registered in the Bahamas. *P&O* have since entered her into the British bareboat register and she is expected to remain on charter to *P&O Portsmouth* until at least 2003.

PRIDE OF CHERBOURG Built as the VIKING VALIANT for Southampton (from 1976 Southampton/Portsmouth and 1984 Portsmouth only) - Cherbourg/Le Havre services. Extensively rebuilt in Bremerhaven in 1986, through the placing of the existing superstructure and rear part of hull on a new front part of hull and from that date generally operated Portsmouth - Le Havre only. In 1989 she was renamed the PRIDE OF LE HAVRE. In 1994 transferred to the Portsmouth - Cherbourg service and renamed the PRIDE OF CHERBOURG.

PRIDE OF HAMPSHIRE Built as the VIKING VENTURER. Details otherwise as the PRIDE OF CHERBOURG. She was renamed the PRIDE OF HAMPSHIRE in 1989. In 1995 she was transferred to the Portsmouth - Cherbourg service.

PRIDE OF LE HAVRE Built as the OLAU HOLLANDIA for *TT-Line* of Germany, to operate for associated company *Olau Line* between Sheerness (Great Britain) and Vlissingen (Netherlands). In May 1994 the service ceased and she was chartered to *P&O European Ferries*, re-registered in Great Britain and renamed the PRIDE OF LE HAVRE. After a brief period on the Portsmouth - Cherbourg service she became a regular vessel on the Portsmouth - Le Havre service.

PRIDE OF PORTSMOUTH Built as the OLAU BRITANNIA for *TT-Line* of Germany, to operate for associated company *Olau Line*. In 1994 she was chartered to *P&O European Ferries*, re-registered in Great Britain and renamed the PRIDE OF PORTSMOUTH. After a brief period on the Portsmouth - Cherbourg service she became a regular vessel on the Portsmouth - Le Havre service from June 1994.

FAST FERRY

| 6 | SUPERSTAR EXPRESS | 5517t | 97 | 36k | 900P | 175C | - | A | Fremantle, AL | MA |

SUPERSTAR EXPRESS Austal Ships 82 catamaran, built for *Star Cruises* of Malaysia for their service between Butterworth and Langkawi. Built as the SUPERSTAR EXPRESS, she was renamed the SUPERSTAR EXPRESS LANGKAWI later in 1997. She was due, in 1998, to circumnavigate the world and to seek to take the Hales Trophy from HOVERSPEED GREAT BRITAIN. However, these plans did not materialise and instead she was chartered to *P&O European Ferries (Portsmouth)* and placed on the Portsmouth - Cherbourg route. She resumed the name SUPERSTAR EXPRESS.

P&O STENA LINE

THE COMPANY *P&O Stena Line* is a British private sector company, 60% owned by the *Peninsular and Oriental Steam Navigation Company* and 40% owned by *Stena Line AB* of Sweden. The new company took over the Dover and Newhaven services of *P&O European Ferries* and *Stena Line* in March 1998. Newhaven services ceased at the end of January 1999.

MANAGEMENT Joint Chairmen: Lord Sterling *(P&O)* and Dan Sten Olsson *(Stena Line)*, **Managing Director:** Russ Peters.

ADDRESS Channel House, Channel View Road, DOVER, Kent CT17 9TJ.

TELEPHONE Administration: +44 (0)1304 863000, **Reservations:** 087 0600 0600 (from UK only), **Fax:** +44 (0)1304 863223, **Telex:** 966266.

INTERNET Email: res38@dial.pipex.com **Website:** http://www.posl.com *(English)*

ROUTE OPERATED Dover - Calais (1 hr 15 mins/1 hr 30 mins; *(1,2,3,4,5,6,7)*; up to 35 per day).

CONVENTIONAL FERRIES

1	P&OSL BURGUNDY	28138t	93	21k	1420P	600C	148T	BA2	Bremerhaven, GY	GB
2	P&OSL CALAIS	26433t	87	22k	2290P	650C	100L	BA2	Bremen-Vegesack, GY	GB
3	P&OSL CANTERBURY	25122t	80	19k	1800P	550C	80T	BA2	Malmö, SW	GB
4	P&OSL DOVER	26433t	87	22k	2290P	650C	100L	BA2	Bremen-Vegesack, GY	GB
5	P&OSL KENT	20446t	80	21k	1825P	460C	64L	BA2	Bremerhaven, GY	GB
6	P&OSL PICARDY	13061t	80	23k	1326P	330C	48L	BA2	Bremerhaven, GY	GB
7	P&OSL PROVENCE	28559t	83	19.5k	2036P	550C	108T	BA2	Dunkerque, FR	GB

P&OSL BURGUNDY Built for *P&O European Ferries* for the Dover - Calais service. When construction started she was due to be a sister vessel to the EUROPEAN HIGHWAY, EUROPEAN PATHWAY and EUROPEAN SEAWAY (see Section 3) called the EUROPEAN CAUSEWAY and operate on the Zeebrugge freight route. However, it was decided that should be completed as a passenger/freight vessel (the design allowed for conversion) and she was launched as the PRIDE OF BURGUNDY. In 1998, transferred to *P&O Stena Line*. In 1998 renamed the P&OSL BURGUNDY.

P&OSL CALAIS Built for *European Ferries* as the PRIDE OF CALAIS for the Dover - Calais service. In 1998, transferred to *P&O Stena Line*. In 1999 renamed the P&OSL CALAIS.

P&OSL CANTERBURY Built as the SCANDINAVIA for *Rederi AB Nordö* of Sweden. After service in the Mediterranean for *UMEF*, she was, in 1981, sold to *SOMAT* of Bulgaria, renamed the TZAREVETZ and used on *Medlink* services between Bulgaria and the Middle East and later on other routes. In 1986 she was chartered to *Callitzis* of Greece for a service between Italy and Greece. In 1988 she was sold to *Sealink*, re-registered in the Bahamas and renamed the FIESTA. She was then chartered to *OT Africa Line*. During autumn 1989 she was rebuilt in Bremerhaven to convert her for passenger use and in March 1990 she was renamed the FANTASIA and placed her on the Dover - Calais service. Later in 1990 she was renamed the STENA FANTASIA. In 1998, transferred to *P&O Stena Line*. In 1999 she was renamed the P&OSL CANTERBURY.

P&OSL DOVER Built for *European Ferries* as the PRIDE OF DOVER for the Dover - Calais service. In 1998, transferred to *P&O Stena Line*. In 1999 renamed the P&OSL DOVER.

P&OSL KENT Built for *European Ferries (Townsend Thoresen)* as the SPIRIT OF FREE ENTERPRISE for the Dover - Calais service, also operating on the Dover - Zeebrugge service during the winter. She was renamed the PRIDE OF KENT in 1987. Sister vessel of the PRIDE OF BRUGES. During winter 1991/92 she was lengthened in Palermo, Italy to give her similar capacity to the PRIDE OF CALAIS and the PRIDE OF DOVER. Now operates Dover - Calais only. In 1998, transferred to *P&O Stena Line*. Later in 1998 renamed the P&OSL KENT.

P&OSL PICARDY Built for *European Ferries (Townsend Thoresen)* as the PRIDE OF FREE ENTERPRISE for the Dover - Calais service, also operating on the Dover - Zeebrugge service during the winter. She was renamed the PRIDE OF BRUGES in 1988 and, following the delivery of the new PRIDE OF CALAIS, she was transferred all year to the Dover - Zeebrugge service. In 1992, after the closure of that routes to passengers, she returned to the Dover - Calais route. Plans to operate her in a freight-only mode in 1997 were changed and she ran as a full passenger vessel. In 1998, transferred to *P&O Stena Line*. Plans to transfer her to the Newhaven - Dieppe route were dropped and she has remained at Dover. In 1999 renamed the P&OSL PICARDY.

P&OSL PROVENCE Built as the STENA JUTLANDICA for *Stena Line* for the Göteborg - Frederikshavn service. In 1996 she was transferred to the Dover - Calais route and renamed the STENA EMPEREUR. In 1998, transferred to *P&O Stena Line*. Later in 1998 renamed the P&OSL PROVENCE.

SEA CONTAINERS FERRIES

THE COMPANY *Sea Containers Ferries Ltd* is a British private sector company, part of the *Sea Containers Group*.

MANAGEMENT Senior Vice President Passenger Transportation: David Benson.

ADDRESS Sea Containers House, 20 Upper Ground, LONDON SE1 9PF.

TELEPHONE Administration: +44 (0)171-805 5000, **Fax:** +44 (0)171-805 5900.

Ferry services in the UK are operated through four subsidiaries - *Argyll and Antrim Steam Packet Company, Hoverspeed Ltd, Sea Containers Ferries Scotland Ltd* and the *Isle of Man Steam Packet Company (IOMSP Co)*. The Dover - Oostende service is a joint venture between *Hoverspeed Ltd* and *Holyman (UK) Ltd*. See also *SeaCat AB* in Section 6. Because of interchange of fast ferries between companies, they are shown in one section at the end. Also *IOMSP Co* and *Sea Containers Ferries Scotland* routes are increasingly becoming integrated and are also shown together.

When you're crossing the water, you could just follow the herd
...or you could try a more civilised approach.

Sea Containers ferry services offer a relaxing and enjoyable alternative to the average ferry crossing. Forget the horrors of being herded in and out of ports, jostling for space and never being sure of a seat. **superseacat** We never compromise on customer service, comfort or safety, no matter how many people are travelling with us. All Sea **seacat** Containers ferry services operate from their own dedicated port and terminal facilities to speed loading and unloading. So why follow the herd when you can journey in style?

DOVER - CALAIS • DOVER - OSTEND • FOLKESTONE - BOULOGNE • NEWHAVEN - DIEPPE • GOTHENBURG - FREDERIKSHAVN
BELFAST - STRANRAER • BELFAST - TROON • LIVERPOOL - DUBLIN • HEYSHAM - BELFAST • HEYSHAM - DOUGLAS
DOUGLAS - LIVERPOOL • DOUGLAS - BELFAST • DOUGLAS - DUBLIN • CAMPBELTOWN - BALLYCASTLE

Sea Containers Passenger Transportation Division, Sea Containers House, 20 Upper Ground, London SE1 9PF
Telephone: 0171-805 5000 Fax: 0171-805 5900 http://www.seacontainers.com

ARGYLL AND ANTRIM STEAM PACKET COMPANY

THE COMPANY The *Argyll and Antrim Steam Packet Company* is a subsidiary of *Sea Containers Ferries* of the UK, part of the *Sea Containers Group*.

MANAGEMENT Managing Director: Hamish Ross, **General Manager:** Diane Poole, **Marketing Manager:** Christina Traill.

ADDRESS 34 Charlotte Street, STRANRAER DG9 7EF.

TELEPHONE Administration: +44 (0)1776 702755, **Reservations:** *From UK:* 08705 523523, *From elsewhere:* +44 (0)1232 313543, **Fax:** +44 (0)1776 705894.

INTERNET Website: http://www.seacontainers.com/ferries/scotland *(English)*

ROUTE OPERATED Campbeltown (Scotland) - Ballycastle (Northern Ireland) (summer only) (3 hrs; *(1)*; 2 per day).

CONVENTIONAL FERRY

1	CLAYMORE	1871t	78	14k	300P	50C	-	AS	Leith, GB	GB

CLAYMORE Built for *Caledonian MacBrayne* for the Oban - Castlebay/ Lochboisdale service, also serving Coll and Tiree between October and May, replacing the IONA (see the PENTALINA B, *Pentland Ferries*). In 1989 she was transferred to the Kennacraig - Port Ellen/Port Askaig (Islay) route, again replacing the IONA. In summer she also operated a weekly service from Port Askaig (Islay) to Colonsay and Oban. She relieved on the Ardrossan - Brodick service during winter 1990. In autumn 1993 she was replaced by the ISLE OF ARRAN and became a spare vessel. Her summer duties in 1994, 1995 and 1996 included Saturday sailings from Ardrossan to Douglas (Isle of Man), returning on Sundays plus standby duties and charter to the *Isle of Man Steam Packet Company* to provide extra sailings between Heysham and Douglas during the TT Season. During the winter she was general relief vessel, spending several months on Islay sailings. In 1997 she was sold to *Sea Containers* to operate for the *Argyll and Antrim Steam Packet Company*. During winters 1997/98 and 1998/99 she was chartered back to *Caledonian MacBrayne* to cover during the refit period.

HOVERSPEED

THE COMPANY *Hoverspeed Ltd* is a British private sector company. It was formed in October 1981 by the merger of *Seaspeed*, a wholly owned subsidiary of the *British Railways Board*, operating between Dover and Calais and Dover and Boulogne and *Hoverlloyd*, a subsidiary of *Broström AB* of Sweden, operating between Ramsgate (Pegwell Bay) and Calais. The Ramsgate - Calais service ceased after summer 1982. In early 1984 the company was sold by its joint owners to a management consortium. In 1986 the company was acquired by *Sea Containers*. It was retained by *Sea Containers* in 1990 following the sale of most of *Sealink British Ferries* to *Stena Line*.

MANAGEMENT Managing Director: Geoffrey Ede, **Marketing Manager:** Steve Boffey.

ADDRESS The International Hoverport, Marine Parade, DOVER, Kent CT17 9TG.

TELEPHONE Administration: +44 (0)1304 865000, **Reservations:** 08705 240241 (from UK only), **Fax:** *Admin:* +44 (0)1304 865087, *Reservations:* +44 (0)1304 240088.

INTERNET Email: info@hoverspeed.co.uk **Website:** http://www.hoverspeed.co.uk *(English)*

ROUTES OPERATED SeaCats: Folkestone - Boulogne (55 mins; *(6)*; up to 6 per day), Dover - Calais (50 mins; *(4)*; up to 6 per day), Dover - Oostende (2 hrs; *(5,7)*; up to 7 per day) (in conjunction with *Holyman (UK) Ltd*), **Summer only*:** Newhaven - Dieppe (2 hrs; *(11)*; up to 3 per day). **Hovercraft:** Dover - Calais (35 mins; *(14,15)*; up to 14 per day). *Note: continuation of this service after 30th September 1999 will depend on its success.

ISLE OF MAN STEAM PACKET COMPANY

THE COMPANY The *Isle of Man Steam Packet Company* is an Isle of Man registered company owned by *Sea Containers Ferries Ltd*.

MANAGEMENT Managing Director: Hamish Ross, **Passenger Marketing Manager:** David Morgan.

ADDRESS PO Box 5, Imperial Buildings, DOUGLAS, Isle of Man IM99 1AF.

TELEPHONE Administration: +44 (0)1624 645645, **Reservations:** *From UK:* 0345 523523, *From elsewhere:* +44 (0)1624 661661, **Fax:** *Admin:* +44 (0)1624 645609, *Reservations:* +44 (0)1624 645697.

INTERNET Email: res@steam-packet.com **Website:** http://www.steam-packet.com *(English)*

ROUTES OPERATED Conventional Ferries: Douglas (Isle of Man) - Heysham (3 hrs 45 mins; *(2,3)*; up to 2 per day), Douglas - Liverpool (4 hrs; *(3)*; irregular), Douglas - Dublin (4 hrs 45 mins; *(2,3)*; irregular). **SeaCats:** Listed with *Sea Containers Ferries Scotland* services below.

CONVENTIONAL FERRIES

2	BEN-MY-CHREE	12504t	98	19k	500P	-	100T	A	Krimpen, NL	IM
3	LADY OF MANN	4482t	76	21k	1000P	130C	0L	S	Troon, GB	IM

BEN-MY-CHREE Built for the *IOMSP Co* and operates mainly between Douglas and Heysham.

LADY OF MANN Built for the *IOMSP Co*. Cars and small vans are side loaded but no ro-ro freight is conveyed. In 1994 replaced by the SEACAT ISLE OF MAN and laid up for sale. She was used in 1995 during the period of the 'TT' motor cycle races between 26th May to 12th June. Later in 1995 she was chartered to *Porto Santo Line* of Madeira for a service from Funchal to Porto Santo. In 1996 she operated throughout the summer, as no SeaCat was chartered. In 1997, she operated for the TT races and then inaugurated a new Liverpool - Dublin service in June, with a weekly Fleetwood - Douglas service until replaced by the SUPERSEACAT TWO in March 1998. In 1998 she operated during the TT race period and was then again chartered to *Porto Santo Line*. During winter 1998/99 she provided back-up to the fast ferries on the Liverpool - Dublin and Douglas - Liverpool routes. She is expected to operate between Douglas and the UK during the TT race period again in summer 1999, some Douglas - Dublin sailings and also a number of special sailings to Fleetwood and Llandudno.

SEA CONTAINERS FERRIES SCOTLAND

THE COMPANY *Sea Containers Ferries Scotland Ltd* is a subsidiary of *Sea Containers Ferries Ltd*.

MANAGEMENT Managing Director: Hamish Ross, **General Manager, Belfast:** Diane Poole, **General Manager, Liverpool-Dublin:** John Burrows.

ADDRESS 34 Charlotte Street, STRANRAER DG9 7EF.

TELEPHONE Administration: +44 (0)1776 702755, **Reservations:** *From UK:* 087055 523523, *From elsewhere:* +44 (0)1232 313543, **Fax:** +44 (0)1776 705894.

INTERNET Website: http://www.seacontainers.com/ferries/scotland *(English)*

ROUTES OPERATED - SEA CONTAINERS IRISH SEA FAST FERRIES SERVICES - IOMSP & SEA CONTAINERS FERRIES, SCOTLAND *All year:* Douglas - Liverpool (2 hrs 30 mins; *(9)*; up to 3 per day), *Seasonal:* Stranraer - Belfast (1 hrs 30 mins; *(10)*; 1 per day), Liverpool - Dublin; (3 hrs 45 mins); *(12)*; 2 per day, Troon - Belfast (2 hrs 30 mins; *(10)*; 2 per day), Heysham - Belfast (4 hrs; *(8)*; 1/2 per day), Douglas - Belfast (2 hrs 45 mins; *(8)*; 3 per week), Douglas - Dublin (2 hrs 45 mins; *(9)*; 3 per week). Note: Belfast - Heysham, Stranraer and Troon services and Liverpool Dublin service are due to finish at the end of September but may be extended. Douglas - Dublin service continues until October, with some services in December.

FAST FERRIES OPERATED BY SEA CONTAINERS COMPANIES IN UK

4	ATLANTIC II	3012t	90	35k	450P	90C	-	BA	Hobart, AL	UY
5	DIAMANT	4305t	96	39k	674P	155C	-	A	Hobart, AL	LX
6	HOVERSPEED GREAT BRITAIN	3003t	90	37k	577P	80C	-	BA	Hobart, AL	GB
7	RAPIDE	4112t	96	39k	674P	155C	-	A	Hobart, AL	LX
8	SEACAT DANMARK	3003t	91	37k	432P	80C	-	BA	Hobart, AL	GB
9	SEACAT ISLE OF MAN	3003t	91	37k	500P	80C	-	BA	Hobart, AL	GB
10	SEACAT SCOTLAND	3003t	91	37k	450P	80C	-	BA	Hobart, AL	GB
11	SUPERSEACAT TWO	4463t	97	37.8k	800P	175C	-	A	Riva Trigoso, IT	IT
12	SUPERSEACAT THREE	4463t	99	37.8k	800P	175C	-	A	Muggiano, IT	IT
13	SUPERSEACAT FOUR	4463t	99	37.8k	800P	175C	-	A	River Trigoso, IT	IT
14	THE PRINCESS ANNE	-	69	50k	360P	55C	-	BA	Cowes, GB	GB
15	THE PRINCESS MARGARET	-	68	50k	360P	55C	-	BA	Cowes, GB	GB

ATLANTIC II Built as SEACAT TASMANIA for *Sea Containers* subsidiary *Tasmanian Ferry Services* of Australia to operate between George Town (Tasmania) and Port Welshpool (Victoria). In 1992 chartered to *Hoverspeed* to operate Dover - Calais and Folkestone - Boulogne services. Returned to Australia after the 1992 summer season but returned to Britain in summer 1993 to operate Dover - Calais and Folkestone - Boulogne services during the summer. She was repainted into *Hoverspeed* livery and renamed the SEACAT CALAIS. In 1994 chartered for five years (with a purchase option) to *Navegacion Atlantida* for *Ferry Linas Argentinas AS* of Uruguay service between Montevideo (Uruguay) - Buenos Aires (Argentina) service and renamed the ATLANTIC II. The purchase option was not taken up and in 1999 she was returned to *Sea Containers*. In summer 1999 to operate between Dover and Calais.

DIAMANT InCat 81m catamaran. Ordered by *Del Bene SA* of Argentina. In 1996, before completion, purchased by the *Holyman Group* and named the HOLYMAN EXPRESS. In 1997 she was renamed the HOLYMAN DIAMANT, transferred to *Holyman Sally Ferries* and in March was introduced onto the Ramsgate - Oostende route. In March 1998 transferred to the Dover - Oostende route, operating for the *Hoverspeed - Holyman (UK)* joint venture, and renamed the DIAMANT.

HOVERSPEED GREAT BRITAIN InCat 74m catamaran. Launched as the CHRISTOPHER COLUMBUS but renamed before entering service. During delivery voyage from Australia, she won the Hales Trophy for the 'Blue Riband' of the Atlantic. She inaugurated a car and passenger service between Portsmouth and Cherbourg, operated by *Hoverspeed*. This service was suspended in early 1991 and later that year she was, after modification, switched to a new service between Dover (Eastern Docks) and Boulogne/Calais, replacing hovercraft. In 1992 operated on Channel routes, including services from Folkestone. During winter 1992/3 she was chartered to *Ferry Lineas* of Argentina, operating between Buenos Aires (Argentina) and Montevideo (Uruguay). She now operates mainly between Folkestone and Boulogne.

RAPIDE InCat 81m catamaran. Built for the *Holyman Group* as the CONDOR 12. In summer 1996 operated by *Condor Ferries*. In 1997 she was renamed the HOLYMAN RAPIDE, transferred to *Holyman Sally Ferries* and in March was introduced onto the Ramsgate - Oostende route. In March 1998 transferred to the Dover - Oostende route, operating for the *Hoverspeed - Holyman (UK)* joint venture, and renamed the RAPIDE.

SEACAT DANMARK InCat 74m catamaran. Christened in 1991 as the HOVERSPEED BELGIUM and renamed HOVERSPEED BOULOGNE before leaving the builders yard. She was the third SeaCat, introduced in 1992 to enable a three vessel service to be operated by *Hoverspeed* across the Channel, including a new SeaCat route between Folkestone and Boulogne (replacing the *Sealink Stena Line* ferry service which ceased at the end of 1991). With the HOVERSPEED FRANCE (now SEACAT ISLE OF MAN) and the HOVERSPEED GREAT BRITAIN she operated on all three Channel routes (Dover - Calais, Dover - Boulogne and Folkestone - Boulogne). In 1993 she was transferred to *SeaCat AB* and renamed the SEACATAMARAN DANMARK and inaugurated a new high-speed service between Göteborg and Frederikshavn. For legal reasons it was not possible to call her the SEACAT DANMARK as intended but in 1995 these problems were resolved and she was renamed the SEACAT DENMARK. From January 1996 transferred to the new joint venture company *ColorSeaCat KS*, jointly with *Color Line* of Norway. During winter 1996/97 she operated on the Dover - Calais route. *ColorSeaCat* did not operate in 1997 and she again operated for *SeaCat AB*. In autumn 1997 she replaced the SEACAT SCOTLAND on the Stranraer - Belfast route. During summer 1998, she operated for the *IOMSP Co*. In 1999 to operate for *Sea Containers Ferries Scotland* between Belfast and Heysham and Belfast and Douglas.

SEACAT ISLE OF MAN InCat 74m catamaran. Built as the HOVERSPEED FRANCE, the second SeaCat. She inaugurated Dover - Calais/Boulogne service in 1991. In 1992 she was chartered to *Sardinia Express* of Italy and renamed the SARDEGNA EXPRESS; she did not operate on the Channel that year. This charter was terminated at the end of 1992 and in 1993 she was renamed the SEACAT BOULOGNE and operated on the Dover - Calais and Folkestone - Boulogne services. In 1994 she was chartered to *IOMSP Co*, renamed the SEACAT ISLE OF MAN and replaced the LADY OF MANN on services between Douglas (Isle of Man) and Britain and Ireland. During winter 1994/5 operated for *SeaCat Scotland* between Stranraer and Belfast. She returned to *IOMSP Co* in June 1995. During spring 1995 she was chartered to *Condor Ferries*; she then was chartered again to *IOMSP Co* and returned to *Sea Containers* in the autumn. In 1996 she was chartered to *ColorSeaCat KS*, renamed the SEACAT NORGE and inaugurated a new service between Langesund (Norway) and Frederikshavn (Denmark). During winter 1996/97 she operated between Dover and Calais. In early 1997 she was again renamed the SEACAT ISLE OF MAN. During summer 1997 she operated for *IOMSP Co*, serving on Liverpool, Dublin and Belfast seasonal services to Douglas (May to September) plus a weekly Liverpool - Dublin service when the LADY OF MANN operated from Fleetwood. In late 1997 she was transferred to the *Hoverspeed* Dover - Calais route and operated on this route throughout 1998. In 1999 she will operate between Douglas and Liverpool and Douglas and Dublin for *IOMSP Co.*

SEACAT SCOTLAND InCat 74m catamaran, the fifth SeaCat to be built. In 1992 she inaugurated a new high-speed car and passenger service for *SeaCat Scotland* on the Stranraer - Belfast route. In autumn 1994 she was chartered to *Q-Ships* of Qatar for services between Doha (Qatar) and Bahrain and Dubai and renamed the Q-SHIP EXPRESS. In spring 1995 she returned to the Stranraer - Belfast service and resumed the name SEACAT SCOTLAND. In autumn 1997 chartered to *Navegacion Atlantida SA* of Uruguay for service between Colonia (Uruguay) and Buenos Aires (Argentina). She returned to the UK in spring 1998 and operated on to the Stranraer - Belfast route. In 1999 she will operate for *Sea Containers Ferries Scotland* between Stranraer and Belfast and Troon and Belfast.

SUPERSEACAT TWO Fincantieri MDV1200 monohull vessel. In 1997 operated on the *Hoverspeed* Dover - Calais route. She was withdrawn from this route at the end of 1997 and in March 1998, she inaugurated a Liverpool - Dublin fast ferry service, operated by *IOMSP Co*. In summer 1999 she will operate for *Hoverspeed* between Newhaven and Dieppe.

SUPERSEACAT THREE, Fincantieri MDV1200 monohull vessel. In 1999 to operate on the Liverpool - Dublin service, operated by *Sea Containers Ferries Scotland*, replacing the SUPERSEACAT TWO.

SUPERSEACAT FOUR Fincantieri MDV 1200 monohull vessel. Usage in 1999 not yet decided.

THE PRINCESS ANNE British Hovercraft Corporation SRN4 type hovercraft built for *Seaspeed*. Built to Mark I specification. In 1978 lengthened to Mark III specification. She underwent complete refurbishment at the beginning of 1999. Operated by *Hoverspeed*.

THE PRINCESS MARGARET British Hovercraft Corporation SRN4 type hovercraft built for *Seaspeed*. Built to Mark I specification. In 1979 lengthened to Mark III specification. She underwent complete refurbishment at the beginning of 1999. Operated by *Hoverspeed*.

Options

| 16 | NEWBUILDING 1 | 4463t | 00 | 37.8k | 800P | 175C | - | A | La Spézia, IT | IT |
| 17 | NEWBUILDING 2 | 4463t | 00 | 37.8k | 800P | 175C | - | A | La Spézia, IT | IT |

NEWBUILDING 1, NEWBUILDING 2 Fincantieri MDV1200 monohull vessels. If the order is confirmed, they are likely to be called the SUPERSEACAT FIVE and the SUPERSEACAT SIX. They could be built at another Fincantieri yard.

SEAFRANCE

THE COMPANY *SeaFrance SA* (previously *SNAT (Société Nouvelle Armement Transmanche)*) is a French state owned company. It is jointly owned by *Société Nationale des Chemins de fer Français (French Railways)* and *Compagnie Générale Maritime Français (French National Shipping Company)*. *SNAT* was established in 1990 to take over the services of *SNCF Armement Naval*, a wholly owned division of *SNCF*. At the same time a similarly constituted body called *Société Proprietaire Navires (SPN)* was established to take over ownership of the vessels. Joint operation of services with *Stena Line* ceased at the end of 1995 and *SeaFrance SA* was formed.

MANAGEMENT Président du Directoire: M Bonnet, **Directeur Sealink Calais:** M Jachet, **Managing Director (UK):** Robin Wilkins.

ADDRESS *France:* 3 rue Ambroise Paré, 75475, PARIS Cedex 10, France, *UK:* Eastern Docks, DOVER, Kent CT16 1JA.

TELEPHONE Administration: *France:* +33 1 55 31 58 92, *UK:* +44 (0)1304 212696, **Reservations:** *France:* +33 3 21 46 80 79, *UK (Passenger):* 0990 711711 (from UK only), *UK*

The Princess Anne *(Philippe Holthof)*

Superferry *(Miles Cowsill)*

(Freight): +44 (0)1304 203030, **Fax:** *France:* +33 1 48 74 62 37, *UK:* +44 (0)1304 240033, **Telex:** 280549.

INTERNET Email: wbl@seafrance.fr **Website:** http://www.seafrance.com *(English)*

ROUTE OPERATED Calais - Dover (1 hr 30 mins; *(1,2,4)*; 15 per day).

CONVENTIONAL FERRIES

1	SEAFRANCE CEZANNE	25122t	80	19.5k	1800P	600C	150T	BA2	Malmö, SW	FR
2	SEAFRANCE MANET	15093t	84	18k	1800P	330C	54T	BA2	Nantes, FR	FR
3•	SEAFRANCE MONET	12962t	74	18k	1800P	425C	51L	BA2	Trogir, YU	BA
4	SEAFRANCE RENOIR	15612t	81	18k	1600P	330C	54T	BA2	Le Havre, FR	FR

SEAFRANCE CEZANNE Built as the ARIADNE for *Rederi AB Nordö* of Sweden. Renamed the SOCA before entering service on *UMEF* freight services (but with capacity for 175 drivers) in the Mediterranean. In 1981 she was sold to *SO Mejdunaroden Automobilen Transport (SOMAT)* of Bulgaria and renamed the TRAPEZITZA. She operated on *Medlink* services between Bulgaria and the Middle East. In 1988 she was acquired by *Sealink British Ferries*, re-registered in the Bahamas and in 1989 renamed the FANTASIA. Later in 1989 she was modified in Bremerhaven, renamed the CHANNEL SEAWAY and, in May, she inaugurated a new freight-only service between Dover (Eastern Docks) and Calais. During winter 1989/90 she was modified in Bremerhaven to convert her for passenger service. In spring 1990 she was renamed the FIESTA, transferred to *SNAT*, re-registered in France and replaced the CHAMPS ELYSEES (now the SEAFRANCE MANET) on the Dover - Calais service. In 1996 she was renamed the SEAFRANCE CEZANNE.

SEAFRANCE MANET Built for *SNCF* as the CHAMPS ELYSEES to operate Calais - Dover and Boulogne - Dover services, later operating Calais - Dover only. In 1990 transferred to the Dieppe - Newhaven service. Chartered to *Stena Sealink Line* in June 1992 when they took over the operation of the service. She was renamed the STENA PARISIEN and carried a French crew. In 1997 the charter was terminated; she returned to *SeaFrance* and was renamed the SEAFRANCE MANET. She replaced the SEAFRANCE MONET.

SEAFRANCE MONET Built as the STENA DANICA for *Stena Line AB* of Sweden for their Göteborg - Frederikshavn service. In 1982, in anticipation of the delivery of a new STENA DANICA, she was renamed the STENA NORDICA. In June 1983 she was taken by *RMT* on a three year charter, introduced onto *RMT's* Oostende - Dover service and re-registered in Belgium. In March 1984 she was renamed the STENA NAUTICA. The charter ended in June 1986 when the PRINS ALBERT re-entered service; she returned to *Stena Line* and was re-registered in The Bahamas. In 1987 she was sold to *SNCF*, re-registered in France, renamed the VERSAILLES and introduced onto the Dieppe - Newhaven service. In May 1992 she was chartered to *Stena Sealink Line*, re-registered in The Bahamas, renamed the STENA LONDONER and re-launched that service, which had abandoned by *SNAT* earlier in the year. In April 1996 she was returned to *SeaFrance*, renamed the SEAFRANCE MONET and entered service in July 1996. In 1997 she was replaced by the SEAFRANCE MANET. She spent the summers of 1997 and 1998 laid up but is used during the winter overhaul period to cover for ships undergoing refits.

SEAFRANCE RENOIR Built for *SNCF* as the COTE D'AZUR for the Dover - Calais service. She also operated Boulogne - Dover in 1985. In 1996 she was renamed the SEAFRANCE RENOIR.

SMYRIL LINE

THE COMPANY *Smyril Line* is a Faroe Islands registered company.

MANAGEMENT Managing Director: Óli Hammer, **Marketing Manager:** Samuel J Arnoldson.

ADDRESS Jonas Bronksgöta 37, PO Box 370, FO-100 TÓRSHAVN, Faroe Islands.

TELEPHONE Administration: +298-315900, **Reservations:** Faroe Islands: +298-315900, **UK:** +44 (0)1224 572615 (*P&O Scottish Ferries*), **Fax:** +298-315707, **Telex:** 81296.

INTERNET Email: office@smyril-line.fo **Website:** http://www.smyril-line.fo *(English, Danish, German)*

ROUTES OPERATED Tórshavn (Faroes) - Hanstholm (Denmark) (31 hrs; *(1)*; 1 per week), Tórshavn - Lerwick (Shetland) (14 hrs; *(1)*; 1 per week) - Bergen (Norway) (via Lerwick) (24 hrs - 27 hrs 30 mins; *(1)*; 1 per week), Tórshavn - Seydisfjordur (Iceland) (15 hrs - 18 hrs; *(1)*; 1 per week) (15 May to 10 September only). Note: Lerwick sailings ceased after the 1992 season but resumed in 1998. The service now operates year round but is restricted to Tórshavn - Hanstholm during winter months.

CONVENTIONAL FERRY

1	NORRÖNA	12000t	73	19k	1050P	300C	44L	BA2	Rendsburg, GY	FA

NORRÖNA Built as the GUSTAV VASA for *Lion Ferry AB* of Sweden, a sister vessel of the NILS DACKE (see the QUIBERON, *Brittany Ferries*). In 1982 the Travemünde - Malmö service ceased and in 1983 she was sold to *Smyril Line* and renamed the NORRÖNA. She was rebuilt in Flensburg, Germany, to increase passenger capacity and in the summer took over services from the SMYRIL of *Strandfaraskip Landsins*. In 1993 Esbjerg replaced Hanstholm as the Danish port and calls at Lerwick (Shetland) ceased. Because the service only operated in the summer period, she has, since purchase, undertaken a number of charters and cruises during the winter months. During autumn 1994 she initially served on the short-lived service between Wismar (Germany) and Newcastle for *North Sea Baltic Ferries* under the name WISMAR II. During the early part of 1996 she was chartered to *Stena Line* to operate between Stranraer and Belfast. In 1998 the Danish port became Hanstholm again and Lerwick sailings resumed. She now operates for *Smyril Line* all year round.

STENA LINE (NETHERLANDS)

THE COMPANY *Stena Line* is the trading name of *Stena Line bv* of The Netherlands, a wholly owned subsidiary of *Stena Line AB* of Sweden. *Stena Line* acquired the previous operator of this route, the Dutch *Stoomvaart Maatschappij Zeeland (Zeeland Steamship Company)* (which had since the start of 1989 traded as *Crown Line*) in summer 1989. Joint operation of the route with *Sealink* ceased in 1990, although *Stena Line Ltd* continue to market the service in the UK and Irish Republic. *Stena Line* is named after its founder, Sten A Olsson.

MANAGEMENT Route Director: Pim de Lange, **Marketing and Sales Director:** Harry Betist.

ADDRESS PO Box 2, 3150 AA, HOEK VAN HOLLAND, Netherlands.

TELEPHONE Administration: +31 (0)174 389333, **Reservations:** +31 (0)174 315811, **Fax:** +31 (0)174 387045, **Telex:** 31272.

INTERNET Website: http://www.stenaline.com *(English, Swedish)*

ROUTE OPERATED Fast Ferry: Hoek van Holland (Netherlands) - Harwich (3 hrs 40 mins; *(1)*; 2 per day).

FAST FERRY

| 1 | STENA DISCOVERY | 19638t | 97 | 40k | 1500P | 375C | 50L | A | Rauma, FI | NL |

STENA DISCOVERY Finnyards HSS1500 built for *Stena Line* to replace two conventional ferries on the Hoek van Holland - Harwich service.

Under Construction

| 2 | NEWBUILDING 1 | 30500t | 99 | 22k | 380P | - | 200T | A | Puerto Real, SP | - |
| 3 | NEWBUILDING 2 | 30500t | 99 | 22k | 380P | - | 200T | A | Puerto Real, SP | - |

NEWBUILDING 1, NEWBUILDING 2 Under construction for *Stena AB*. May be chartered to *Stena Line bv* to operate between Hoek van Holland and Harwich, providing back-up to the STENA DISCOVERY and replacing the existing freight vessels. At the time of going to press, this has not been confirmed. Delivery may not be until 2000, at least for the second vessel.

STENA LINE (UK)

THE COMPANY *Stena Line* is the trading name of *Stena Line Ltd*, a Swedish owned British registered private sector company. It was purchased (as *Sealink UK Ltd*) from the state owned *British Railways Board* in summer 1984 by *British Ferries Ltd*, a wholly owned subsidiary of *Sea Containers* of Bermuda. In 1990 most services and vessels were purchased from *Sea Containers* by *Stena Line AB* of Sweden - although the Isle of Wight vessels and services were excluded. In late 1990 the trading name was changed to *Sealink Stena Line*, in 1993 to *Stena Sealink Line* and in 1996 to *Stena Line*. In 1998, Dover and Newhaven services were transferred to *P&O Stena Line*.

MANAGEMENT Chief Executive: Bo Severed (Stena Line AB, Sweden).

ADDRESS Charter House, Park Street, ASHFORD, Kent TN24 8EX.

TELEPHONE Administration: +44 (0)1233 647022, **Reservations:** 0990 707070 (from UK only), **Fax:** +44 (0)1233 202361.

INTERNET Website: http://www.stenaline.com *(English, Swedish)*

ROUTES OPERATED Conventional Ferries: Stranraer - Belfast (3 hrs; *(2,4)*; up to 6 per day (Note: these services are primarily for freight but passengers and cars are carried on some (and, on certain dates, all) sailings), Holyhead - Dublin (3 hrs 45 mins; *(3)*; 2 per day); Fishguard - Rosslare (3 hrs 30 mins; *(1)*; 2 per day). **Fast Ferries:** Stranraer - Belfast (1 hrs 45 mins; *(7)*; 5 per day), Holyhead - Dun Laoghaire (1 hr 39 mins; *(5)*; up to 5 per day), Fishguard - Rosslare (1 hr 39 mins; *(6)*; up to 5 per day).

CONVENTIONAL FERRIES

1	KONINGIN BEATRIX	31189t	86	20k	2100P	500C	75L	BA	Krimpen, NL	GB
2	STENA CALEDONIA	12619t	81	19.5k	1000P	280C	56T	BA2	Belfast, GB	GB
3	STENA CHALLENGER	18523t	90	18k	500P	480C	100T	BA2	Rissa, NO	GB
4	STENA GALLOWAY	12175t	80	19k	1000P	280C	56T	BA2	Belfast, GB	GB

KONINGIN BEATRIX Built as the for *Stoomvaart Maatschappij Zeeland* of The Netherlands for their Hoek van Holland - Harwich service (trading as *Crown Line*). In 1989 transferred to *Stena Line bv*. In June 1997 chartered by *Stena Line bv* to *Stena Line Ltd* and used on the Fishguard - Rosslare service. In August 1997, transferred to the British flag.

STENA CALEDONIA Built as the ST DAVID for the Holyhead - Dun Laoghaire and Fishguard - Rosslare services. It was originally planned that she would replace the chartered STENA NORMANDICA (5607t, 1975) but it was subsequently decided that an additional large vessel was required for the Irish Sea routes. Until 1985 her normal use was, therefore, to substitute for other Irish Sea vessels as necessary (including the Stranraer - Larne route) and also to operate additional summer services on the Holyhead - Dun Laoghaire route. During the spring of 1983 she operated on the Dover - Calais service while the ST CHRISTOPHER (now the STENA ANTRIM) was being modified. From March 1985 she operated between Dover and Oostende, a service which ceased in December 1985 with the decision of *RMT* to link up with *Townsend Thoresen*. During the early part of 1986 she operated between Dover and Calais and then moved to the Stranraer - Larne route where she became a regular vessel. In 1990 she was renamed the STENA CALEDONIA. In September 1996 she became mainly a freight-only vessel (with a maximum passenger capacity of 100) but passengers are carried on certain sailings and when the STENA VOYAGER is unavailable and the passenger capacity is increased accordingly.

STENA CHALLENGER Built for *Stena Rederi AB* of Sweden and chartered to *Stena Sealink Line* for Dover - Calais and Dover - Dunkerque freight services. Her hull was constructed and launched in Landskrona, Sweden and towed to Norway for fitting out. In 1992 she was switched to the Dover (Eastern Docks) - Dunkerque freight services. From summer 1994 until summer 1996 she operated passenger services between Dover and Calais. In summer 1996 she was transferred to the Holyhead - Dublin freight-only route, replacing sister ship, the STENA TRAVELLER (now the TT-TRAVELLER). Cars and passengers are now carried on all sailings.

STENA GALLOWAY Built as the GALLOWAY PRINCESS for the Stranraer - Larne (now Belfast) service. In 1990 renamed the STENA GALLOWAY. In September 1996 she became mainly a freight-only vessel (with a maximum passenger capacity of 100) but passengers are carried on certain sailings and when the STENA VOYAGER is unavailable. The passenger capacity is increased accordingly.

FAST FERRIES

5	STENA EXPLORER	19638t	96	40k	1500P	375C	50L	A	Rauma, FI	GB
6	STENA LYNX III	4113t	96	45k	677P	181C	-	A	Hobart, AL	BA
7	STENA VOYAGER	19638t	96	40k	1500P	375C	50L	A	Rauma, FI	GB

STENA EXPLORER Finnyards HSS1500 ('High-speed Sea Service') built for *Stena Line*. Operates on the Holyhead - Dun Laoghaire route.

STENA LYNX III InCat 81m catamaran. Chartered new by *Del Bene* of Argentina to *Stena Line* in June 1996 and named the STENA LYNX III. Initially used on the Dover - Calais service. Since summer 1997 she operated between Newhaven and Dieppe. In 1998 transferred to *P&O Stena Line* and was renamed the ELITE. She was then renamed the P&O STENA ELITE (although only carrying the name ELITE on the bow). In 1998 she was transferred back to *Stena Line*, renamed the STENA LYNX III and placed on the Fishguard - Rosslare service, replacing the STENA LYNX (3231t, 1993).

STENA VOYAGER Finnyards HSS1500 built for *Stena Line*. Operates on the Stranraer - Belfast route.

SWANSEA CORK FERRIES

THE COMPANY *Swansea Cork Ferries* is a company established in 1987 to re-open the Swansea - Cork service abandoned by *B&I Line* in 1979. It was originally jointly owned by *West Glamorgan County Council, Cork Corporation, Cork County Council* and *Kerry County Council*. The service did not operate in 1989 but resumed in 1990. In 1993 the company was acquired by *Strintzis Lines* of Greece. In 1999 it was purchased from *Strintzis Lines* by a consortium of Irish businessmen.

MANAGEMENT Managing Director: Thomas Hunter McGowan, **Sales Manager:** Alec Maguire.

ADDRESS 52 South Mall, CORK, Republic of Ireland.

TELEPHONE Administration: *Head Office:* +353 (0)21 276000, *Cork Ferry Port:* +353 (0)21 378036, **Reservations:** *IR:* +353 (0)21 271166, *UK:* +44 (0)1792 456116, **Fax:** *IR - Admin:* +353 (0)21 275814, *IR - Reservations:* +353 (0)21 275061, *UK:* +44 (0)1792 644356.

MANY YEARS SERVING CORK — DIRECTLY! —

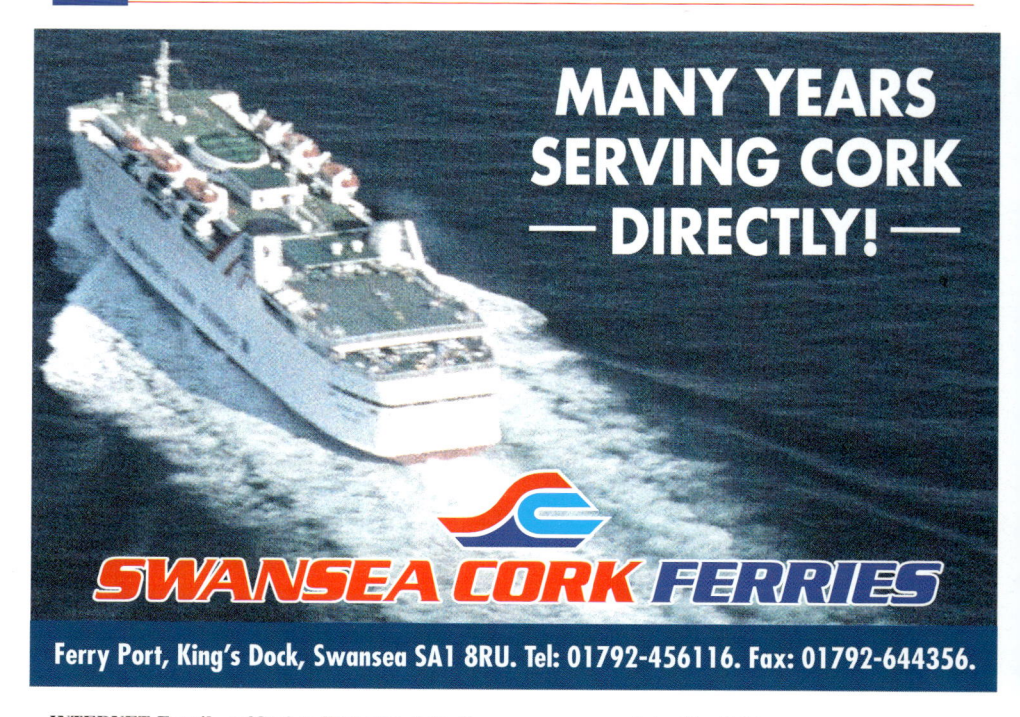

SWANSEA CORK FERRIES

Ferry Port, King's Dock, Swansea SA1 8RU. Tel: 01792-456116. Fax: 01792-644356.

INTERNET Email: scf@iol.ie **Website:** http://www.swansea-cork.ie *(English)*

ROUTE OPERATED Swansea - Cork (10 hrs; *(1)*; 1 per day or alternate days, according to season). Note: Due to tidal restrictions at Swansea, the service operates to Pembroke Dock on a few days each year.

CONVENTIONAL FERRY

1	SUPERFERRY	14797t	72	21k	1400P	350C	50L	BA2	Hashihama, JA	GR

SUPERFERRY Built as the CASSIOPEIA for *Ocean Ferry KK* of Japan. In 1976 the company became *Ocean Tokyu Ferry KK* and she was renamed the IZU NO 3. She was used on the service between Tokyo (Honshu) - Tokushima (Shikoko) - Kokura (Kyshu). In 1991 she was sold to *Strintzis Lines* and briefly renamed the IONIAN EXPRESS. Following major rebuilding, she was renamed the SUPERFERRY and used on their services between Greece and the Greek islands. In 1993 chartered to *Swansea Cork Ferries*. She will operate the 1999 season on charter to the new owners.

SECTION 2 - DOMESTIC SERVICES
ARGYLL & BUTE COUNCIL

THE COMPANY *Argyll & Bute Council* is a British local government authority.

MANAGEMENT Area Manager: N Brown.

ADDRESS Kilbowie House, Gallanach Road, OBAN PA34 4PF.

TELEPHONE Administration: +44 (0)1631 562125, **Reservations:** +44 (0)1852 300252, **Fax:** +44 (0)1631 566728.

ROUTES OPERATED Seil - Luing (5 mins; *(1)*; frequent service), Port Askaig (Islay) - Feolin (Jura) (5 mins; *(2)*; approx hourly).

VESSELS

1	BELNAHUA	35t	72	8k	40P	5C	1L	BA	Campbeltown, GB	GB
2	EILEAN DHIURA	86t	98	9k	50P	13C	1L	BA	Bromborough, GB	GB

BELNAHUA Built for *Argyll County Council* for the Seil - Luing service. In 1975, following local government reorganisation, transferred to *Strathclyde Regional Council*. In 1996, transferred to *Argyll & Bute Council*.

EILEAN DHIURA Built to replace the *Western Ferries (Argyll)* SOUND OF GIGHA on the Islay - Jura route. *Serco-Denholm Ltd* manage and operate this vessel on behalf of the *Argyll & Bute Council*.

ARRANMORE ISLAND FERRY SERVICES

THE COMPANY *Arranmore Island Ferry Services* is an Irish Republic company, supported by *Údarás na Gaeltachta (The Gaeltacht Authority)*, a semi-state owned body responsible for tourism and development in the Irish speaking areas of The Irish Republic. The operation is also known as *Maoin-Na-Farraige* (literally 'sea treasure' or 'sea wealth').

MANAGEMENT Managing Director: Cornelius Bonner.

ADDRESS Bridge House, Leabgarrow, ARRANMORE, County Donegal, Republic of Ireland.

TELEPHONE Administration & Reservations: +353 (0)75 20532, **Fax:** + 353 (0)75 20750.

ROUTE OPERATED Burtonport (County Donegal) - Leabgarrow (Arranmore Island) (20 mins; *(1,2,3,4)*; up to 8 per day (summer), 5 per day (winter)).

VESSELS

1	ÁRAINN MHÓR	64t	72	8k	138P	4C	-	B	Port Glasgow, GB	GB
2	COLL	69t	74	8k	152P	6C	-	B	Port Glasgow, GB	GB
3	MORVERN	64t	73	8k	138P	4C	-	B	Port Glasgow, GB	GB
4	RHUM	69t	73	8k	164P	6C	-	B	Port Glasgow, GB	GB

ÁRAINN MHÓR Built as the KILBRANNAN for *Caledonian MacBrayne*. Used on a variety of routes until 1977, she was then transferred to the Scalpay (Harris) - Kyles Scalpay service. In 1990 she was replaced by the CANNA and, in turn, replaced the CANNA in her reserve/relief role. In 1992 sold to *Arranmore Island Ferry Services* and renamed the ÁRAINN MHÓR.

COLL Built for *Caledonian MacBrayne*. For several years she was employed mainly in a relief capacity. In 1986 she took over the Tobermory (Mull) - Kilchoan service from a passenger only vessel; the conveyance of vehicles was not inaugurated until 1991. In 1996 she was transferred to the Oban - Lismore route. In 1998 she was sold to *Arranmore Island Ferry Services*.

MORVERN Built for *Caledonian MacBrayne*. After service on a number of routes she was, after 1979, the main vessel on the Fionnphort (Mull) - Iona service. In 1992 replaced by the LOCH BUIE and became a spare vessel. In 1995 sold to *Arranmore Island Ferry Services*.

RHUM Built for *Caledonian MacBrayne*. Until 1987, she was used primarily on the Claonaig - Lochranza (Arran) service. After that time she served on various routes. In 1994 she inaugurated a new service between Tarbert (Loch Fyne) and Portavadie. In 1997 operated between Kyles Scalpay and Scalpay until the opening of the new bridge on 16th December 1997. In 1998 she was sold to *Arranmore Island Ferry Services*.

BERE ISLAND FERRIES

THE COMPANY *Bere Island Ferries Ltd* is an Irish Republic private sector company.

MANAGEMENT Operator: C Harrington.

ADDRESS Ferry Lodge, West End, BERE ISLAND, County Cork, Republic of Ireland.

TELEPHONE Administration: +353 (0)27 75009, **Reservations:** Not applicable.

INTERNET Email: tjb@indigo.ie.

ROUTE OPERATED Castletownbere (County Cork) - Bere Island (10 mins; *(1,2)*; up to 10 per day).

VESSELS

1	F.B.D. DUNBRODY	139t	60	8k	107P	18C	-	BA	Hamburg, GY	IR
2	MISNEACH	30t	78	7k	80P	4C	-	B	New Ross, IR	IR

F.B.D. DUNBRODY Built as the BERNE-FARGE for the service between Berne and Farge, across the River Weser in Germany. Subsequently she was sold to *Elbe Clearing* of Germany, renamed the ELBE CLEARING 12 and used as a floating platform for construction works in the Elbe. In 1979 she was sold to *Passage East Ferry Company* and renamed the F.B.D. DUNBRODY. Withdrawn in January 1998 and became a spare vessel. Later in 1998 she was sold to *Bere Island Ferries*.

MISNEACH Built for *Arranmore Island Ferry Services* of the Irish Republic and used on their Burtonport - Arranmore service. In 1992 sold to *Bere Island Ferries*. In 1993 inaugurated a car ferry service between Castletownbere and Bere Island. Now reserve vessel.

CALEDONIAN MACBRAYNE

THE COMPANY *Caledonian MacBrayne* Limited is a British state owned company, the responsibility of the Secretary of State for Scotland. Until 1990 it was part of the state owned Scottish Transport Group (formed in 1969). *Caledonian MacBrayne* Limited as such was formed in 1973 by the merger of the *Caledonian Steam Packet Company Ltd* (which had been formed in 1889) and *David MacBrayne Ltd* (whose origins go back to 1851). The company has more vessels sailing under the British flag than any other.

MANAGEMENT Managing Director: Capt J A B Simkins, **Marketing Manager:** Mike Blair.

ADDRESS The Ferry Terminal, GOUROCK PA19 1QP.

TELEPHONE Administration: +44 (0)1475 650100, **Vehicle Reservations:** 0990 650000 (from UK only), **Fax: Admin:** +44 (0)1475 637607, *Vehicle Reservations:* +44 (0)1475 635235.

INTERNET Email: mike.blair@calmac.co.uk **Website:** http://www.calmac.co.uk *(English)*

ROUTES OPERATED *All year vehicle ferries (frequencies are for summer):* Ardrossan - Brodick (Arran) (55 mins; *(2)*; up to 6 per day), Largs - Cumbrae Slip (Cumbrae) (10 mins; *(13,20)*; every 30 or 15 mins), Wemyss Bay - Rothesay (Bute) (30 mins; *(11,12,25,27)*; up to 22 per day), Colintraive

Lord of the Isles *(Brian Maxted)*

St Sunniva *(Miles Cowsill)*

- Rhubodach (Bute) (5 mins; *(16)*; frequent service), Tarbert (Loch Fyne) - Portavadie (20 mins; *(8)*; up to 11 per day), Gourock - Dunoon (20 mins; *(11,12,27)*; hourly service with extras at peaks), Kennacraig - Port Ellen (Islay) (2 hrs 15 mins; *(7)*; 1 or 2 per day), Kennacraig - Port Askaig (Islay) (2 hrs; *(7)*; 1 or 2 per day), Tayinloan - Gigha (20 mins; *(19)*; hourly with some gaps), Oban - Lismore (50 mins; *(26)*; up to 4 per day), Oban - Colonsay (2 hrs 10 mins; *(4,7,10)*; 3 per week), Oban - Craignure (Mull) (40 mins; *(10)*; two hourly), Oban - Coll (2 hrs 45 mins (direct), 4 hrs 50 mins (via Tiree); *(4 (summer), 24 (winter))*; up to 5 per week), Oban - Tiree (3 hrs 30 mins (direct), 4 hrs 15 mins (via Coll *(4 (summer), 24 (winter))*; up to 5 per week), Oban - Castlebay (Barra) (5 hrs (direct); *(4 (summer), 24 (winter))*; 4 per week), Oban - Lochboisdale (South Uist) (5 hrs (direct), 7 hrs (via Barra); *(4 (summer), 24 (winter))*; 5 per week), Otternish (North Uist) - Leverburgh (Harris) (1 hr 10 mins; *(14)*; 3-4 per day), Lochaline - Fishnish (Mull) (15 mins; *(17)*; up to 16 per day), Sconser (Skye) - Raasay (15 mins; *(21)*; up to 10 per day), Uig (Skye) - Tarbert (Harris) (1 hr 45 mins; *(6)*; 1 or 2 per day), Uig (Skye) - Lochmaddy (North Uist) (1 hr 45 mins; *(6)*; 1 or 2 per day), Ullapool - Stornoway (Lewis) (2 hrs 40 mins; *(9)*; up to 3 per day). ***All year passenger and restricted vehicle ferries (frequencies are for summer):*** Fionnphort (Mull) - Iona (5 mins; *(15)*; frequent), Ballycastle (Northern Ireland) - Rathlin Island (40 mins; *(3)*; 2 per day). Note: although these services are operated by vehicle ferries, special permission is required to take a vehicle on the ferry and tourist vehicles are not conveyed. ***All year passenger only ferries (frequencies are for summer):*** Mallaig - Eigg - Muck - Rum - Canna - Mallaig (passenger only) (round trip 7 hrs (all islands); *(23)*; at least 1 sailing per day - most islands visited daily). ***Summer only vehicle ferries:*** Claonaig - Lochranza (Arran) (30 mins; *(22)*; up to 10 per day), Kennacraig - Port Askaig - Colonsay - Oban (3 hrs 35 mins; *(7)*; 1 per week), Tobermory (Mull) - Kilchoan (35 mins; *(18)*; up to 11 per day), Mallaig - Armadale (Skye) (cars and passengers) (30 mins; *(24)*; up to 7 per day), Mallaig - Lochboisdale (3 hrs 15 mins); *(24)*; 1 per week), Mallaig - Castlebay (3 hrs 45 mins); *(24)*; 1 per week. ***Winter only passenger and restricted vehicle ferries:*** Mallaig - Armadale (Skye) (30 mins; *(23)*; up to 2 per day), Tarbert - Lochranza (1 hr; *(varies)*; 1 per day). ***Clyde Cruising*** In addition to car and passenger services, the following cruises are operated in the Clyde between May and September; parts of these cruises are sometimes normal car/passenger services: Gourock - Dunoon - Largs - Rothesay - Tighnabruaich - Tarbert (Loch Fyne)(*(11,12,27)*; 2 per week (only one per week to Tarbert), Gourock - Dunoon - Rothesay - Millport (*(11,12,27)*; 1 per week).

VESSELS

1	BRUERNISH	69t	73	8k	164P	6C	-	B	Port Glasgow, GB	GB
2	CALEDONIAN ISLES	5221t	93	15k	1000P	120C	-	BA	Lowestoft, GB	GB
3	CANNA	69t	73	8k	140P	6C	-	B	Port Glasgow, GB	GB
4	CLANSMAN	5499t	98	-	634P	90C	-	BA	Appledore, GB	GB
5	EIGG	69t	75	8k	75P	6C	-	B	Port Glasgow, GB	GB
6	HEBRIDEAN ISLES	3040t	85	15k	507P	68C	-	BAS	Selby, GB	GB
7	ISLE OF ARRAN	3296t	84	15k	659P	68C	-	BA	Port Glasgow, GB	GB
8	ISLE OF CUMBRAE	169t	77	8.5k	138P	15C	-	BA	Troon, GB	GB
9	ISLE OF LEWIS	6753t	95	18k	680P	123C	-	BA	Port Glasgow, GB	GB
10	ISLE OF MULL	4719t	88	15k	1000P	80C	-	BA	Port Glasgow, GB	GB
11	JUNO	902t	74	14k	531P	40C	-	AS	Port Glasgow, GB	GB
12	JUPITER	898t	74	14k	531P	40C	-	AS	Port Glasgow, GB	GB
13	LOCH ALAINN	396t	97	10k	150P	24C	-	BA	Buckie, GB	GB
14	LOCH BHRUSDA	246t	96	8k	150P	18C	-	BA	Bromborough, GB	GB
15	LOCH BUIE	295t	92	8k	250P	9C	-	BA	St Monans, GB	GB
16	LOCH DUNVEGAN	550t	91	9k	150P	36C	-	BA	Port Glasgow, GB	GB
17	LOCH FYNE	550t	91	9k	150P	36C	-	BA	Port Glasgow, GB	GB
18	LOCH LINNHE	206t	86	8k	199P	12C	-	BA	Hessle, GB	GB
19	LOCH RANZA	206t	87	8k	199P	12C	-	BA	Hessle, GB	GB
20	LOCH RIDDON	206t	86	8k	199P	12C	-	BA	Hessle, GB	GB

21	LOCH STRIVEN	206t	86	8k	199P	12C	-	BA	Hessle, GB	GB
22	LOCH TARBERT	211t	92	8k	149P	18C	-	BA	St Monans, GB	GB
23	LOCHMOR	175t	79	10k	129P	-	-	C	Troon, GB	GB
24	LORD OF THE ISLES	3504t	89	16k	506P	56C	-	BAS	Port Glasgow, GB	GB
25	PIONEER	1088t	74	16k	356P	33C	-	AS	Leith, GB	GB
26	RAASAY	69t	76	8k	75P	6C	-	B	Port Glasgow, GB	GB
27	SATURN	899t	78	14k	531P	40C	-	AS	Troon, GB	GB

BRUERNISH Until 1980 she served on a variety of routes. In 1980 she inaugurated ro-ro working between Tayinloan and the island of Gigha and served this route until June 1992 when she was replaced by the LOCH RANZA and became a relief vessel. In summer 1994 she operated as secondary vessel on the Tobermory (Mull) - Kilchoan service for one season only. In December 1996 she started a vehicle ferry service between Ballycastle (on the North West coast of Northern Ireland) and Rathlin Island under charter; the route became a *Caledonian MacBrayne* operation in April 1997 - see the CANNA. In 1997 she operated on the Tarbert - Portavadie service and in 1998 on the Oban - Lismore service. In 1999 she is likely to be a spare vessel.

CALEDONIAN ISLES Built for the Ardrossan - Brodick (Arran) service and has to date not operated on any other route.

CANNA She was the regular vessel on the Lochaline - Fishnish (Mull) service. In 1986 she was replaced by the ISLE OF CUMBRAE and until 1990 she served in a relief capacity in the north, often assisting on the Iona service. In 1990 she replaced the KILBRANNAN (see the ÁRAINN MHÓR, *Arranmore Island Ferry Services*) on the Kyles Scalpay (Harris) - Scalpay service (replaced by a bridge in autumn 1997). In spring 1997 she was transferred to the Ballycastle - Rathlin Island route.

CLANSMAN Built to replace the LORD OF THE ISLES on the Oban - Coll and Tiree and Oban - Castlebay and Lochboisdale service. She also serves as winter relief vessel on the Stornoway, Tarbert, Lochmaddy, Mull, Islay and Brodick services.

EIGG Since 1976 she was employed mainly on the Oban - Lismore service. In 1996 she was transferred to the Tobermory (Mull) - Kilchoan route, very occasionally making special sailings to the Small Isles (Canna, Eigg, Muck and Rum) for special cargoes. In 1999 she is expected to be a spare vessel.

HEBRIDEAN ISLES Built for the Uig - Tarbert/Lochmaddy service. She was used initially on the Ullapool - Stornoway and Oban - Craignure/Colonsay services pending installation of link-span facilities at Uig, Tarbert and Lochmaddy. She took up her regular role in May 1986. Since May 1996 she has no longer operated direct services between Tarbert and Lochmaddy, this role being taken on by the new Harris - North Uist services of the LOCH BHRUSDA. In 1999 Berneray replaced Otternish as the southern terminal, following the opening of a causeway between North Uist and Berneray in autumn 1998.

ISLE OF ARRAN Built for the Ardrossan - Brodick service. In 1993 transferred to the Kennacraig - Port Ellen/Port Askaig service, also undertaking the weekly Port Askaig - Colonsay - Oban summer service. Until 1997/98 she also relieved on the Brodick, Coll/Tiree, Castlebay/Lochboisdale, Craignure and Tarbert/Lochmaddy routes in winter.

ISLE OF CUMBRAE Built for the Largs - Cumbrae Slip (Cumbrae) service. In 1986 she was replaced by the LOCH LINNHE and the LOCH STRIVEN and transferred to the Lochaline - Fishnish (Mull) service. She used to spend most of the winter as secondary vessel on the Kyle of Lochalsh - Kyleakin service; however this ceased following the opening of the Skye Bridge in 1995. In 1997 she was transferred to the Colintraive - Rhubodach service but returned to Lochaline for part of the winter. In 1998 operated on the Colintraive - Rhubodach service. In summer 1999 she is to be transferred to the Tarbert - Portavadie service.

ISLE OF LEWIS Built to replace the SUILVEN on the Ullapool - Stornoway service. Largest vessel ever to operate on Clyde or Western Isles routes and has never operated on any other service.

ISLE OF MULL Built for the Oban - Craignure (Mull) service. She also operates the Oban - Colonsay service and until 1997/98 was the usual winter relief vessel on the Ullapool - Stornoway service. She has also deputised on the Oban - Castlebay/Lochboisdale and Oban - Coll/Tiree routes.

JUNO, JUPITER, SATURN Built for the Gourock - Dunoon, Gourock - Kilcreggan and Wemyss Bay - Rothesay services. The JUPITER has been upgraded to Class III standard for the Ardrossan - Brodick service. Before 1986, the JUNO and JUPITER operated mainly on the Gourock - Dunoon and Gourock - Kilcreggan (now withdrawn) services and the SATURN on the Wemyss Bay - Rothesay service. Since 1986 they have usually rotated on a four weekly basis on the three services. They are all used on the summer cruise programme. Since 1996 they rotate weekly on the Dunoon and Rothesay services plus cruising.

LOCH ALAINN Built for the Lochaline - Fishnish service. Launched as the LOCH ALINE but renamed the LOCH ALAINN before entering service. After a brief period on the service she was built for, she was transferred to the Colintraive - Rhubodach route. She was transferred to the Largs - Cumbrae Slip service in summer 1998.

LOCH BHRUSDA Built to inaugurate a new Otternish (North Uist) - Berneray - Leverburgh (Harris) service. Note: 'Bhrusda' is pronounced "Vroosda".

LOCH BUIE Built for the Fionnphort (Mull) - Iona service to replace the MORVERN (see *Arranmore Island Ferry Services*) and obviate the need for a relief vessel in the summer. Due to height restrictions, loading arrangements for vehicles taller than private cars are bow only. Only islanders' cars and service vehicles (eg mail vans, police) are carried; no tourist vehicles are conveyed.

LOCH DUNVEGAN Built for the Kyle of Lochalsh - Kyleakin service. On the opening of the Skye Bridge in October 1995 she was withdrawn from service and put up for sale. In autumn 1997, returned to service on the Lochaline - Fishnish route. In 1998 she was due to be transferred to the Colintraive - Rhubodach route but this was delayed due to problems in providing terminal facilities. She operated on the Clyde and between Mallaig and Armadale during the early summer and spent the rest of the summer laid up. In 1999 it is expected that she will finally take over the Colintraive - Rhubodach route.

LOCH FYNE Built for the Kyle of Lochalsh - Kyleakin service (see the LOCH DUNVEGAN). In autumn 1997, she also served on the Lochaline - Fishnish route and was transferred to this route as regular vessel in 1998.

LOCH LINNHE Until 1997, used mainly on the Largs - Cumbrae Slip (Cumbrae) service. Until winter 1994/95 she was usually used on the Lochaline - Fishnish service during the winter. Since then she had relieved on various routes in winter. In summer 1998 she operated mainly on the Tarbert - Portavadie route. In 1999 she is expected to operate on the summer only Tobermory - Kilchoan service.

LOCH RANZA Built for the Claonaig - Lochranza (Arran) seasonal service and used a relief vessel in the winter. In 1992 she was replaced by the LOCH TARBERT and transferred to the Tayinloan - Gigha service.

LOCH RIDDON Until 1997 she was used almost exclusively on the Colintraive - Rhubodach service. In 1997, she was transferred to the Largs - Cumbrae Slip service.

LOCH STRIVEN Used mainly on the Largs - Cumbrae Slip service until 1997. In winter 1995/6 and 1996/67 she was used on the Tarbert - Portavadie and Claonaig - Lochranza routes. In 1997 she took over the Sconser - Raasay service.

LOCH TARBERT Built for the Claonaig - Lochranza service. She has been the regular winter vessel on the Largs - Cumbrae Slip route since winter 1994/5 and is also the winter relief vessel for the Otternish - Leverburgh route.

LOCHMOR Built for the passenger only 'Small Isles' service from Mallaig to Eigg, Muck, Rum and Canna with, until 1997, weekly summer cruises to Kyle of Lochalsh. She also maintains the winter restricted passenger-only service between Mallaig and Armadale. She can convey a small vehicle for the islands as cargo but this service is not available to tourists.

LORD OF THE ISLES Built to replace the CLAYMORE on the Oban - Castlebay and Lochboisdale services and also the COLUMBA (1420t, 1964) on the Oban - Coll and Tiree service. She took over Mallaig - Armadale and Mallaig - Outer Isles service in July 1998 but returned to her previous routes during the winter period. In summer 1999 will again operate from Mallaig.

PIONEER Built to operate on the West Loch Tarbert - Port Ellen service (see the PENTALINA B, *Pentland Ferries*). When the IONA was at last able to operate this service in 1978 (following the move to Kennacraig) the PIONEER was transferred to the Mallaig - Armadale service, operating as a relief vessel in the winter on Upper Clyde and Small Isles routes. In 1989 she was replaced at Mallaig by the IONA and became the company's spare vessel, replacing the GLEN SANNOX (1269t, 1957). Since summer 1995 she has undertaken Wemyss Bay - Rothesay and Rothesay - Largs - Brodick sailings. She serves as a Clyde and Small Isles relief vessel in the winter replacing the JUNO, JUPITER, SATURN and LOCHMOR for annual overhaul. In 1998 she opened the Mallaig - Armadale/Outer Isles service and temporarily operated between Oban and Craignure before returning to the Clyde in July. In summer 1999 she is expected to operate on the Clyde, solely on the Wemyss Bay - Rothesay route.

RAASAY Built for and used primarily on the Sconser (Skye) - Raasay service. In 1997 she was replaced by the LOCH STRIVEN and became a spare/relief vessel. In 1999 she is likely to operate on the Oban - Lismore service.

SATURN As the JUNO and JUPITER. In earlier days operated mainly on the Wemyss Bay - Rothesay service.

Caledonian MacBrayne also operates the ULVA, a 35 ft motor vessel built in 1958 and carrying up to 28 passengers. She tenders to the LOCHMOR at Eigg, Muck and Rum.

Under Construction

| 28 | NEWBUILDING 1 | - | 00 | - | 200P | 14C | - | BA | Troon, GB | GB |
| 29 | NEWBUILDING 2 | - | 00 | - | 650P | 110C | - | BA | Port Glasgow, GB | GB |

NEWBUILDING 1 Under construction to replace the LOCHMOR on the Mallaig - Small Isles service. Although a vehicle ferry, cars will not be normally be carried. The ro-ro facility will be used for the carriage of agricultural machinery and livestock and it will be possible to convey a vehicle on the ferry from which goods can be unloaded directly onto local transport rather than transhipping at Mallaig. Ramps are to be provided at each island and the practice of tendering at Eigg, Muck and Rum will cease, the ULVA being disposed of.

NEWBUILDING 2 Under construction to replace the HEBRIDEAN ISLES on the Uig - Tarbert and Uig - Lochmaddy services. The HEBRIDEAN ISLES is likely to replace the PIONEER as the spare vessel for the fleet.

COMHAIRLE NAN EILEAN SIAR

THE COMPANY *Comhairle Nan Eilean Siar* (formerly the *Western Isles Council*) is a British municipal authority.

ADDRESS Council Offices, Sandwick Road, STORNOWAY, Isle of Lewis HS1 2BW.

TELEPHONE Administration: +44 (0)1851 703773, Extn 440 **Reservations:** +44 (0)1878 720261, **Fax:** +44 (0)1851 706426.

INTERNET Email: mmaciver@w-iles.gov.uk **Website:** http://www.open.gov.uk/westile/wiichome.htm *(English)*

ROUTES OPERATED Car Ferries: Ludaig (South Uist) - Eriskay (30 mins; *(3)*; 3 per day (minimum)) (additional services operate during the summer). **Passenger Only Ferry:** Ludaig (South Uist) - Eriskay (15 mins; *(1)*; 3 per day), Ludaig (South Uist) - Eoligarry (Barra) (40 mins; *(1)*; 2 per day).

VESSELS

1p	ALLASDALE LASS	-	98	12k	50P	0C	0T	-	Stornoway, GB	GB
2•	EILEAN BHEARNARAIGH	67t	83	7k	35P	4C	1T	BA	Glasgow, GB	GB
3	EILEAN NA H-OIGE	69t	80	7k	35P	4C	1T	BA	Stornoway, GB	GB

ALLASDALE LASS Owned and operated by *G V MacLeod Ltd* on behalf of *Comhairle Nan Eilean Siar*. Operates passenger only sailings between Ludaig and Eriskay and Barra.

EILEAN BHEARNARAIGH Built for *Western Isles Islands Council* for their Otternish (North Uist) - Berneray service. Since 1996 she has been operated by *Caledonian MacBrayne* in conjunction with the LOCH BHRUSDA on the service between Otternish and Berneray. During the winter she is laid up. Following the opening of a causeway between North Uist and Berneray in early 1999, she is now relief vessel for the Ludaig - Eoligarry route.

EILEAN NA H-OIGE Built for *Western Isles Islands Council* (from 1st April 1996 the *Western Isles Council* and from 1st January 1998 *Comhairle Nan Eilean Siar*) for their Ludaig - Eriskay service.

CROSS RIVER FERRIES

THE COMPANY *Cross River Ferries Ltd* is an Irish Republic company, jointly owned by *Marine Transport Services Ltd* of Cobh and *Arklow Shipping Ltd* of Arklow, County Wicklow.

MANAGEMENT Operations Manager: Edward Perry.

ADDRESS Atlantic Quay, COBH, County Cork, Republic of Ireland.

TELEPHONE Administration: +353 (0)21 811223, **Reservations:** Not applicable, **Fax:** +353 (0)21 812645.

ROUTE OPERATED Carrigaloe (near Cobh, on Great Island) - Glenbrook (Co Cork) (4 mins; *(1,2)*; frequent service (one or two vessels used according to demand).

VESSELS

1	CARRIGALOE	225t	70	8k	200P	27C	-	BA	Newport (Gwent), GBIR
2	GLENBROOK	225t	71	8k	200P	27C	-	BA	Newport (Gwent), GBIR

CARRIGALOE, GLENBROOK Built as the KYLEAKIN and the LOCHALSH for *David MacBrayne Ltd* (later *Caledonian MacBrayne*) for the Kyle of Lochalsh - Kyleakin service. In 1991 replaced by the LOCH DUNVEGAN and the LOCH FYNE and sold to *Marine Transport Services Ltd* who renamed them the CARRIGALOE and the GLENBROOK respectively. They entered service in March 1993.

GLENELG - KYLERHEA FERRY

THE COMPANY The *Glenelg - Kylerhea Ferry* is privately operated.

MANAGEMENT Ferry Master: R MacLeod.

ADDRESS Corriehallie, Inverinate, KYLE IV40 8HD.

TELEPHONE Administration: +44 (0)1599 511302, **Reservations:** +44 (0)1599 511302, **Fax:** +44 (0)07070 600845.

ROUTE OPERATED *Easter - October only:* Glenelg - Kylerhea (Skye) (10 mins; *(1)*; frequent service).

VESSEL

1	GLENACHULISH		44t	69	9k	12P	6C	-	BSt	Troon, GB	GB

GLENACHULISH Built for the *Ballachulish Ferry Company* for the service between North Ballachulish and South Ballachulish, across the mouth of Loch Leven. In 1975 the ferry was replaced by a bridge and she was sold to *Highland Regional Council* and used on a relief basis on the North Kessock - South Kessock and Kylesku - Kylestrome routes. In 1984 she was sold to the operator of the Glenelg - Kylerhea service. She is the last turntable ferry in operation.

THE HIGHLAND COUNCIL

THE COMPANY *The Highland Council* (previously *Highland Regional Council*) is a British local government authority.

MANAGEMENT Ferry Manager: J McAuslane.

ADDRESS Ferry Cottage, Ardgour, FORT WILLIAM.

TELEPHONE Administration: *Corran:* +44 (0)1855 841243, *Fort William:* +44 (0)1397 772483, **Reservations:** Not applicable, **Fax:** +44 (0)1855 841243,.

ROUTES OPERATED Vehicle Ferries: Corran - Ardgour (5 mins; *(2,3)*; half hourly), **Passenger Only Ferry:** Fort William - Camusnagaul (10 mins; *(1)*, frequent).

VESSELS

1p	CAILIN AN AISEAG	-	80	7.5k	26P	0C	0L	-	Buckie, GB	GB
2	MAID OF GLENCOUL	166t	75	8k	116P	16C	-	BA	Ardrossan, GB	GB
3	ROSEHAUGH	150t	67	8.5k	150P	18C	-	BA	Berwick on Tweed, GB	GB

CAILIN AN AISEAG Built for *Highland Regional Council* and used on the Fort William - Camusnagaul service.

MAID OF GLENCOUL Built for *Highland Regional Council* for the service between Kylesku and Kylestrome. In 1984 the ferry service was replaced by a bridge and she was transferred to the Corran - Ardgour service. In April 1996, ownership transferred to *The Highland Council.*

ROSEHAUGH Built for *Ross and Cromarty County Council* for the service between South Kessock and North Kessock (across the Beauly Firth, north of Inverness). In 1975, ownership was transferred to *Highland Regional Council.* In 1982 a bridge was opened and she was transferred to the Corran - Ardgour route. Following the arrival of the MAID OF GLENCOUL in 1984 she has been the reserve vessel. In April 1996, ownership transferred to *The Highland Council.*

ISLES OF SCILLY STEAMSHIP COMPANY

THE COMPANY *Isles of Scilly Steamship Company* is a British private sector company.

MANAGEMENT Group Operations Manager: R Johns, **Marketing Manager:** J Hoelen.

ADDRESS *Scilly:* PO Box 10, Hugh Town, ST MARY'S, Isles of Scilly TR21 0LJ, *Penzance:* Steamship House, Quay Street, PENZANCE, Cornwall, TR18 4BD.

TELEPHONE Administration & Reservations: *Scilly:* +44 (0)1720 422357, *Penzance:* +44 (0)1736 334220, **Fax:** *Scilly:* +44 (0)1720 422192, *Penzance:* +44 (0)1736 351223.

INTERNET Email: sales@islesofscilly-travel.co.uk **Website:** http://www.islesofscilly-travel.co.uk *(English)*

ROUTES OPERATED Penzance - St Mary's (Isles of Scilly) (2 hrs 40 mins; *(1,3)*; 1 per day). **Freight services:** St Mary's - Tresco/St Martin's/St Agnes/Bryher; *(2)*; irregular).

VESSELS

1	GRY MARITHA	550t	81	10.5k	12P	5C	1L	C	Kolvereid, NO	GB
2	LYONESSE LADY	50t	91	9k	12P	1C	0L	A	Fort William, GB	GB
3p	SCILLONIAN III	1256t	77	15.5k	600P	-	-	C	Appledore, GB	GB

GRY MARITHA Built for *Gjofor* of Norway. In design she is a coaster rather than a ferry. In 1990 sold to *Isles of Scilly Steamship Company*. She operates a freight and passenger service all year (conveying all residents' cars and other vehicles to and from the islands - tourist cars are not conveyed). During the winter she provides the only sea passenger service to the islands, the SCILLONIAN III being laid up.

LYONESSE LADY Built for inter-island ferry work.

SCILLONIAN III Built for the Penzance - St Mary's service. She operates from Easter to late autumn and is laid up in the winter. Last major conventional passenger/cargo ferry built for UK waters and probably Western Europe. Extensively refurbished during winter 1998/99.

ORKNEY FERRIES

THE COMPANY *Orkney Ferries Ltd* (previously the *Orkney Islands Shipping Company*) is a British company, owned by *The Orkney Islands Council*.

MANAGEMENT Operations Director: R S Moore, **Ferry Services Manager:** A Learmonth.

ADDRESS Shore Street, KIRKWALL, Orkney KW15 1LG.

TELEPHONE Administration: +44 (0)1856 872044, **Reservations:** +44 (0)1856 872044, **Fax:** +44 (0)1856 872921, **Telex:** 75475.

INTERNET Website: http://www.orkneyislands.com/travel/orkfer *(English)*

ROUTES OPERATED Kirkwall (Mainland) to Eday (1 hr, 15 mins), Westray (1 hr 25 mins), Sanday (1 hr 25 mins), Stronsay (1 hr 35 mins), Papa Westray (1 hr 50 mins), North Ronaldsay (2 hrs 30 mins) ('North Isles service') (timings are direct from Kirkwall - sailings via other islands take longer; *(1,2,9)*; 1 per day except Papa Westray which is twice weekly and North Ronaldsay which is weekly), Pierowall (Westray) - Papa Westray (25 mins; *(4)*; up to six per day (passenger only)), Kirkwall - Shapinsay (25 mins; *(7)*; 6 per day), Houton (Mainland) to Lyness (Hoy) (35 mins; *(6)*; 5 per day), Flotta (35 mins; *(6)*; 4 per day) and Graemsay (25 mins; *(6)*; weekly) ('South Isles service') (timings are direct from Houton - sailings via other islands take longer), Tingwall (Mainland) to Rousay (20 mins; *(3)*; 6 per day), Egilsay (30 mins; *(3)*; 5 per day) and Wyre (20 mins; *(3)*; 5 per day) (timings are direct from Tingwall - sailings via other islands take longer), Stromness (Mainland) to Moaness

(Hoy) (25 mins; *(5)*; 2/3 per day) and Graemsay (25 mins; *(5)*; 2/3 per day) (passenger/cargo service - cars not normally conveyed).

VESSELS

1	EARL SIGURD	771t	90	12k	190P	26C	-	BA	Bromborough, GB	GB
2	EARL THORFINN	771t	90	12k	190P	26C	-	BA	Bromborough, GB	GB
3	EYNHALLOW	79t	87	9.5k	95P	8C	-	BA	Bristol, GB	GB
4p	GOLDEN MARIANA	33t	73	9.5k	40P	0C	-	-	Bideford, GB	GB
5	GRAEMSAY	82t	96	10k	73P	1C	-	C	Troon, GB	GB
6	HOY HEAD	358t	94	9.8k	125P	18C	-	BA	Bideford, GB	GB
7	SHAPINSAY	199t	89	9.5k	91P	12C	-	BA	Hull, GB	GB
8	THORSVOE	400t	91	10.5k	96P	16C	-	BA	Campbeltown, GB	GB
9	VARAGEN	950t	89	12k	144P	33C	5L	BA	Selby, GB	GB

EARL SIGURD, EARL THORFINN Built to inaugurate ro-ro working on the 'North Isles' service (see above).

EYNHALLOW Built to inaugurate ro-ro services from Tingwall (Mainland) to Rousay, Egilsay and Wyre. In 1991 she was lengthened by 5 metres, to increase car capacity.

GOLDEN MARIANA Passenger only vessel. Generally operates feeder service between Pierowall (Westray) and Papa Westray.

GRAEMSAY Built to operate between Stromness (Mainland), Moaness (Hoy) and Graemsay. Designed to offer an all year round service to these islands, primarily for passengers and cargo.

HOY HEAD Built to replace the THORSVOE on the 'South Isles' service (see above).

SHAPINSAY Built for the service from Kirkwall (Mainland) to Shapinsay.

THORSVOE Built for the 'South Isles' service (see above). In 1994 replaced by new HOY HEAD and became the main reserve vessel for the fleet.

VARAGEN Built for *Orkney Ferries*, a private company established to start a new route between Gills Bay (Caithness, Scotland) and Burwick (South Ronaldsay, Orkney). However, due to problems with the terminals it was not possible to maintain regular services. In 1991, the company was taken over by *OISC* and the VARAGEN became part of their fleet, sharing 'North Isles' services with the EARL SIGURD and the EARL THORFINN and replacing the freight vessel ISLANDER (494t, 1969).

P&O SCOTTISH FERRIES

THE COMPANY *P&O Scottish Ferries* is British private sector company, a subsidiary of the *Peninsular and Oriental Steam Navigation Company*. The name was changed from *P&O Ferries* to *P&O Scottish Ferries* in 1989.

MANAGEMENT Managing Director: Terry Cairns, **Marketing Director:** Scott Colegate.

ADDRESS PO Box 5, Jamieson's Quay, ABERDEEN AB9 8DL.

TELEPHONE Administration: +44 (0)1224 589111 **Reservations:** +44 (0)1224 572615, **Fax:** +44 (0)1224 574411.

INTERNET Email: passenger@poscottishferries.co.uk **Website:** http://www.poscottishferries.co.uk *(English)*

ROUTES OPERATED Scrabster - Stromness (Orkney) (1 hr 45 mins; *(2)*; up to 3 per day)), Aberdeen - Lerwick (Shetland) (direct) (14 hrs; *(1,3)*; up to 4 per week), Aberdeen - Stromness (8 hrs (day), 14 hrs (night)) - Lerwick (8 hrs; *(3)*; 1 per week (2 per week June, July and August)).

VESSELS

1	ST CLAIR	8696t	71	19k	600P	160C	30L	A	Bremerhaven, GY	GB
2	ST OLA	4833t	71	16k	500P	140C	12L	BA	Papenburg, GY	GB
3	ST SUNNIVA	6350t	71	16k	400P	199C	28L	A	Helsingør, DK	GB

ST CLAIR Built as the TRAVEMÜNDE for *Gedser-Travemünde Ruten* for their service between Gedser (Denmark) and Travemünde (Germany). In 1981 she was sold to *Prekookeanska Plovidba* of Yugoslavia, renamed the NJEGOS and used on their services between Yugoslavia, Greece and Italy. In 1984 chartered to *Sally Line* for use on their Ramsgate - Dunkerque service. In 1985 she was taken on a two year charter by *Brittany Ferries*, renamed the TREGASTEL and moved to the Plymouth - Roscoff service. In 1987 she was purchased and re-registered in France. In 1989 she was replaced by the QUIBERON and transferred to *Truckline Ferries* for their Poole - Cherbourg service. In 1991 she was renamed the TREG and sold to *P&O Scottish Ferries*. Following a major refit she was, in 1992, renamed the ST CLAIR and in March 1992 introduced onto the Aberdeen - Lerwick service, replacing the previous ST CLAIR (4468t, 1965). In addition to operating between Aberdeen and Lerwick, in 1993 she inaugurated a weekly peak season Lerwick - Bergen (Norway) service; this service last operated in 1997.

ST OLA Built as the SVEA SCARLETT for *Stockholms Rederi AB Svea* of Sweden and used on the *SL (Skandinavisk Linjetrafik)* service between København (Tuborg Havn) and Landskrona (Sweden). In 1980 she was sold to *Scandinavian Ferry Lines* of Sweden and *Dampskibsselskabet Øresund A/S* of Denmark (jointly owned). Initially she continued to serve Landskrona but later that year the Swedish terminal became Malmö. In 1981 she operated on the Helsingborg - Helsingør service for a short while, after which she was withdrawn and laid up. In 1982 she was sold to *Eckerö Linjen* of Finland, renamed the ECKERÖ and used on services between Grisslehamn (Sweden) and Eckerö (Åland Islands). In 1991 she was sold to *P&O Scottish Ferries* and renamed the ST OLA. In March 1992 she replaced the previous ST OLA (1345t, 1974) on the Scrabster - Stromness service.

ST SUNNIVA Built as the DJURSLAND for *Jydsk Færgefart* of Denmark for their service between Grenaa (Jylland) and Hundested (Sjælland). In 1974 she was replaced by a larger vessel called DJURSLAND II (4371t, 1974) and switched to the company's other route, between Juelsminde (Jylland) and Kalundborg (Sjælland), being renamed the LASSE II. In 1979 she was sold to *P&O Ferries*, renamed the N F PANTHER ('N F' standing for *'Normandy Ferries'*) and became the third vessel on the Dover - Boulogne service. Sold to *European Ferries* in 1985 and in summer 1986 replaced (with sister vessel NF TIGER (4045t, 1972)) by the FREE ENTERPRISE IV (5049t, 1969) and FREE ENTERPRISE V (5044t, 1970). In 1987 sold to *P&O Scottish Ferries*, renamed the ST SUNNIVA, converted to an overnight ferry and introduced onto the Aberdeen - Lerwick service, supplementing ST CLAIR and also providing a weekly Aberdeen - Stromness - Lerwick and return service (twice weekly in high summer).

PASSAGE EAST FERRY

THE COMPANY *Passage East Ferry Company Ltd* is an Irish Republic private sector company.

MANAGEMENT Managing Director: Derek Donnelly. **Operations Manager:** Conor Gilligan.

ADDRESS Barrack Street, PASSAGE EAST, Co Waterford, Republic of Ireland.

TELEPHONE Administration: +353 (0)51 382480, **Reservations:** Not applicable, **Fax:** +353 (0)51 382598.

INTERNET Email: passageferry@tinet.ie

ROUTE OPERATED Passage East (County Waterford) - Ballyhack (County Wexford) (7 mins; *(1)*; frequent service).

Superior accommodation with spectacular sea views.

*S*ail with us to Orkney and Shetland and we'll spoil you all the way. Enjoy high standards of comfort and service on the way to these unspoilt islands as well as spectacular views from the sea of the coastline, wild yet gentle and inviting in its solitude.

Our vessels St Clair, St Ola and St Sunniva are as much a part of the local scene as the seabirds and the seals and ensure the perfect start to your island adventure.

Choose from hotel inclusive holidays, mini-cruises, motorist holidays or day excursions. Our regular sailing prices start from £14.50. Whichever you decide, you'll find us more than accommodating.

If you would like more information please see your local travel agent or contact P&O Scottish Ferries, Jamieson's Quay, Aberdeen, AB11 5NP. Telephone: (01224) 572615.

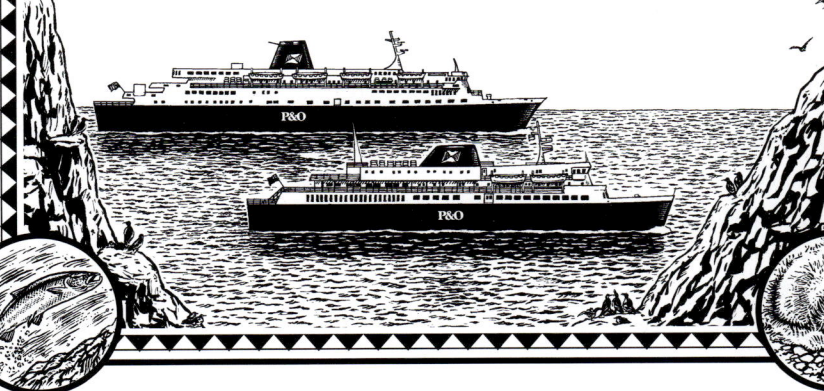

P&O Scottish Ferries

VESSEL

1	EDMUND D	300t	68	9k	250P	30C	-	BA	Dartmouth, GB	IR

EDMUND D Built as the SHANNON HEATHER for *Shannon Ferry Ltd* and used on their service between Killimer (County Clare) and Tarbert (County Kerry). Withdrawn from regular service in 1996 and, in 1997, sold to *Passage East Ferry* and renamed the EDMUND D. She entered service in January 1998.

PENTLAND FERRIES

THE COMPANY *Pentland Ferries* is a UK private sector company.

MANAGEMENT No information is available.

ADDRESS St Margaret's Hope, SOUTH RONALDSAY, Orkney.

TELEPHONE No information is available.

ROUTE OPERATED Summer only: Gills Bay (Scotland) - Burwick (South Ronaldsay, Orkney). It is hoped to start operations in spring 1999.

CONVENTIONAL FERRY

1	PENTALINA B	1908t	70	16k	250P	47C	-	BAS	Troon, GB	GB

PENTALINA B Built for *David MacBrayne*. She was actually built to operate the Islay service. However, shortly after the order was placed, plans to build a new pier at Redhouse, near the mouth of West Loch Tarbert, were abandoned, so she was not able to operate on this route until *Caledonian MacBrayne* acquired the *Western Ferries'* pier in deeper water at Kennacraig in 1978. She operated on the Gourock - Dunoon service in 1970 and 1971, between Mallaig and Kyle of Lochalsh and Stornoway in 1972 and between Oban and Craignure in 1973. From 1974 until 1978 she operated mainly on the Oban to Castlebay/Lochboisdale service and in addition the winter Oban - Coll/Tiree route. From 1978 until 1989 she operated mainly on the Islay service. In 1989 she was replaced by the CLAYMORE and then replaced the PIONEER as the summer Mallaig - Armadale vessel. Full ro-ro working was introduced on the route in 1994 and she also operated a twice weekly sailing between Mallaig, Lochboisdale and Castlebay and, in 1997, a weekly Mallaig - Coll and Tiree sailing. She was withdrawn in October 1997 and sold to *Pentland Ferries*. In 1998 she was renamed the PENTALINA B. In spring 1998 she was chartered back to *Caledonian MacBrayne* to operate between Oban and Craignure following the breakdown of the ISLE OF MULL. Services are now planned to start in spring 1999.

RED FUNNEL FERRIES

THE COMPANY *Red Funnel Ferries* is the trading name of the *Southampton Isle of Wight and South of England Royal Mail Steam Packet Public Limited Company*, a British private sector company. The company was acquired by *Associated British Ports* (owners of Southampton Docks) in 1989.

MANAGEMENT Managing Director: A M Whyte, **Marketing Director:** Ms O H Glass.

ADDRESS 12 Bugle Street, SOUTHAMPTON SO14 2JY.

TELEPHONE Administration: +44 (0)1703 333042, **Reservations:** +44 (0)1703 334010, **Fax:** +44 (0)1703 639438.

INTERNET Email: admin@redfunnel.co.uk **Website:** http://www.redfunnel.co.uk *(English)*

ROUTES OPERATED Conventional Ferries: Southampton - East Cowes (55 mins; *(1,2,3)*; hourly). **Fast Passenger Ferries:** Southampton - Cowes (20 mins; *(4,5,6)*; every half hour).

Red Jet 3 and **Red Falcon** *(John Hendy)*

Eilean Na-H-Oige *(Brian Maxted)*

CONVENTIONAL FERRIES

1	RED EAGLE	3028t	96	13k	900P	140C	16L	BA	Port Glasgow, GB	GB
2	RED FALCON	2881t	94	13k	900P	140C	16L	BA	Port Glasgow, GB	GB
3	RED OSPREY	2881t	94	13k	900P	140C	16L	BA	Port Glasgow, GB	GB

RED EAGLE, RED FALCON, RED OSPREY Built for the Southampton - East Cowes service.

FAST PASSENGER FERRIES

4p	RED JET 1	168t	91	32.5k	138P	0C	0L	-	Cowes, GB	GB
5p	RED JET 2	168t	91	32.5k	138P	0C	0L	-	Cowes, GB	GB
6p	RED JET 3	180t	98	32.5k	190P	0C	0L	-	Cowes, GB	GB
7p	SHEARWATER 5	62t	80	32k	67P	0C	0L	-	Messina, IT	GB
8p•	SHEARWATER 6	62t	82	32k	67P	0C	0L	-	Messina, IT	GB

RED JET 1, RED JET 2, RED JET 3 FBM Marine catamarans built for the Southampton - Cowes service.

SHEARWATER 5 Rodriquez RHS40 hydrofoil built for the Southampton - Cowes service. Now a reserve vessel.

SHEARWATER 6 Rodriquez RHS40 hydrofoil built for the Southampton - Cowes service. Withdrawn and laid up in 1998.

SEABOARD MARINE (NIGG)

THE COMPANY *Seaboard Marine (Nigg) Ltd* is a British private company.

MANAGEMENT Managing Director: Andrew Thoms, **Marketing Manager:** Robert McCrae.

ADDRESS Cliff House, Cadboll, TAIN, Ross-shire.

INTERNET Email: seaboard@zetnet.co.uk

TELEPHONE Administration: +44 (0)1862 871254, **Reservations:** +44 (0)1862 871254, **Fax:** +44 (0)1862 871231.

ROUTE OPERATED Cromarty - Nigg (Ross-shire) (10 mins; *(1)*; half hourly).

VESSEL

1	CROMARTY ROSE	28t	87	8k	50P	2C	-	B	Ardrossan, GB	GB

CROMARTY ROSE Built for *Seaboard Marine (Nigg) Ltd*.

SHANNON FERRY LTD

THE COMPANY *Shannon Ferry Ltd* is an Irish Republic private company owned by six families on both sides of the Shannon Estuary.

MANAGEMENT Managing Director: J J Meehan.

ADDRESS Ferry Terminal, KILLIMER, County Clare, Republic of Ireland.

TELEPHONE Administration: +353 (0)65 9053124, **Reservations:** Not applicable, **Fax:** +353 (0)65 9053125.

INTERNET Email: sferry@iol.ie **Website:** http://www.euroka.com/ferries/tarbert.html *(English, German, French, Italian)*.

ROUTE OPERATED Killimer (County Clare) - Tarbert (County Kerry) (20 mins; *(1,2)*; hourly (half hourly during July and August).

VESSELS

1	SHANNON DOLPHIN	501t	95	10k	350P	52C	-	BA	Appledore, GB	IR
2	SHANNON WILLOW	360t	78	10k	300P	44C	-	BA	Bowling, GB	IR

SHANNON DOLPHIN, SHANNON WILLOW Built for *Shannon Ferry Ltd.*

SHETLAND ISLANDS COUNCIL

THE COMPANY *Shetland Islands Council* is a British Local Government authority.

MANAGEMENT Director of Marine Operations: Capt G H Sutherland, FNI, MRIN, **Divisional Manager - Ferry Operations:** Capt M J Hogan.

ADDRESS Port Administration Building, Sella Ness, MOSSBANK, Shetland ZE2 9QR.

TELEPHONE Administration: +44 (0)1806 244216, 244262, 244252, **Reservations:** +44 (0)1957 722259, **Fax:** +44 (0)1806 242237, **Voice Banks:** +44 (0)1426 980317 (Bressay), +44 (0)1426 983633 (Fair Isle, Foula), +44 (0)1426 980209 (Unst/Fetlar), +44 (0)1426 983633 (Whalsay), +44(0)1426 980735 (Yell), **Telex:** 75142 Sulvoe G.

INTERNET Email: marine.ferries@shetland.gov.uk **Website:** http://www.shetland-news.co.uk/tourism/time.html#one *(English)*

ROUTES OPERATED Toft (Mainland) - Ulsta (Yell) (20 mins; *(1,5)*; up to 26 per day), Gutcher (Yell) - Belmont (Unst) (10 mins; *(3)*; 30 per day), Gutcher (Yell) - Oddsta (Fetlar) (25 mins; *(4)*; 6 per day), Lerwick (Mainland) - Maryfield (Bressay) (5 mins; *(10)*; 19 per day), Laxo (Mainland) - Symbister (Whalsay) (30 mins; *(8,12)*; 17 per day), Vidlin (Mainland) - Symbister (Whalsay) (30-45 mins; *(8,12)*; operates when weather conditions preclude using Laxo), Lerwick (Mainland) - Out Skerries (3 hrs; *(2)*; 2 per week), Vidlin (Mainland) - Out Skerries (1 hrs 30 mins; *(2)*; 7 per week), Grutness (Mainland) - Fair Isle (3 hrs; *(6)*; 2 per week), West Burrafirth (Mainland) - Papa Stour (40 mins; *(9)*; 7 per week), Foula - Walls (Mainland) (3 hrs; *(11)*; 2 per week).

VESSELS

1	BIGGA	274t	91	11k	96P	21C	4L	BA	St Monans, GB	GB
2	FILLA	130t	83	9k	12P	6C	1T	A	Flekkefjord, NO	GB
3	FIVLA	230t	85	11k	95P	15C	4L	BA	Troon, GB	GB
4	FYLGA	147t	75	8.5k	93P	10C	2L	BA	Tórshavn, FA	GB
5	GEIRA	226t	88	10.8k	95P	15C	4L	BA	Hessle, GB	GB
6	GOOD SHEPHERD IV	76t	86	10k	12P	1C	0L	C	St Monans, GB	GB
7	GRIMA	147t	74	8.5k	93P	10C	2L	BA	Bideford, GB	GB
8	HENDRA	225t	82	11k	100P	18C	4L	BA	Bromborough, GB	GB
9	KOADA	35t	69	8k	12P	1C	0L	C	Bideford, GB	GB
10	LEIRNA	420t	93	10k	100P	20C	4L	BA	Greenock, GB	GB
11	NEW ADVANCE	21t	96	8.7k	12P	1C	-	C	Penryn, GB	GB
12	THORA	147t	75	8.5k	93P	10C	2L	BA	Tórshavn, FA	GB

BIGGA Used on the Toft (Mainland) - Ulsta (Yell) service.

FILLA Used on the Lerwick (Mainland) - Out Skerries and Vidlin (Mainland) - Out Skerries services. At other times she operates freight and charter services around the Shetland Archipelago. She resembles a miniature oil rig supply vessel. Passenger capacity is 20 in summer.

FIVLA Used on the Gutcher (Yell) - Belmont (Unst) service.

FYLGA Used on the Gutcher (Yell) - Oddsta (Fetlar) service.

GEIRA Used on the Toft (Mainland) - Ulsta (Yell) service.

GOOD SHEPHERD IV Used on the service between Grutness (Mainland) and Fair Isle. Vehicles conveyed by special arrangement and generally consist of agricultural vehicles.

GRIMA Used on the Lerwick (Mainland) - Maryfield (Bressay) service until 1992 when she was replaced by the LEIRNA and became a spare vessel.

HENDRA Used on the Laxo (Mainland) - Symbister (Whalsay) service.

KOADA Built as an inshore trawler and bought by the shareholders on Fair Isle to operate to Shetland and named the GOOD SHEPHERD III. In 1986 the service was taken over by *Shetland Islands Council* and she was replaced by GOOD SHEPHERD IV. She was however acquired by the *Shetland Islands Council* and renamed the KOADA. She now operates between West Burrafirth (Mainland) and Papa Stour (operation to Foula having ceased following the delivery of the NEW ADVANCE). Car carrying capacity used occasionally.

LEIRNA Built for *Shetland Islands Council* for the Lerwick - Maryfield (Bressay) service.

NEW ADVANCE Built for the Foula service. Although built in Penryn, she was completed at Stromness in Orkney. She has a Cygnus Marine GM38 hull and is based on the island where she can be lifted out of the water. Vehicle capacity is to take new vehicles to the island - not for tourist vehicles. Mainland ports used are Walls and Scalloway.

THORA Sister vessel to the FYLGA and the GRIMA. After a period as a spare vessel, in 1998 she took over the Laxo - Symbister service from the withdrawn KJELLA.

STRANGFORD LOUGH FERRY SERVICE

THE COMPANY The *Strangford Ferry Lough Service* is operated by the *DOE (Department of the Environment) (Northern Ireland)*, a UK Department of State.

MANAGEMENT Ferry Manager: D Pedlow.

ADDRESS Strangford Lough Ferry Service, STRANGFORD, Co Down BT30 7NE.

TELEPHONE Administration: +44 (0)1396 881637, **Reservations:** Not applicable, **Fax:** +44 (0)1396 881249.

ROUTE OPERATED Strangford - Portaferry (County Down) (10 mins; *(1,2)*; half hourly).

VESSELS

1	PORTAFERRY FERRY	151t	62	9k	200P	18C	-	BA	Pembroke, GB	GB
2	STRANGFORD FERRY	186t	69	10k	263P	20C	-	BA	Cork, IR	GB

PORTAFERRY FERRY Built as the CLEDDAU KING for *Pembrokeshire County Council* (from 1974 *Dyfed County Council*) for their service between Hobbs Point (Pembroke Dock) and Neyland. Following the opening of a new bridge, the service ceased and, in 1976, she was sold to *DOE (Northern Ireland)* and renamed the PORTA FERRY. In 1990 she was renamed the PORTAFERRY FERRY.

STRANGFORD FERRY Built for *Down County Council*. Subsequently transferred to the *DOE (Northern Ireland)*.

VALENTIA ISLAND FERRIES

THE COMPANY *Valentia Island Ferries Ltd* is an Irish Republic private sector company.

MANAGEMENT Manager: Richard Foran.

ADDRESS VALENTIA ISLAND, County Kerry, Republic of Ireland.

TELEPHONE Administration: +353 (0)66 76141, **Reservations:** Not applicable, **Fax:** +353 (0)66 76377.

INTERNET Email: reforan@indigo.ie **Website:** http://www.euroka.com/ferries/valentia.html *(English)*

ROUTE OPERATED Reenard (Co Kerry) - Knightstown (Valentia Island) (5 minutes;*(1)*; frequent service, 1st April - 30th September).

VESSEL

1	GOD MET ONS III	95t	63	-	95P	18C	-	BA	Millingen, NL		IR

GOD MET ONS III Built for *FMHE Res* of the Netherlands for a service across the River Maas between Cuijk and Middelaar. In 1987 a new bridge was opened and the service ceased. She was latterly used on contract work in the Elbe and then laid up. In 1996 acquired by *Valentia Island Ferries* and inaugurated a car ferry service to the island. Note: this island has never had a car ferry service before. A bridge was opened at the south end of the island in 1970; before that a passenger/cargo service operated between Reenard Point and Knightstown.

WESTERN FERRIES

THE COMPANY *Western Ferries (Clyde) Ltd* is a British private sector company.

MANAGEMENT Managing Director: Kenneth C Cadenhead.

ADDRESSES Hunter's Quay, DUNOON PA23 8HJ.

TELEPHONE Administration: +44 (0)1369 704452, **Reservations:** Not applicable, **Fax:** +44 (0)1369 706020.

ROUTE OPERATED McInroy's Point (Gourock) - Hunter's Quay (Dunoon) (20 mins; *(1,2,3,4,5)*; half hourly).

VESSELS

1	SOUND OF SANDA	403t	61	10k	220P	37C	-	BA	Arnhem, NL	GB
2	SOUND OF SCALPAY	403t	61	10k	220P	37C	-	BA	Arnhem, NL	GB
3	SOUND OF SCARBA	175t	60	7k	200P	22C	-	BA	Åmål, SW	GB
4	SOUND OF SHUNA	244t	62	7k	200P	25C	-	BA	Åmål, SW	GB
5	SOUND OF SLEAT	466t	61	10k	296P	30C	-	BAS	Hardinxveld, NL	GB

SOUND OF SANDA Built as the G24 for *Amsterdam City Council* and operated from Centraal Station to the other side of the River Ijs. In 1996 purchased by *Western Ferries* and renamed the SOUND OF SANDA.

SOUND OF SCALPAY Built as the G23 for *Amsterdam City Council*. In 1995 sold to *Western Ferries* and renamed the SOUND OF SCALPAY.

SOUND OF SCARBA Built as the ÖLANDSSUND III for *Rederi AB Ölandssund* of Sweden for service between Revsudden on the mainland and Stora Rör on the island of Öland. Following the opening of a new bridge near Kalmar, about 4 miles to the South, the ferry service ceased. In 1973 she was sold to *Western Ferries*, renamed the SOUND OF SCARBA and joined the SOUND OF SHUNA their

McInroy's Point - Hunter's Quay service. Now relief vessel and also used on contract work in the Clyde estuary.

SOUND OF SHUNA Built as the ÖLANDSSUND IV for *Rederi AB Ölandssund* of Sweden (see the SOUND OF SCARBA above). In 1973 she was sold to *Western Ferries*, renamed the SOUND OF SHUNA and, with the SOUND OF SCARBA, inaugurated the McInroy's Point - Hunter's Quay service. Now a relief vessel.

SOUND OF SLEAT Built as the DE HOORN for the service between Maassluis and Rozenburg, across the 'Nieuwe Waterweg' (New Waterway) in The Netherlands. In 1988 she was purchased by *Western Ferries* and renamed the SOUND OF SLEAT.

WIGHTLINK

THE COMPANY *Wightlink* is a British private sector company, owned by *CINVen Ltd*, a venture capital company. The routes and vessels were previously part of *Sealink* but were excluded from the purchase of most of the *Sealink* operations by *Stena Line AB* in 1990. They remained in *Sea Containers* ownership until purchased by *CINVen*.

MANAGEMENT Chairman: Michael Aiken, **Head of Marketing:** Janet Saville.

ADDRESS PO Box 59, PORTSMOUTH PO1 2XB.

TELEPHONE Administration: +44 (0)1705 812011, **Reservations:** 0990 827744 (from UK only), +44 (0)1705 812011 (from overseas), **Fax:** +44 (0)1705 855257, **Telex:** 86440 WIGHTLG.

INTERNET Email: info@wightlink.co.uk **Website:** http://www.wightlink.co.uk *(English)*

ROUTES OPERATED Conventional Ferries: Lymington - Yarmouth (Isle of Wight) (approx 30 mins; *(1,2,3)*; half hourly), Portsmouth - Fishbourne (Isle of Wight) (approx 35 mins; *(4,5,6,7)*; half hourly or hourly depending on time of day). **Fast Passenger Ferries:** Portsmouth - Ryde (Isle of Wight) (passenger only) (approx 15 mins; *(8,9)*; half hourly/hourly).

CONVENTIONAL FERRIES

1	CAEDMON	763t	73	9.5k	520P	58C	6L	BA	Dundee, GB	GB
2	CENRED	761t	73	9.5k	520P	58C	6L	BA	Dundee, GB	GB
3	CENWULF	761t	73	9.5k	520P	58C	6L	BA	Dundee, GB	GB
4	ST CATHERINE	2036t	83	12.5k	769P	142C	12L	BA	Leith, GB	GB
5	ST CECILIA	2968t	87	12.5k	769P	142C	12L	BA	Selby, GB	GB
6	ST FAITH	3009t	90	12.5k	769P	142C	12L	BA	Selby, GB	GB
7	ST HELEN	2983t	83	12.5k	769P	142C	12L	BA	Leith, GB	GB

CAEDMON Built for Portsmouth - Fishbourne service. In 1983 transferred to the Lymington - Yarmouth service.

CENRED, CENWULF Built for Lymington - Yarmouth service.

ST CATHERINE, ST CECILIA, ST FAITH, ST HELEN Built for the Portsmouth - Fishbourne service.

FAST PASSENGER FERRIES

8p	OUR LADY PAMELA	312t	86	28.5k	410P	0C	0L	Hobart, AL	GB
9p	OUR LADY PATRICIA	312t	86	28.5k	410P	0C	0L	Hobart, AL	GB

OUR LADY PAMELA, OUR LADY PATRICIA InCat 30 m catamarans. Built for the Portsmouth - Ryde service.

St Helen *(Miles Cowsill)*

WOOLWICH FREE FERRY

THE COMPANY The *Woolwich Free Ferry* is operated by the *London Borough of Greenwich*, a British municipal authority.

MANAGEMENT Principal Engineer (Ferry): Eur Ing C Thew, **Ferry Manager:** Capt P Deeks.

ADDRESS New Ferry Approach, Woolwich, LONDON SE18 6DX.

TELEPHONE Administration: +44 (0)181-312 5583, **Reservations:** Not applicable, **Fax:** +44 (0)181-316 6096.

ROUTE OPERATED Woolwich - North Woolwich (free ferry) (5 mins; *(1,2,3)*; 9 mins (weekdays - two ferries in operation), 16 mins (weekends - one ferry in operation). Note: one ferry always in reserve/under maintenance.

VESSELS

1	ERNEST BEVIN	1214t	63	8k	310P	32C	6L	BA	Dundee, GB	GB
2	JAMES NEWMAN	1214t	63	8k	310P	32C	6L	BA	Dundee, GB	GB
3	JOHN BURNS	1214t	63	8k	310P	32C	6L	BA	Dundee, GB	GB

ERNEST BEVIN, JAMES NEWMAN, JOHN BURNS Built for the *London County Council* who operated the service in 1963. In 1965 ownership was transferred to the *Greater London Council*. Following the abolition of the *GLC* in April 1986, ownership was transferred to the *Department of Transport*. The *London Borough of Greenwich* operate the service on their behalf. An alternative loading is 6 x 18m articulated lorries cars and 14 cars; lorries of this length are too long for the nearby northbound Blackwall Tunnel.

SECTION 3 - FREIGHT ONLY FERRIES
ARGOMANN FERRY SERVICE

THE COMPANY *ArgoMann Ferry Service GmbH* is a joint venture between *Argo Reederei* of Germany and *Mann & Son (London) Ltd* of Great Britain.

MANAGEMENT Joint Managing Directors: Mr D R Adler (Germany), Mr F A Hatchard (UK), **Marketing Director (UK):** Roger G Gibbs.

ADDRESS *Germany:* Argo Reederei RA&S, 2800 BREMEN 1, Am Wall 187/189, Germany, ***UK:*** Mann & Son (London) Ltd, The Naval House, Kings Quay Street, HARWICH CO12 3JJ.

TELEPHONE Administration & Reservations: *(Germany):* +49 (0)421 363070, *(UK):* +44 (0)1255 245200, **Fax:** *(Germany):* +49 (0)421 321575, *(UK):* +44 (0)1255 245219, **Telex:** *(UK):* 98229.

INTERNET Email: enquiry@manngroup.comuk argoline@aol.com

Website: http://www.ArgoMann.com *(English)*

ROUTE OPERATED Harwich (Navy Yard) *(dep: 22.00 Fri:)* - Cuxhaven *(arr: 17.00 Sat, dep: 19.00 Sat)* - Tallinn *(arr: 15.00 Mon, dep: 21.00 Mon)* - Turku *(arr: 08.00 Tue, dep: 17.30 Tue)* - Bremerhaven *(arr: 18.00 Thu, dep: 21.00 Thu)* - Harwich *(arr: 16.00 Fri)*; *(1)*; one per week.

VESSEL

1	ESTRADEN	18205t	99	20k	12P		130C	160T	A	Rauma, FI	FI

Built for *Rederi Ab Engship* of Finland and chartered to *ArgoMann*. To be renamed the AMAZON.

BELFAST FREIGHT FERRIES

THE COMPANY *Belfast Freight Ferries* is a British private sector company owned by *Scruttons plc* of London. *Scruttons* is now owned by *Cenargo*, owners of *Merchant Ferries*.

MANAGEMENT General Manager: Alan Peacock, **Operations Director:** Trevor Wright.

ADDRESS Victoria Terminal 1, Dargan Road, BELFAST BT3 9LJ.

TELEPHONE Administration: +44 (0)1232 770112, **Reservations:** *Belfast:* +44 (0)1232 770112, *Heysham:* +44 (0)1524 855988, **Fax:** +44 (0)1232 781217.

ROUTE OPERATED Heysham *(dep: 06.30, 10.30, 18.30, 22.30)* - Belfast *(dep: 06.30, 10.30, 18.30, 22.30)*; (8 hrs; *(1,2,3,4)*; 4 per day).

VESSELS

1	MERCHANT BRAVERY	9368t	78	17k	12P	-	106T	A	Oslo, NO	BA
2	MERCHANT BRILLIANT	9368t	79	17k	12P	-	106T	A	Kyrksæterøra, NO	BA
3	MERLE	9088t	85	15k	12P	-	80T	A	Galatz, RO	BA
4	SPHEROID	7171t	71	16k	12P	-	55T	A	Sharpsborg, NO	IM

MERCHANT BRAVERY Launched as the STEVI for *Steineger & Wiik* of Norway and, on delivery, chartered to *Norient Line* of Norway, being renamed the NORWEGIAN CRUSADER. In 1980 chartered to *Ignazio Messina* of Italy for Mediterranean service and renamed the JOLLY GIALLO. In 1982 the charter ended and she was briefly renamed the NORWEGIAN CRUSADER before being purchased by *Ignazio Messina* and resuming the name JOLLY GIALLO. In 1993 sold to *Merchant Ferries*, renamed the MERCHANT BRAVERY and placed on the Heysham - Warrenpoint (Dublin since 1995) service. In 1999 chartered to *Belfast Freight Ferries*.

MERCHANT BRILLIANT Built as the NORWEGIAN CHALLENGER *for Steineger & Wiik* of Norway and chartered to *Norient Line* of Norway. In 1982, chartered to *Ignazio Messina* of Italy for Mediterranean service and renamed the JOLLY BRUNO. Later in 1982 she was purchased by *Ignazio Messina*. In 1993 sold to *Merchant Ferries*, renamed the MERCHANT BRILLIANT and placed on the Heysham - Warrenpoint (Dublin since 1995) service. In 1999 chartered to *Belfast Freight Ferries*.

MERLE Built as the BALDER STEN for *K/S A/S Balder RO/RO No 2* of Norway (part of the *Parley Augustsson* group). In 1995 acquired by *Navrom* of Romania and renamed the BAZIAS 3. In 1991 chartered to *Sally Ferries* for the Ramsgate - Oostende freight service and subsequently purchased by a joint *Sally Ferries/Romline* company. In 1993 renamed the SALLY EUROROUTE and re-registered in The Bahamas. In October 1996 she was chartered to *Belfast Freight Ferries* and renamed the MERLE. In 1997 *Sally Ferries'* interests in her were purchased by *Jacobs Holdings*.

SPHEROID Built as the STARMARK for *Avermoi Oy* of Finland. In 1981 sold to *Manta Line* of Greece for Mediterranean and deep sea service and renamed the RORO TRADER. In 1985 she was sold to *Oceanwide Shipping* for charter and renamed the NIEKIRK. In 1986 chartered to *Belfast Freight Ferries* and in 1987 sold to them and renamed the SPHEROID.

COBELFRET FERRIES

THE COMPANY Cobelfret Ferries nv is a Belgian private sector company, a subsidiary of *Cobelfret nv* of Antwerpen.

MANAGEMENT Operations Manager (Belgium): Marc Vandersteen, **UK: *Purfleet, Dagenham and Sheerness services:*** Cobelfret Ferries UK Ltd - **General Manager:** Phil Tomkins, ***Immingham Services:*** Exxtor Shipping Services Ltd - **Director & General Manager:** Jeffe Baker.

ADDRESS *Belgium:* Sneeuwbeslaan 14, B-2610 ANTWERP, Belgium, ***UK Purfleet:*** Purfleet Thames Terminal Ltd, London Road, PURFLEET, Essex RM19 1RF, ***UK Immingham:*** Exxtor Shipping Services Ltd, PO Box 40, Manby Road, IMMINGHAM, South Humberside DN40 3EG.

TELEPHONE Administration: *Belgium:* +32 (0)3 829 9011, ***UK:*** +44 (0)1708 865522, **Reservations: *Belgium:*** +32 (0)50 547200, ***UK (Purfleet Services):*** +44 (0)1708 891199, ***(Immingham Services):*** +44 (0)1469 551341, **Fax: *Belgium - Admin):*** +32 (0)3 237 7646, ***Belgium - Reservations:*** +32 (0)50 545348, ***UK - Admin:*** +44 (0)1708 866418, ***UK - Reservations (Purfleet):*** +44 (0)1708 890853, ***UK - Reservations (Immingham):*** +44 (0)1469 573739.

INTERNET Website: http://www.cobelfret.com *(Not yet active)*

ROUTES OPERATED

Zeebrugge *(dep: 02.00, 07.00, 10.00 14.00, 18.30, 22.00)* - Purfleet *(dep: 02.00, 05.30, 09.00, 15.00, 18.00, 21.00)* (8 hrs; *(3,4,5,6,8,9,10,12,13)*, 6 per day), Zeebrugge *(dep: 18.00)* - Immingham *(dep: 18.00)* (14 hrs; *(4,6,11)*; 1 per day), Sheerness *(dep: 09.00 Sat)* - Oostende *(arr: 1800 Sat, dep: 2359 Sat)* - Purfleet *(arr: 0800 Sun)*; *(4,5,6,12,13)*; 1 per week), Zeebrugge - Dagenham (contract service for Ford Motor Company) (8 hrs 30 mins; *(3,4,5,12,13)*), Rotterdam *(dep: 17.30)* - Immingham *(dep: 17.30)* (14 hrs; *(1,7)*; 1 per day).

VESSELS

1	AMANDINE	14715t	78	14.5k	12P	-	150T	A	Kiel, GY	GB
2	CELESTINE	23986t	96	17.8k	24P	654C	156T	A	Sakaide, JA	PA
3	CLEMENTINE	23986t	97	17.8k	24P	654C	156T	A	Sakaide, JA	LX
4	CYMBELINE	11886t	92	14.5k	10P	790C	130T	A2	Dalian, CH	LX
5	EGLANTINE	10030t	89	14.5k	10P	790C	120T	A2	Dalian, CH	LX
6	LOVERVAL	10931t	78	17k	12P	675C	112T	A2	Lödöse, SW	LX
7	LYRA	12817t	78	15k	12P	-	145T	A	Kiel, GY	AT

Clementine *(John Bryant)*

Dart 5 *(Nick Widdows)*

8	MAERSK ANGLIA	6862t	77	14.5k	0P	60C	75T	A2	Ishikawajima, JA	IM
9	RODONA	6568t	80	15k	6P	-	82T	A	Karlskrona, SW	SW
10	SAPPHIRE	6568t	80	15k	6P	-	82T	A	Karlskrona, SW	SW
11	STENA SHIPPER	12337t	79	18.5k	12P	-	70T	A2	Papenburg, GY	BA
12	SYMPHORINE	10030t	88	14.5k	10P	790C	130T	A2	Dalian, CH	LX
13	UNDINE	11854t	91	14.5k	10P	790C	130T	A2	Dalian, CH	LX

AMANDINE Built as the MERZARIO PERSIA for *Merzario Line* of Italy and used on services between Italy and the Middle East. In 1986 she was chartered to *Grimaldi* of Italy and renamed the PERSIA, continuing on Middle East services. In 1988 she was sold to *Eimskip* of Iceland and renamed the BRUARFOSS. She was used on their service between Reykjavik, Immingham, Hamburg and Rotterdam. In 1996, the ro-ro service was replaced by a container only service and she was withdrawn. She was renamed the VEGA and was placed a number of short term charters including *Suardiaz* of Spain and *Fred. Olsen Lines*. In 1998, she was sold to *Cobelfret* and renamed the AMANDINE.

CELESTINE Built for *Cobelfret*. In 1996 chartered to the British *Ministry of Defence* and renamed the R.F.A. SEA CRUSADER. In 1999, she maybe returned to *Cobelfret* and resume the name CELESTINE. At the time of going to press, she was still on charter to the M.O.D.

CLEMENTINE, CYMBELINE, EGLANTINE Built by *Cobelfret*. Currently used on the Zeebrugge - Purfleet and Zeebrugge - Dagenham (Ford) services.

LOVERVAL Built as the VALLMO for the *Johansson Group* of Sweden and undertook a variety of charters. In 1982 she was sold to *Cobelfret* and renamed the MATINA. In 1984 renamed the LOVERVAL. Currently used on the Zeebrugge - Purfleet and Zeebrugge - Immingham services.

LYRA Built as the MERZARIO ARABIA for *Merzario Line* of Italy and used on services between Italy and the Middle East. In 1986 she was chartered to *Ignazio Messina* of Italy and renamed the JOLLY OCRA, continuing on Middle East services. In 1987, she was chartered to *Lloyd Triestino Line* of Italy and renamed the DUINO. In 1988 she was sold to *Eimskip* of Iceland, renamed the LAXFOSS and used on their services from Iceland to the UK, Netherlands and Germany. In 1996, the ro-ro service was replaced by a container only service and she was withdrawn. She was chartered to *Nordana Line* of Denmark and renamed the SILKEBORG. In 1997 she was renamed the LYRA and briefly chartered to *Dart Line* and used on their Dartford - Zeebrugge service. Later in 1997 she was chartered to *Exxtor Ferries* to operate between Immingham and Rotterdam. When the service was taken over by *Cobelfret* later in the year, the charter was transferred to them and she continues to operate between Immingham and Rotterdam.

MAERSK ANGLIA Built as the ADMIRAL CARIBE for *Admiral Shipping* for services between the USA and Venezuela. In 1982 she was sold to *CGM* of France and used on service between France and the Middle East; she was renamed the SAINT REMY. In 1986 she was sold to *Norfolk Line* for their Brit Line Immingham - Esbjerg service and renamed the DUKE OF ANGLIA. In 1989 *Norfolk Line* was acquired by *Maersk Line* and she was transferred to associated company *Kent Line* for their Dartford - Zeebrugge service. In 1990 she was chartered to the *Ford Motor Company* for conveyance of privately owned trailers between Dagenham and Zeebrugge and was renamed MAERSK ANGLIA. In 1995 *Cobelfret* took over the operation of this service. Currently used on the Zeebrugge - Purfleet service.

RODONA Built as the BALDER DONA for *Dag Engström* of Sweden and undertook a number of charters in the Caribbean and Mediterranean. In 1984 she was renamed the RODONA and chartered to *Seaboard Shipping* of the USA and used on Caribbean services. In 1987 she was chartered to the *Ford Motor Company* for conveyance of privately owned trailers between Dagenham and Zeebrugge. In 1995 *Cobelfret* took over the operation of this service. Currently used on the Purfleet - Zeebrugge service.

SAPPHIRE Built as the BALDER VINGA for *Dag Engström* of Sweden and undertook a number of charters in the Caribbean and Mediterranean. In 1984 she was renamed the ROVINGA and chartered to *Seaboard Shipping* of the USA and used on Caribbean services. In 1985 she was renamed the AZUA. In 1987 she briefly reverted to the name ROVINGA before being renamed the SAPPHIRE and chartered to the *Ford Motor Company* for conveyance of privately owned trailers between Dagenham and Zeebrugge. In 1995 *Cobelfret* took over the operation of this service. Currently used on the Purfleet - Zeebrugge service.

STENA SHIPPER Built as the NESTOR for *Nestor Reederei* of Germany and chartered out. In 1984 she was renamed the NESTOR 1 but in 1985 she resumed the name NESTOR. In 1986 she was chartered to *Nile Dutch Line* and operated between Northern Europe and West Africa. In 1989 the charter terminated and she was renamed the NESTOR; the following year she was chartered to *Stream Line*, renamed the CARIBBEAN STREAM and placed on service between Europe and South America. This charter ended in 1991 and she resumed the name NESTOR. In 1994 she was purchased by *Stena Rederi AB*, renamed the STENA SHIPPER and chartered to *Cobelfret*. Currently used on the Zeebrugge - Immingham service.

SYMPHORINE Built *Cobelfret*. Currently used on the Purfleet - Zeebrugge service.

UNDINE Built for *Cobelfret*. Currently used on the Zeebrugge - Purfleet and Zeebrugge - Dagenham (Ford) services.

Under Construction

14	CATHERINE	23986t	99	18k	12P		635C	188T	A	Kobe, JA	LX
15	CELANDINE	23986t	99	18k	12P		635C	188T	A	Kobe, JA	LX
16	MELUSINE	23986t	99	18k	12P		635C	188T	A	Kobe, JA	LX
17	VALENTINE	23986t	99	18k	12P		635C	188T	A	Kobe, JA	LX

CATHERINE, CELANDINE, MELUSINE, VALENTINE Under construction for charter to *Cobelfret*. Similar to the CLEMENTINE.

COMMODORE FERRIES

THE COMPANY *Commodore Ferries (CI) Ltd* is a Guernsey private sector company.

MANAGEMENT Managing Director: Jeff Vidamour.

ADDRESS PO Box 10, New Jetty Offices, White Rock, St Peter Port, GUERNSEY GY1 3AF.

TELEPHONE Administration & Reservations: +44 (0)1481 728620, **Fax:** +44 (0)1481 728521.

ROUTE OPERATED Portsmouth *(dep: 09.30, 20.30)* - Guernsey *(dep: 04.00, 18.00)* (12 hrs) - Jersey *(dep: 08.00, 22.00)* (8 hrs; *(1,2)*; 2 per day). Also Saturday charter from Jersey to St Malo for *Morvan Fils*.

INTERNET Email: bds.ferry.1@aol.com

VESSELS

1	COMMODORE GOODWILL	11166t	96	18.3k	12P	-	95T	A	Vlissingen, NL	BA
2	ISLAND COMMODORE	11166t	95	18.3k	12P	-	95T	A	Vlissingen, NL	BA

COMMODORE GOODWILL, ISLAND COMMODORE Built for *Commodore Ferries*.

Under construction

3	COMMODORE CLIPPER	13460t	99	19k	480P	250C	105T	A	Krimpen, NL	BA

COMMODORE CLIPPER Ro-pax vessel under construction to operate between Portsmouth and The Channel Islands. She will replace one of the two *Commodore* ro-ro vessels as well as replacing the

Commodore Ferries

Using purpose built roll-on roll-off vessels, Commodore Ferries operate twice daily sailings between Portsmouth and the Channel Islands. This enables us to offer the best and most frequent freight service on this route. With this commitment one can begin to understand why we are entrusted to carry the major part of all cargo to and from the Channel Islands.

Our service is tailored to the needs of our customers, and we can accommodate all types of vehicles including both ambient and refrigerated trailers, rigids, cars and out of gauge cargo.

Please give us a call for full details of our schedules and rate structures.

Two new ro-ro vessels:
- m.v. Island Commodore   - Length 126 metres   - Plugs for 40 refrigerated trailers
- m.v. Commodore Goodwill - Capacity 94 x 12 metre trailers - 12 driver's cabins

Commodore Ferries,
P.O. Box 10, New Jetty Offices,
White Rock, St. Peter Port, Guernsey GY1 3AF
Tel. 01481 728620   Fax. 01481 728521

Telephone: (01481) 728620

HAVELET in providing a conventional ship passenger facility to the islands as back-up to the *Condor Ferries* passenger service.

DART LINE

THE COMPANY *Dart Line Ltd* is a British private sector company owned by *Jacobs Holdings plc*. It took over the Dartford - Vlissingen service from *Sally Ferries* in 1996.

MANAGEMENT Managing Director: Simon Taylor, **Marketing Director:** Kevin Miller.

ADDRESS Crossways Business Park, Thames Europort, DARTFORD, Kent DA2 6PJ.

TELEPHONE Administration & **Reservations:** +44 (0)1322 281122, **Fax:** +44 (0)1322 281133.

INTERNET Email: sales@dartline.co.uk **Website:** http://www.dartline.co.uk *(English)*

ROUTES OPERATED Dartford *(dep: 09.00 Tue-Fri, 10.00 Sun, 21.00 daily)* - Vlissingen *(dep: 10.00 Tue-Fri, 11.00 Sun, 21.00 daily)* (9 hrs; *(5,6)*; 2 per day), Dartford *(dep: 03.00 Tue-Fri, 0500 Sat, Sun, 08.00 Tue-Fri, 20.00 daily)* - Zeebrugge *(dep: 09.00 Tue-Fri, 16.00 Mon-Sat, 21.00 daily)* (9 hrs; *(1,2,4)*; 3 per day).

VESSELS

1	DART 1	9071t	84	15k	12P	-	100T	A	Galatz, RO		RO
2	DART 2	9082t	84	15k	12P	-	100T	A	Galatz, RO		RO
3	DART 4	9088t	85	15k	12P	-	100T	A	Galatz, RO		BA
4	DART 5	9082t	86	15k	12P	-	100T	A	Galatz, RO		RO
5	DART 6	7606t	98	17k	12P	-	88T	A	Huelva, SP		ES
6	DART 7	7800t	98	17k	12P	-	88T	A	Huelva, SP		ES

DART 1 Built as the BALDER FJORD for *K/S A/S Balder RO/RO No 2* of Norway. In 1986 acquired by *Navrom* of Romania and renamed the BAZIAS 1. In 1990 transferred to *Romline* of Romania and subsequently sold to *Octogon Shipping* of Romania. In 1996 chartered to *Ignazio Messina* of Italy and later renamed the JOLLY ARANCIONE. In late 1997 chartered to *Dart Line* and renamed the DART 1. Charter expected to end later in 1999.

DART 2 Built as the BALDER HAV for *K/S A/S Balder RO/RO No 2* of Norway. In 1985 acquired by *Navrom* of Romania, renamed the BAZIAS 2 and used on Mediterranean services. In 1995 chartered to *Dart Line* and renamed the DART 2. Operations began in 1996. Later in 1996 she was sold to *Jacobs Holdings*.

DART 4 Built as the BALDER BRE for *K/S A/S Balder RO/RO No 2* of Norway. Later in 1985 acquired by *Navrom* of Romania and renamed the BAZIAS 4. In 1991 chartered to *Sally Ferries* for the Ramsgate - Oostende freight service and subsequently purchased by a joint *Sally Ferries/Romline* company. In 1993 renamed the SALLY EUROLINK and re-registered in The Bahamas. In 1997 *Sally Ferries*' interests in her were purchased by *Jacobs Holdings*. She was later transferred to *Dart Line* and renamed the DART 4. In 1998 she was chartered to *Belfast Freight Ferries*. She returned to *Dart Line* in February 1999. To operate on Vlissingen route later in 1999.

DART 5 Launched as the BALDER RA for *K/S A/S Balder RO/RO No 2* of Norway. On completion acquired by *Navrom* of Romania, renamed the BAZIAS 5 and used on Mediterranean services; subsequently transferred to *Romline* of Romania. In 1995 she was chartered to *Grimaldi* of Italy and renamed the PERSEUS; she was later chartered to *Sudcargos* of France. In 1996 she was chartered to *Dart Line* and renamed the DART 5. To operate on Vlissingen route later in 1999.

DART 6 Built as the VARBOLA for *Estonian Shipping Company*. On completion, chartered to *Dart Line* and placed on the Dartford - Vlissingen route. In 1999 she was renamed the DART 6. Charter expected to end later in 1999

DART 7 Built as the LEMBITU for *Estonian Shipping Company*. On completion chartered *P&O*

European Ferries (Irish Sea) and placed on their Liverpool Dublin route whilst the BUFFALO was being lengthened (renamed EUROPEAN LEADER on re-entry to service). In autumn 1998 she was chartered to *Dart Line* and placed on the Dartford - Vlissingen route. In 1999 she was renamed the DART 7. Charter expected to end later in 1999.

Dart Line also owns the MERLE, on charter to *Belfast Freight Ferries* and listed under that company. She is known within the *Jacobs* organisation as the DART 3, although she has never carried that name.

REPLACEMENT SHIPS UNDERGOING MODIFICATION

7	DART 8	22748t	80	18k	12P	-	190T	A	Sakaide, BA	BA
8	DART 9	22748t	80	18k	12P	-	190T	A	Sakaide, BA	BA
9	DART 10	22748t	80	18k	12P	-	190T	A	Sakaide, BA	BA

DART 8, DART 9 and DART 10. Built as the XI FENG KOU, GU BEI KOU, ZHANG JIA KOU. Deep sea ro-ro/container ships built for *China Merchant Steam Navigation Company* (chartered to *China Ocean Shipping Company*) of the People's Republic of China for service between China and the USA, Australia and New Zealand. In 1999, purchased by *Jacobs Holdings*. Being converted in China to short sea ro-ro specification, including the fitting of a stern ramp (replacing the quarter ramp) and accommodation for 12 drivers. To be delivered during Summer 1999. *The Dart 8* and *Dart 9* will enter service on *Dart Line's* Dartford - Zeebrugge service, replacing the existing vessels. No decision has yet been made on the third vessel.

DELOM

THE COMPANY *Delom SA* is a French private sector company.

ADDRESS 16 quai Francois Maillol, F-34200 SETE, France.

TELEPHONE Administration: +33 4 67 51 66 20 **Fax:** +33 4 07 74 22 91.

ROUTE OPERATED Dunkerque - Dover (3 hrs; *(1)*; irregular). The vessel is used on charter to *Farmers Ferries* to operate special services for the carriage of livestock. She is expected to operate some sailings for general traffic on days she is not required for livestock.

VESSEL

1	CAP AFRIQUE	‡1583t	78	13.5k	12P	-	50T	A	Niigata, JA	KE

CAP AFRIQUE Built as the CATHERINE SCHIAFFINO for *Schiaffino Line* of France and chartered out, generally operating on services in the Mediterranean. In 1983 she was transferred to the company's own service between Dover and Oostende; in 1984 the British terminal moved to Ramsgate. In 1989 she was renamed the SAINT CHARLES. In 1990 she was chartered to *Sally Ferries* took over the service. She was later sold to *Delom* and in 1991 she was renamed the CAP AFRIQUE. She undertook a number of charters and was also used on *Delom's* own services between France and Tunisia. In 1996 she was moved to Dunkerque and began a number of charters conveying livestock from Dover. In 1997 she returned to Mediterranean service but returned to Dunkerque in autumn 1998 and the livestock trade resumed. In 1999 she is expected to convey ordinary traffic on a commercial basis when not required for livestock.

DFDS LINER DIVISION

THE COMPANY *DFDS Liner Division* is one of the trading names of the freight division of *DFDS A/S*, a Danish private sector public company. See also *DFDS Tor Line* (Swedish services).

MANAGEMENT Managing Director UK: Ebbe Pedersen.

ADDRESS Scandinavia House, Parkeston Quay, HARWICH CO12 4QG.

TELEPHONE Administration & Reservations: +44 (0)1255 242242, **Fax:** +44 (0)1255 244310, **Telex:** 98582.

ROUTES OPERATED

Immingham *(dep: 15.00 Mon, 21.00 Tue, 01.00 Thu, 07.00 Fri, 23.00 Sat)* - Esbjerg *(dep: 18.00 Mon, 21.00 Tue, 04.00 Thu, 19.00 Fri, 16.00 Sat)* (21 hrs; *(3,4)*; 5 per week) (under the name of *DFDS North Sea Line*), Immingham *(dep: 07.00 Sun, 19.00 Tue, 01.00 Fri)* - Cuxhaven *(dep: 18.00 Mon, 23.00 Wed, 05.00 Sat)* (22 hrs; *(1)*; 3 per week) (under the name of *DFDS Elbe-Humber RoLine*), Harwich *(dep: 23.00 Sun, 20.00 Wed, 20.00 Fri)* - Esbjerg *(dep: 20.00 Tue, 21.00 Thu, 23.00 Sat)* (20 hrs; *(2)*; 3 per week (complemented by sailings from passenger vessel DANA ANGLIA giving 6/7 per week)) (under the name of *DFDS North Sea Line*).

VESSELS

1	DANA CIMBRIA	12189t	86	17k	12P	-	150T	A	Frederikshavn, DK	DK
2	DANA FUTURA	18469t	96	20k	12P	-	170T	AS	Donanda, IT	IT
3	DANA MAXIMA	17068t	78	17k	12P	-	210T	A	Osaka, JA	DK
4	DANA MINERVA	21213t	78	18k	0P	-	171T	A	Oskarshamn, SW	DK

DANA CIMBRIA Launched as the MERCANDIAN EXPRESS II and immediately bare-boat chartered to *DFDS* for their North Sea freight services, being renamed the DANA CIMBRIA. Purchased by *DFDS* in 1989. Until 1996, generally used on Immingham and North Shields - Esbjerg services; between 1996 and 1998 she operated between Immingham and Esbjerg. In 1998 she was transferred to the Immingham - Cuxhaven service.

DANA FUTURA Built for *DFDS* to operate between Harwich and Esbjerg.

DANA MAXIMA Built for *DFDS* for their North Sea services. Until 1996, generally used on Grimsby and North Shields - Esbjerg services. Now mainly operates between Immingham and Esbjerg. In summer 1995 she was lengthened to increase trailer capacity.

DANA MINERVA Built as the BANDAR ABBAS EXPRESS for *A/S Skarhamns Oljetransport* of Norway and chartered out. In 1980 renamed the SAUDI EXPRESS. During the early eighties she undertook a number of charters including *Mideastcargo* for services between Europe and the Middle East, *Atlanticargo* for services from Europe to USA and Mexico and *OT West Africa Line* from Europe to West Africa. In 1983 she was chartered to *Ignazio Messina* of Italy, renamed the JOLLY AVORIO and used on services from Italy to the Middle East. In 1986 this charter ended and she briefly reverted to the name the SAUDI EXPRESS before being chartered again to *OT West Africa Line* and renamed the KARAWA. In 1987 she was sold to *Fred. Olsen Lines* who renamed her the BORACAY; she operated between Norway and Northern Europe. In 1998 she was sold to *DFDS*, renamed the DANA MINERVA and placed on the Immingham - Esbjerg route.

DFDS TOR LINE

THE COMPANY *DFDS Tor Line* is one of the trading names of the freight division of *DFDS A/S*, a Danish private sector company. See also *DFDS Liner Division* (Danish services). Services of *Fred. Olsen Lines* of Norway (trading as *Fred. Olsen North Sea Line*) were taken over in January 1999. The joint service with *Stena Line AB* between Göteborg and Harwich is now marketed as *Stena Tor Line*.

MANAGEMENT Managing Director: Oddbjörn Fastesson, **Marketing Director:** Eric Nilsson, **General Manager UK:** Brian Thompson.

ADDRESS *Sweden:* PO Box 8888, 402 74 GÖTEBORG, Sweden, *UK:* Nordic House, Western Access Road, Immingham Dock, IMMINGHAM, South Humberside DN40 2LZ.

TELEPHONE Administration & Reservations: *Sweden:* +46 (0)31 650800, *UK:* +44 (0)1469 575231, **Fax:** *Sweden:* +46 (0)31 547014, *UK:* +44 (0)1469 552690.

INTERNET Website: http://www.torline.se *(Swedish, English)*

ROUTES OPERATED Service pattern before all three new ships have been delivered: Harwich *(dep: 14.00 Sun, 14.00 Sat (via Immingham))* - Göteborg *(dep: 19.00 Wed (via Immingham), 21.00 Fri)* (36 hrs (direct), 63/75 hrs (via Immingham; 2 per week), Immingham *(dep: 23.59 Sun, 20.00 Mon-Thu, 13.00 Sat)* - Göteborg *(dep: 23.59 Sun, 19.00 Mon-Thu, 14.00 Sat)* (32-37 hrs; 6 per week). **Service pattern after all three new ships have been delivered:** Göteborg - Harwich (36 hrs; 3 per week), Göteborg *(dep: 23.00)* - Immingham *(dep: 04.00)* - (24 hrs; 6 per week), **Service pattern throughout:** Immingham *(dep: 15.00 Sun, 17.00 Mon-Fri)* - Rotterdam *(dep: 18.00 Mon-Sat)* (14 hrs 30 mins; 6 per week), Göteborg *(dep: 03.00 Sun, Tue-Sat)* - Gent (Belgium) *(dep: 21.00 Sun, Mon, Wed-Sat)* (42 hrs; 6 per week). **Norway services:** *Circuit 1* Oslo *(dep: 15.00 Mon)* - Bamble *(dep: 21.00 Mon)* - Kristiansand *(dep: 10.00 Tue)* - Hamburg *(arr: 12.00 Wed, dep: 14.00 Wed)* - Bamble *(arr: Thu)* - Oslo *(arr: 0.700 Fri, dep: 14.00 Fri)* - Hamburg *(arr: 19.00 Sat, dep: 23.59 Sat)* - Oslo *(arr: 07.00 Mon)*, *Circuit 2* Oslo *(dep: Mon)* - Larvik *(dep: 10.00 Tue)* - Frederikstad *(dep: 16.00 Tue)* - Oslo *(dep: 15.30 Wed)* - Kristiansand *(dep: 04.00 Thu)* - Felixstowe *(arr: 08.00 Fri, dep: 21.00 Fri)* - **Rotterdam** *(dep: 16.00 Sat)* - Kristiansand *(dep: 17.00 Sun)* - Oslo *(arr: 07.00 Mon)*, *Circuit 3* Oslo *(dep: Mon)* - Bamble *(dep: 11.00 Tue)* - Herøya *(dep: 16.00 Tue)* - Oslo *(dep: 15.30 Wed)* - Kristiansand *(dep: 04.00 Thu)* - Immingham *(arr: 08.00 Fri, dep: 21.00 Fri)*, Zeebrugge *(dep: 17.00 Sat)* - Oslo *(arr: 07.00 Mon)*, *Circuit 4* Oslo *(dep: 15.30 Fri)* - Herøya *(dep: 23.59 Fri)* - Kristiansand *(dep: 10.00 Sat)* - **Rotterdam** *(arr: 07.30 Mon)* - Immingham *(arr: 08.00 Tue, dep: 17.00 Tue)* - **Rotterdam** *(dep: 16.00 Wed)* - Larvik *(arr: 21.00 Thu)* - Oslo *(arr: 07.00 Fri)*. Note: Circuit 1 does not call in the UK ports. Services not calling at UK ports are strictly outside the scope of this book but are included for the sake of completeness.

VESSELS

1	BRITTA ODEN	16950t	79	15k	12P	180C	183T	A	Landskrona, SW	SW
2	DANA HAFNIA	11125t	79	16k	12P	400C	121T	A2	Lödöse, SW	DK
3	EVA ODEN	16950t	79	15k	12P	180C	183T	A	Landskrona, SW	SW
4	STENA GOTHICA	14406t	75	16k	12P	-	150T	A	Sandefjord, NO	SW
5	TOR ANGLIA	17492t	77	15k	12P	-	206T	A	Kiel, GY	NL
6	TOR BELGIA	21491t	78	18k	12P	200C	224T	AS	Dunkerque, FR	SW
7	TOR BRITANNIA	24196t	99	21.1k	12P	-	230T	A	Ancona, IT	DK
8	TOR CALEDONIA	14424t	77	16k	12P	-	160T	A	Frederikstad, NO	DK
9	TOR DANIA	21850t	78	18k	12P	200C	224T	AS	Dunkerque, FR	DK
10	TOR FLANDRIA	33652t	81	19k	12P	300C	240T	A	Malmö, SW	SW
11	TOR GOTHIA	12259t	71	17k	12P	-	130T	A	Sandefjord, NO	NL
12	TOR HOLLANDIA	12254t	73	15.5k	12P	-	130T	A	Sandefjord, NO	NL

13	TOR HUMBRIA	20165t	78	18.5k	0P	-	178T	A	Oskarshamn, SW	NO
14	TOR NORVEGIA	12494t	75	19k	12P	-	142T	A	Florø, NO	NO
15	TOR SCANDIA	33652t	81	19k	12P	300C	240T	A	Malmö, SW	SW
16	TOR SELANDIA	24196t	98	21.1k	12P	-	230T	A	Ancona, IT	DK
17	TOR SUECIA	24196t	99	21.1k	12P	-	230T	A	Ancona, IT	DK
18	TRANSLUBECA	24727t	90	20k	84P	-	175T	A	Gdansk, PO	GY

BRITTA ODEN Built as the BRITTA ODEN for *AB Norsjöfrakt* (later *Bylock & Norsjöfrakt*) of Sweden and chartered to *Oden Line* of Sweden for North Sea services, in particular associated with the export of Volvo cars and trucks from Göteborg. In 1980 *Oden Line* was taken over by *Tor Lloyd AB*, a joint venture between *Tor Line* and *Broströms AB* and the charter transferred to them, moving to *Tor Line* in 1981 when *DFDS* took over. In 1987 she was enlarged and on re-entry into service in early 1988 was renamed the TOR SCANDIA and became regular vessel on the Göteborg - Gent (Belgium) service. In 1998 renamed the BRITTA ODEN. When the second and third newbuildings are delivered, she and sister vessel, EVA ODEN will be replaced by the TOR BELGIA and the TOR DANIA.

DANA HAFNIA Built as the LINNÉ and chartered to *OT Africa Line* for services between Italy and Libya. In 1985 sold and renamed the BELINDA; she was employed on a variety of charters including *DFDS* and *Stena Line* until 1988 when she was sold to *Dannebrog* of Denmark and renamed the NORDBORG. Chartering continued, including *Kent Line* and *DFDS* again, and in 1993 she was chartered to *Cobelfret*. In 1994 she was sold to *DFDS* and renamed the DANA HAFNIA. Initially operated on *Tor Line* services but in 1995 transferred to *DFDS* to operate between Harwich and Esbjerg. Following delivery of the DANA FUTURA in 1996 she was transferred to the Immingham - Cuxhaven service. In 1998 she was replaced by the DANA CIMBRIA and was due to be transferred to *DFDS Baltic Line* TO operate between Fredericia (Denmark) - København - Klaípeda (Lithuania). However, following the collapse of the Russian economy, she was, instead, chartered to *Cobelfret Ferries*. In 1999 she was transferred to *DFDS Tor Line*.

EVA ODEN Built as the EVA ODEN. In 1988 renamed the TOR BELGIA. Otherwise as the BRITTAN ODEN. In 1998 she was renamed the EVA ODEN. When the second and third newbuildings are delivered, she and sister vessel BRITTA ODEN will be replaced by the TOR BELGIA and the TOR DANIA.

STENA GOTHICA Built as the MELBOURNE TRADER for *Australian National Line* for services in Australia. She was of the same design as *Tor Line's* TOR GOTHIA class. In 1987 sold to *Forest Shipping*. In 1988 she was chartered to *Elbe-Humber RoLine* and renamed the RAILRO 2. Later in 1988 she was sold to *Stena Line*, renamed the STENA PROJECT and was then chartered by them to *CoTuNav* of Tunisia and renamed the MONAWAR L. In 1990, following the start of a joint *Stena Line/Tor Line* service between Göteborg and Harwich (operated by *Tor Line*) she was renamed the STENA GOTHICA, lengthened by 31m and chartered to *Tor Line*. Generally used on the Göteborg - Immingham/Harwich service. When all three newbuildings have been delivered, she will operate between Göteborg and Harwich.

TOR ANGLIA Built as the MERZARIO GALLIA and chartered to *Merzario Line* of Italy for services between Italy and Saudi Arabia. In 1981 she was chartered to *Wilhelmsen*, renamed the TANA and used between USA and West Africa. In 1983 she was chartered to *Salenia AB* of Sweden and renamed the NORDIC WASA. In 1987 she had a brief period on charter to *Atlantic Marine* as the AFRICAN GATEWAY and in 1988 she was sold to *Tor Line* and renamed the TOR ANGLIA. In 1989 an additional deck was added. In recent years she has operated on the Göteborg - Gent service but in late 1998 she was switched to the Immingham - Rotterdam service.

TOR BELGIA Built as the VILLE DU HAVRE for *Société Française de Transports Maritimes* of France. Between 1979 and 1981 she was chartered to *Foss Line*, renamed the FOSS HAVRE and operated between Europe and the Middle East. In 1987 she was renamed the KAMINA. In 1990 she was

THE NORTH SEA CARRIER

For more than 30 years we have built transport systems specially adapted to our customers' needs. With daily departures from Immingham, Harwich, Rotterdam, Ghent and Gothenburg we are able to offer high frequency, reliability and cost-effective transport solutions.

As from January 1999 we have taken over The North Sea Line from Fred. Olsen. The Norwegian traffic to/from ports in Great Britain, Germany and Belgium is a complement to our other services.

Visit us at http://www.torline.se.

DFDS TOR LINE
THE NORTH SEA CARRIER

Immingham	Phone: +44 1469 575231
Rotterdam	Phone: +31 10 428 36 00
Ghent	Phone: +32 9 269 12 69
Gothenburg	Phone: +46 31 65 08 00
Oslo	Phone: +47 23 10 61 00

chartered to *Maersk Line* of Denmark, renamed the MAERSK KENT and used on *Kent Line* services between Dartford and Zeebrugge. In 1992 she was chartered to and later purchased by *Tor Line* and renamed the TOR BRITANNIA. In 1994 she was lengthened by 23.7m. In 1999 she was renamed the TOR BELGIA. She will be transferred from the Göteborg - Immingham route to the Göteborg - Gent route.

TOR BRITANNIA Built for *DFDS Tor Line*. To operate on the Göteborg - Immingham route. Delivery expected in June 1999.

TOR CALEDONIA Built for charter to *Tor Line* for freight service between Sweden and UK/Netherlands. She was a lengthened version of the TOR GOTHIA class, these vessels being lengthened in the same year. In 1982 she served with the British Falkland islands Task Force. In 1984 she was chartered to *Grimaldi* of Italy, renamed the GOTHIC WASA. Later that year she was renamed the GALLOWAY but in 1985 she was returned to *Tor Line* and renamed the TOR CALEDONIA. In 1988 she was purchased by *DFDS* and in 1990 she was lengthened by 26m. Generally operated on the Göteborg - Immingham/Harwich route. When all three newbuildings have been delivered, she will operate between Göteborg and Harwich.

TOR DANIA Built as the VILLE DE DUNKERQUE for *Société Française de Transports Maritimes* of France. Between 1979 and 1981 she was chartered to *Foss Line*, renamed the FOSS DUNKERQUE and operated between Europe and the Middle East. In 1986 she was chartered to *Grimaldi* of Italy and renamed the G AND C EXPRESS. In 1988 she was briefly chartered to *Elbe-Humber RoLine* and renamed the RAILRO. She was then chartered to *DFDS* where she was renamed the DANIA HAFNIA. The following year she was chartered to *Maersk Line* of Denmark, renamed the MAERSK ESSEX and used on *Kent Line* services between Dartford and Zeebrugge. In 1992 she was chartered to and later purchased by *DFDS* and renamed the TOR DANIA. In 1993 she was renamed the BRIT DANIA but later in the year reverted to her original name. She was generally used on the Harwich - Esbjerg service, working in consort with the passenger ferry DANIA ANGLIA (see *DFDS Seaways*). In 1994 she was lengthened by 23.7m. and chartered to *Tor Line*. In 1999 she will be transferred from the Göteborg - Immingham route to the Göteborg - Gent route.

TOR FLANDRIA Built as the FINNCLIPPER for the *Johansson Group* of Sweden and chartered out. In 1983 she was sold to *Zenit Shipping* and renamed the ZENIT CLIPPER. She was chartered to *Foss Line* and used on services between Northern Europe and the Middle East. In 1986 she was sold to *Crowley American Transport* of the USA and chartered to the US Military. She was reamed the AMERICAN FALCON and used for military transport purposes across the world. In 1998 sold to *Stena Rederi* and was renamed the STENA PARTNER. She was then chartered to *Tor Line* and renamed the TOR FLANDRIA, part of her charter conditions are that she be purchased at the end of the five year charter period.. She is used on the Göteborg - Gent route.

TOR GOTHIA Built for *Tor Line*. Lengthened in 1977. She was usually used on the Immingham - Rotterdam service.

TOR HOLLANDIA Built as the TOR DANIA for charter to *Tor Line*. In 1975 she was chartered to *Salenrederierna* for service in the Middle East and renamed the BANDAR ABBAS EXPRESS. In 1977 she was lengthened and, in 1978, returned to *Tor Line* and resumed the name TOR DANIA. Purchased by *Tor Line* in 1986. In 1992 she was renamed the TOR DAN and in 1993 the TOR HOLLANDIA. She was usually used on the Immingham - Rotterdam service. In January 1999, she was transferred to former *Fred. Olsen Lines North* sea services.

TOR HUMBRIA Built as the EMIRATES EXPRESS for *A/S Skarhamns Oljetransport* of Norway and chartered to *Mideastcargo* for services between Europe and the Middle East. In 1981 chartered to *OT West Africa Line* for services between Europe and West Africa and renamed the ABUJA EXPRESS. In 1983 chartered to *Foss Line*, renamed the FOSSEAGLE and returned to Middle East service. In 1985 she was renamed the FINNEAGLE, chartered briefly to *Finncarriers* and then to

FERRIES OF THE BRITISH ISLES & NORTHERN EUROPE

Fred. Olsen Lines. In 1987 they purchased her and renamed her the BORAC. In 1999 purchased by *DFDS Tor Line* and renamed the TOR HUMBRIA.

TOR NORVEGIA Built as the BALDUIN for *Fred. Olsen Lines*. 1999 purchased by *DFDS Tor Line* and renamed the TOR NORVEGIA. She is used on the former *Fred. Olsen Lines* services.

TOR SCANDIA Built as the KUWAIT EXPRESS for the *Johansson Group* of Sweden and chartered to *NYK Line* of Japan for services between Japan and the Arabian Gulf. In 1983 she was sold to *Zenit Shipping* and renamed the ZENIT EXPRESS. She was chartered to *Foss Line* and used on services between Northern Europe and the Middle East. In 1984 she was sold to *Crowley American Transport* of the USA and chartered to the US Military. She was renamed the AMERICAN CONDOR and used for military transport purposes across the world. In 1998 sold to *Stena Rederi* and was renamed the STENA PORTER. She was sold to *Tor Line* and renamed the TOR SCANDIA. She is used on the Göteborg - Gent route.

TOR SELANDIA Built for *DFDS Tor Line*. She operates on the Göteborg - Immingham route.

TOR SUECIA Built for *DFDS Tor Line*. To operate on the Göteborg - Immingham route. Delivery expected in April 1999.

TRANSLUBECA 'Ro-pax' vessel build for *Poseidon Schiffahrt* of Germany to operate between Lübeck and Helsinki. In 1995 she inaugurated a new Lübeck - Turku service. In 1997 *Poseidon Schiffahrt* was acquired by *Finnlines*. In 1998 she operated between Helsinki and Travemünde. In 1999 she was chartered to *DFDS Tor Line*.

FALCON SEAFREIGHT

THE COMPANY *Falcon Seafreight* is operated by *Falcon Distribution Group Limited*, a UK company.

ADDRESS Folkestone Port, FOLKESTONE, Kent CT20 1QH.

TELEPHONE Administration & Reservations: +44 (0)1303 221456, **Fax:** +44 (0)1303 248709.

ROUTES OPERATED Folkestone *(dep: 06.00, 10.00, 13.30, 20.00, 22.00)* - Boulogne *(dep: 03.00, 06.00, 10.45, 16.15, 19.00)* (2 hrs 15 mins; *(1,2)*; 5 per day).

VESSELS

1	PICASSO	5689t	77	16k	12P	-	64T	A	Hamburg, GY	CI
2	PURBECK	6507t	78	17.5k	58P	-	57T	BA	Le Havre, FR	BA

PICASSO Built as the WUPPERTAL for *J A Reinecke* of Germany and chartered out. In 1978 she was renamed the CANAIMA but the following year she resumed her original name. Charters included *North Sea Ferries*, with spells on both the Ipswich - Rotterdam and Hull - Zeebrugge services, *Tor Lloyd* and *DFDS*. In 1987 she was renamed the BEAVERDALE. She had a number of further charters, including *North Sea Ferries* where she operated from 1989 to 1991 between Middlesbrough and Zeebrugge. In 1991 she was purchased by *Sea Containers*, renamed the POKER and chartered out. In 1995 she was briefly chartered to *Mannin Line* to operate between Great Yarmouth and IJmuiden (Netherlands). Later that year she was renamed the PICASSO and chartered to *DFDS*. In 1996 she was transferred to *Hoverspeed Falcon Sea Freight* (a joint venture between *Hoverspeed* and *Falcon Distribution*) and introduced onto the Folkestone - Boulogne route. In early 1998, *Hoverspeed* ceased to have commercial involvement in the service but continued to crew the vessel, which remains owned by *Sea Containers*. She was chartered to *Falcon Seafreight*. In summer 1998 the charter was terminated and she was laid up. Later in 1998, she was chartered again, in order to operate a two ship service. She began operating in 1999. Withdrawn from service in late March 1999.

PURBECK Built for *Truckline Ferries* for their Cherbourg - Poole service. In 1986 she was lengthened to increase vehicle capacity by 34%. In 1992 transferred to the Roscoff - Plymouth and Santander -

Plymouth services. In 1994 she was sold to *Channel Island Ferries* (parent company of *British Channel Island Ferries*) to operate freight services between Poole and The Channel Islands. Later in 1994, chartered to *Commodore Ferries* following the cessation of *BCIF*'s operations. In 1995 she was chartered to *Sally Ferries* for use on their Dartford - Vlissingen service until replaced by the *Dart 5* later in the year. During summer 1996 she was chartered to *Irish Ferries* to operate supplementary freight services between Dublin and Holyhead. In autumn 1996 she returned to *Sally Ferries* and in 1997 she was transferred to *Holyman Sally Ferries*. She was chartered to *Truckline Ferries* in summer 1997 to operate between Portsmouth and Caen. Later in 1997, she was chartered to *Gaelic Ferries* to inaugurate a new Cork - Cherbourg service. During the French truckers' blockade in late 1997, she operated between Cork and Santander (Spain). In 1998 she was chartered to *Falcon Seafreight*.

FINANGLIA FERRIES

THE COMPANY *Finanglia Ferries* is a joint operation between *Finncarriers Oy Ab*, a Finnish private sector company and *Andrew Weir Shipping*, (owners of the *United Baltic Corporation*), a British private sector company.

MANAGEMENT Managing Director: J Ashley, **Sales Manager:** Miss C M Cotton.

ADDRESSES *UK:* 8 Heron Quay, LONDON E14 4JB, *Finland:* PO Box 197, Porkkalankatu 7, FIN-00181 HELSINKI, Finland.

TELEPHONE Administration & Reservations: *UK:* +44 (0)171-519 7300, *Finland:* +358 (0)10 34350, **Fax:** *UK:* +44 (0)171-536 0255, *Finland:* +358 (0)10 3435200, **Telex:** *Finland:* 1001743.

ROUTES OPERATED Felixstowe - Helsinki (Finland) - Hamina (Finland) (4 days; *(1,2,5,6,7)*; 2 per week northbound, 3 per week southbound), Hull - Helsinki - Hamina (5 days; *(3,4)*; 1 per week). Note: Finland - Hull service operates via Felixstowe on southward journey giving additional southward sailing. Vessels operate on weekly, two and three weekly cycles and are sometimes moved between routes.

VESSELS

1	BALTIC EAGLE	14738t	79	18k	12P	-	116T	A	Rauma, FI	IM
2	BALTIC EIDER	20865t	89	19k	0P	-	180T	A	Ulsan, SK	IM
3	FINNBIRCH	14059t	78	17k	0P	-	174T	A	Ulsan, SK	SW
4	FINNFOREST	15525t	78	17k	0P	-	174T	A	Ulsan, SK	SW
5	FINNRIVER	20172t	79	16.5k	0P	-	136T	Q	Ichihara, JA	SW
6	FINNROSE	20169t	78	19k	0P	-	136T	Q	Ichihara, JA	SW
7	TRANSBALTICA	21224t	90	19k	0P	-	182T	A	Ulsan, SK	CY

BALTIC EAGLE Built for *United Baltic Corporation*.

BALTIC EIDER Built for *United Baltic Corporation*.

FINNBIRCH Laid down as the STENA PROSPER and completed as the ATLANTIC PROSPER for *Stena Rederi* and chartered to *ACL* of Great Britain for service between Britain and Canada. In 1981 chartered to *Merzario Line* of Italy for services between Italy and Saudi Arabia and renamed, initially, the STENA IONIA and then the MERZARIO IONIA. Later the same year she reverted to the name STENA IONIA and was chartered to *OT West Africa Line* for services between Europe and Nigeria. In 1985 she was renamed the STENA GOTHICA and used on *Stena Portlink* services. In 1988 she was chartered to *Bore Line* of Finland and renamed the BORE GOTHICA. In 1992 chartered to *Finncarriers*. In 1996 renamed the FINNBIRCH. In 1997 she began operating a service between Hull and Zeebrugge on charter to *P&O North Sea Ferries* in the course of her normal two week circuit from Finland.

Ferries of the British Isles & Northern Europe

125

Tor Flandria *(C.G. De Bijl)*

European Highlander *(Gordon Hislip)*

Dart Line - Dartford Terminal *(Dart Line)*

FINNFOREST Laid down as the STENA PROJECT and completed as ATLANTIC PROJECT for *Stena Rederi* and chartered to *ACL* (see above). In 1981 chartered to *Merzario Line* of Italy for services between Italy and Saudi Arabia and renamed the MERZARIO HISPANIA. In 1983 returned to *Stena Line* and renamed the STENA HISPANIA. In 1984 chartered to *Kotka Line* of Finland, renamed the KOTKA VIOLET and used on their services between Finland, UK and West Africa. This charter ended in 1985 and she was again named the STENA HISPANIA. In 1986 she was renamed the STENA BRITANNICA and used on *Stena Portlink* (later *Stena Tor Line*) service between Sweden and Britain. In 1988 she was chartered to *Bore Line* of Finland, renamed the BORE BRITANNICA and used on services between Finland and Britain. In 1992 chartered to *Finncarriers*. In 1997 renamed the FINNFOREST. In 1997 she began operating a service between Hull and Zeebrugge on charter to *P&O North Sea Ferries* in the course of her normal two week circuit from Finland.

FINNRIVER Built as the VASALAND for *Boström AB* of Sweden and chartered to *EFFOA* of Finland for services between Scandinavia and Mediterranean ports. In 1983 chartered to *Swedish Orient Line* for similar services and renamed the HESPERUS. In 1986 chartered to *Finncarriers* and renamed the CELIA. In 1996 the charter was extended for a further five years and she was renamed the FINNROVER.

FINNROSE Built as the TIMMERLAND for *Boström AB* of Sweden and chartered to *EFFOA* of Finland for services between Scandinavia and Mediterranean ports. In 1984 chartered to *Swedish Orient Line* for similar services and renamed the HEKTOS. In 1986 chartered to *Finncarriers* and renamed the CORTIA. In 1996 the charter was extended for a further five years and she was renamed the FINNROSE.

TRANSBALTICA Built as the AHLERS BALTIC the for *Ahlers Line* and chartered to *Finncarriers*. In 1995 acquired by *Poseidon Schiffahrt AG* of Germany and renamed the TRANSBALTICA. She continued to be chartered to *Finncarriers* and was acquired by them when they purchased *Poseidon Schiffahrt AG* in 1997.

UNDER CONSTRUCTION

| 8 | NEWBUILDING 1 | 12000t | 00 | 21k | 0P | - | 158T | A | Jinling, CH | - |
| 9 | NEWBUILDING 1 | 12000t | 00 | 21k | 0P | - | 158T | A | Jinling, CH | - |

NEWBUILDING 1, NEWBUILDING 2 Under construction for *Nordic Forest Terminals* of Sweden to operate for *Finncarriers* between Finland and the UK.

ISLE OF MAN STEAM PACKET COMPANY

THE COMPANY, MANAGEMENT, ADDRESS AND TELEPHONE See Section 1.

ROUTE OPERATED No dedicated freight service is now operated. All freight is conveyed on the ro-pax vessel BEN-MY-CHREE. See *Sea Containers Ferries*, Section 1.

VESSEL

| 1• | PEVERIL | 5254t | 71 | 16k | 12P | - | 40T | A | Kristiansand, NO | IM |

PEVERIL Built as the HOLMIA for *Rederi AB Silja* of Finland. She was used on *Silja Line* cargo and ro-ro services between Norrtälje (Sweden) and Turku (Finland). In 1973 she was sold and renamed the A S D METEOR. Later that year she was sold to *P&O Ferries* for their joint Heysham - Belfast service with *Sealink* and renamed the PENDA. In 1980 she was renamed the N F JAGUAR and transferred to freight services between Southampton and Le Havre. In 1981 she was chartered to *IOMSP Co* for a Douglas - Liverpool freight service and in 1983 she was demise chartered by *James Fisher* of Barrow and chartered to *IOMSP Co*; she was renamed the PEVERIL. The freight service was switched to Heysham in 1985. The charter ended in December 1992 and she was purchased by the *IOMSP Co*. She was replaced by the BELARD in 1997 and was laid up but was chartered to *Irish Ferries* in November 1997 to operate between Rosslare and Pembroke. In 1998 the BELARD was sold and she returned to service. She was replaced by the ro-pax ferry BEN-MY-CHREE in August 1998 and laid up.

MERCHANT FERRIES

THE COMPANY *Merchant Ferries* is a British private sector company, owned by *Cenargo*. The 50% share owned by *The Mersey Docks and Harbour Co* was sold to *Cenargo* in 1997.

MANAGEMENT General Manager: Richard Harrison.

ADDRESS North Quay, Heysham Harbour, MORCAMBE, Lancs LA3 2UL.

TELEPHONE Administration: +44 (0)1524 855018, **Reservations:** +44 (0)1524 855018, **Fax:** +44 (0)1524 852527.

INTERNET Email: Merchant.Ferries@btinternet.com

ROUTE OPERATED Heysham *(dep: 06.30, 24.00)* - Dublin *(dep: 12.00, 19.00)* (8 hrs; *(2,3)*; 1 per day). *Merchant Ferries* also operate a passenger/freight service from Liverpool to Dublin. See Section 1.

VESSELS

1	MERCHANT VENTURE	6056t	79	17k	12P	-	55T	A	Castelo, PL	IM
2	RIVER LUNE	7765t	83	15k	12P	-	100T	A	Galatz, RO	BA
3	SAGA MOON	7746t	84	15k	12P	-	75T	A	Travemünde, GY	GI

MERCHANT VENTURE Built as the FARMAN and chartered to *GNMTC* of Italy for Mediterranean services. In 1982 she was sold to *Medlines* for similar service and renamed the MED ADRIATICO. In 1985 she was sold, renamed the ARGENTEA and chartered to *SGMAT*, continuing to operate in the Mediterranean. In 1987 sold to *Cenargo* and chartered to *Merchant Ferries* who renamed her first the MERCHANT ISLE and then the MERCHANT VENTURE. She was purchased by *Merchant Ferries* in 1993. Until 1993 she was used on the Fleetwood - Warrenpoint service; in 1993 the UK terminal was moved to Heysham and in 1995 the Irish terminal was moved to Dublin. In autumn 1998 she was placed on the charter market.

RIVER LUNE Built for *Almira Shipping* of Liberia (part of the Norwegian *Balder* group) as the BALDER VIK and initially used on services between Italy and the Middle East. Subsequently she was employed on a number of charters including *North Sea Ferries* and *Norfolk Line*. In 1986 she was acquired by *Navimpex* of Romania, renamed the BAZIAS 7 and initially used on Mediterranean and Black Sea services. In 1987 she was chartered to *Kent Line* for service between Chatham and Zeebrugge. In 1988 she was sold to *Stena Rederi AB* of Sweden and chartered for service between Finland and Germany. In 1989 she was briefly renamed the STENA TOPPER before being further renamed the SALAR. During the ensuing years she undertook a number of charters. In 1993 she briefly resumed the name STENA TOPPER before being chartered to *Belfast Freight Ferries* and renamed the RIVER LUNE. In October 1996 she was sold to *Belfast Freight Ferries*. In 1999 she was chartered to associated company *Merchant Ferries*.

SAGA MOON Built as the LIDARTINDUR for *Trader Line* of the Faroe Islands for services between Tórshavn and Denmark. In 1986 chartered to *Belfast Freight Ferries* renamed the SAGA MOON. In 1990 she was sold to *Belfast Freight Ferries*. In 1995 she was lengthened by 18m to increase trailer capacity from 52 to 72 units and trade cars from 25 to 50. The lift was replaced by an internal fixed ramp. In 1998 she was chartered to associated company *Merchant Ferries*.

NOR-CARGO

THE COMPANY *Nor-Cargo AS* is a Norwegian company jointly owned by *Ofotens og Vesteraalen Dampskipsselskab, Det Stavangerske Dampskipsselskab* and *Troms Fylkes Dampskipsselskab. Nor-Cargo Ltd* is a British registered subsidiary company.

ADDRESS *Norway:* Pir-Senteret, N-7005 TRONDHEIM, Norway, *UK:* 1 Prince Albert Gardens, GRIMSBY DN31 3HT.

TELEPHONE Administration & Bookings: *Norway:* +47 73 54 50 00, *UK:* +44 (0)1472 240241, **Fax:** *Norway:* +47 73 54 50 01, *UK:* +44 (0)1472 240250.

INTERNET Email: Info@Nor-Cargo.com **Website:** http://www.nor-cargo.demon.co.uk/

ROUTES OPERATED Circuit 1: Bergen *(dep: Sat)* - Tananger *(dep: Sun)* - Stavanger *(dep: Sun)* - Aberdeen *(arr: Mon)* - Grimsby *(arr/dep: Tue)* - Aberdeen *(dep: Wed)* - Tananger *(arr: Thu)* / Stavanger *(arr: Thu)* - Sandnes *(arr: Thu)* - Håvik *(arr: Fri)* - Haugesund *(arr: Fri)* - Bergen *(arr: Sat)* (1 week; *(1)*; weekly), **Circuit 2:** Bergen *(dep: Mon)* - Håvik *(dep: Tue)* - Stavanger *(dep: Tue)* - Amsterdam *(arr: Thu/dep: Fri)* - Aberdeen *(arr/dep: Sat)* - Stavanger *(arr: Sun)* - Bergen *(arr: Mon)* (1 week; *(3)*; weekly).

VESSELS

1	COMETA	4610t	81	16k	0P	-	26T	AS	Rissa, NO	NO
2	NORDHAV	5846t	80	15k	12P	-	67T	A	Kraljevica, YU	NO
3	TUNGENES	4234t	79	15.5k	0P	-	29T	AS	Rissa, NO	NO

COMETA Built for *Nor-Cargo*.

NORDHAV Built as the CRES for *Losinjska Plovidba* of Yugoslavia (later Croatia) and used on Mediterranean services. In 1998 she was sold to *Nor-Cargo* and renamed the NORDHAV. She is due to operate additional sailings between Bergen and Amsterdam via Aberdeen and Immingham but has not yet entered service.

TUNGENES Built for *Nor-Cargo*. Launched as the ERIC JARL but renamed the ASTREA before entering service. In 1986 she sank and, after raising and refitting she was, in 1992, renamed the TUNGENES.

Nor-Cargo also operate a lo-lo service between Grimsby and the West Coast of Norway using cargo vessels NORDJARL (3698t, 1985 (ex ICE PEARL, 1995)), NORDKYN (2503t, 1979) and NORDVÆR (2731t, 1986 (ex VICTORIAHAMN, 1993)). The service leaves Grimsby every Saturday, arriving back on Friday three weeks later.

NORFOLKLINE

THE COMPANY *Norfolkline* (before 1 January 1999 *Norfolk Line*) is a Dutch private sector company owned by *A P Møller Finance* of Denmark.

MANAGEMENT Managing Director: D G Sloan, **Deputy Managing Director:** D V J M Blom, **Marketing Manager:** R A Meijer, **General Manager UK:** E J Green.

ADDRESS *Netherlands:* Kranenburgweg 211, 2583 ER SCHEVENINGEN, Netherlands. *UK:* Norfolk House, The Dock, FELIXSTOWE, Suffolk IP11 8UY.

TELEPHONE Administration: *Netherlands:* +31 (0)70 352 74 00, *UK:* +44 (0)1394 673676, **Reservations:** *Netherlands:* +31 (0)70 352 74 71, *Felixstowe:* +44 (0)1394 603630, *Immingham:* +44 (0)1469 571122, **Fax:** *Netherlands:* +31 (0)70 354 93 30, *UK:* +44 (0)1394 603673.

INTERNET Email: info@norfolkline.com **Website:** http://www.norfolkline.com (*English*)

ROUTES OPERATED Felixstowe *(dep: 06.00, 12.00, 18.00, 23.00)* - Scheveningen *(dep: 07.00, 14.00, 19.00, 23.59)* (7 hrs; *(1,2,3,4)*; 4 per day), Scheveningen *(dep: 14.00 Sat, 19.00 Sat)* - Esbjerg *(dep: 13.00 Sat, 20.00 Sun)* (20 hrs; *(1,3)*; 2 per week), Immingham - Esbjerg (22 hrs; 5 per week), Harwich - Esbjerg (21 hrs; 6/7 per week). UK - Denmark services operated in conjunction with *DFDS* who provide all vessels.

VESSELS

1	BOLERO	9983t	85	14.5k	12P	-	72T	A	Wismar, GY	RO
2	MAERSK EXPORTER	13017t	96	18.6k	12P	-	122T	A	Shimizu, JA	NL
3	MAERSK FLANDERS	7199t	78	15k	12P	-	80T	A	Tokyo, JA	NL
4	MAERSK IMPORTER	13017t	96	18.6k	12P	-	122T	A	Shimizu, JA	NL

BOLERO Launched as the SPIEGELBURG. On completion, delivered as the TUZLA to *NavRom* of Romania for Mediterranean service was also chartered to various operators. In 1996 chartered to *Seatruck Ferries* and renamed the BOLERO. In summer 1997 chartered to *EstLine* to operate between Stockholm and Tallinn. In autumn 1997, chartered to *Norfolkline*. In 1998 sold to *Octogon Shipping* of Romania.

MAERSK EXPORTER, MAERSK IMPORTER Built for *Norfolkline*.

MAERSK FLANDERS Built as the ADMIRAL ATLANTIC for *Admiral Shipping* of the USA for Caribbean service. In 1983 she was chartered to *Portlink* for North Sea services. In 1984 sold to Swedish interests and renamed the ROMIRA. In 1986 she was sold to *Norfolkline*, renamed the DUKE OF FLANDERS and used on their services between Great Yarmouth and Esbjerg (Denmark), Immingham and Esbjerg and Immingham and Cuxhaven. In 1990 she was renamed MAERSK FLANDERS.

Under Construction

5	NEWBUILDING 1	c13000t	99	18.6k	12P	-	122T	A	Guangzhou, CH	NL
6	NEWBUILDING 2	c13000t	00	18.6k	12P	-	122T	A	Guangzhou, CH	NL

NEWBUILDING 1, NEWBUILDING 2 Under construction to replace the BOLERO and the MAERSK FLANDERS. Similar in design to the MAERSK EXPORTER and MAERSK IMPORTER.

ORCARGO

THE COMPANY *Orcargo* is a UK registered private sector company.

MANAGEMENT Managing Director: D Laidlow, **Marketing Manager:** Ken Brookman.

ADDRESS Norlantic House, Grainshore, KIRKWALL, Orkney WK15 1RE.

TELEPHONE Administration & Reservations: +44 (0)1856 873838, **Fax:** +44 (0)1856 876521.

INTERNET Website: http://www.orkneyislands.com/orcargo *(English)*

ROUTE OPERATED Invergordon *(dep: 03.30 Tue-Sat, 20.00 Sun)* - Kirkwall *(dep: 17.30 Mon-Fri, 08.00 Sun)* (9 hrs; *(1)*; 6 per week) (passengers can be carried subject to availability).

VESSEL

1	CONTENDER	2292t	73	15k	12P	-	12T	AS	Le Havre, FR	GB

CONTENDER Built as the ANTINEA for *Union Industrielle & Maritime* of France. In 1983 sold to *Euroline SpA* of Italy and renamed the FERRUCCIA. In 1986 she was sold to *White Star Enterprises* of Italy and renamed and INDIANA and in 1988 to *Quay Shipping* of the Bahamas and renamed the INDIANA I. In 1992 she was sold to *Orcargo* and renamed the CONTENDER.

P&O EUROPEAN FERRIES (IRISH SEA)

THE COMPANY, MANAGEMENT AND ADDRESS See Section 1.

TELEPHONE Administration: +44 (0)1253 615700, **Reservations:** *Ardrossan:* +44 (0)1292 469 211, *Cairnryan:* +44 (0)1581 200663, *Dublin:* +353(0)1 855 7001, *Fleetwood:* +44 (0)1253 615755, *Larne:* +44 (0)1574 8722001, *Liverpool:* +44 (0)151 820 1441, *Rosslare:* +353(0)1 855 7001. Fax: *Cairnryan:* +44 (0)1581 200282, *Larne:* +44 (0)1574 272477, *Fleetwood:* +44 (0)1253 615740.

Website: http://www.poef.com *(English)*

ROUTES OPERATED Ardrossan *(02.30 Mon-Sat, 16.15 Tue-Sat)* - Larne *(dep: 11.45 Tue-Fri, 19.00 Sun-Fri, 10.00 Sat)* (4 hrs 15 mins; *(1,3,9)*; 2 per day), Cairnryan *(dep: 02.30, 03.30, 04.00*, 07.30, 11.30*, 15.30, 17.30, 19.30*, 23.30)* - Larne *(dep: 03.30, 08.00*, 11.30, 13.00, 15.30*, 21.30, 22.00, 23.59)* (*operated by passenger vessel) (2 hrs 15 mins; *(1,5,9)*; up to 9 per day), Fleetwood *(dep: 10.00 Sun, Tue-Fri, 22.00)* - Larne *(dep: 10.00 Sun, Tue-Fri, 22.00)* (7 hrs; *7,8*); 2 per day), Liverpool *(dep: 05.00 Tue-Fri, 10.00 Tue-Sat, 22.00 daily)* - Dublin *(dep: 10.00 Tue-Sat, 17.00 Tue-Fri, 22.00 daily)* (8 hrs; *(2,4, CELTIC STAR - see late news)*; 3 per day), Rosslare *(dep: 22.00 Tue, 21.30 Thu, 16.00 Sat)* - Cherbourg *(dep: 22.00 Wed, 19.00 Fri, 14.00 Sun)* (18 hrs; *(6)*; 3 per week). Vessels are sometimes moved between routes. A limited number of ordinary passengers is conveyed on the day sailings between Fleetwood and Larne, all sailings between Rosslare and Cherbourg and 10.00 (22.00 Sun) Liverpool - Dublin and Dublin - Liverpool sailings under the 'Value Route' branding.

VESSELS

1	EUROPEAN ENDEAVOUR	8097t	78	18.4k	107P	-	46L	BA2	Bremerhaven, GY	BD
2	EUROPEAN ENVOY	18653t	79	18.2k	107P	-	125T	A	Tamano, JA	BD
3	EUROPEAN HIGHLANDER	5897t	77	15k	12P	-	71T	A	Bremerhaven, GY	BA
4	EUROPEAN LEADER	12879t	75	17k	50P	-	110T	A	Hamburg, GY	BD
5	EUROPEAN NAVIGATOR	9085t	77	18k	42P	-	70T	A	Korneuburg, AU	BD
6	EUROPEAN PATHFINDER	8023t	75	18.5k	52P	-	72T	BA	Bremerhaven, GY	BD
7	EUROPEAN PIONEER	14387t	75	17.7k	76P	-	123T	A	Hamburg, GY	BD
8	EUROPEAN SEAFARER	10957t	75	18k	50P	-	98T	A	Hamburg, GY	BD
9	EUROPEAN TRADER	8007t	75	18k	54P	-	55L	BA2	Bremerhaven, GY	BA

EUROPEAN ENDEAVOUR Built as the EUROPEAN ENTERPRISE for *European Ferries*. In 1988 she was renamed the EUROPEAN ENDEAVOUR. She was used on freight services between Dover and Calais and Dover and Zeebrugge. If space was available, a small number of passengers was sometimes conveyed on the Zeebrugge service, although the sailings were not advertised for passengers. This ceased with the withdrawal of passenger services on this route at the end of 1991. During the summer period she provided additional freight capacity on the Dover - Calais service and has also served on other routes. In autumn 1995 she was transferred to the Cairnryan - Larne service. In 1998 accommodation was raised to provide extra freight capacity. In March 1999 began also operating to Ardrossan.

EUROPEAN ENVOY Built as the IBEX for *P&O* for *Pandoro* Irish sea services. In 1980 chartered to *North Sea Ferries*, renamed the NORSEA and used on the Ipswich - Rotterdam service. In 1986 she was renamed the NORSKY. In 1995 she returned to *Pandoro* and was re-registered in Bermuda. Later in 1995 she resumed her original name of IBEX. An additional deck was added in 1996. In late 1997 she was renamed the EUROPEAN ENVOY. She is used on the Liverpool - Dublin service.

EUROPEAN HIGHLANDER Built as the SALAHALA and chartered to *Gilnavi* of Italy for Mediterranean services. In 1990 she was purchased by *Cenargo* and chartered to *Merchant Ferries* who renamed her the MERCHANT VALIANT. She was used on the Fleetwood - Warrenpoint service until 1993 when she was chartered to *Pandoro* and placed on their Ardrossan - Larne service. Purchased by *P&O* in 1995 and renamed the LION. In early 1998 renamed the EUROPEAN HIGHLANDER.

EUROPEAN LEADER Built for *Stena Line* as the BUFFALO and due to be chartered to *P&O* for *Pandoro* Irish Sea services. Before completion she was purchased by *P&O*. In 1989 she was lengthened by 12.5m and in 1998 she was further lengthened by 15m and renamed the EUROPEAN LEADER. She is now used on the Liverpool - Dublin service.

EUROPEAN NAVIGATOR Launched as the STENA TRADER but entered service as the GOYA for *United Baltic Corporation* of Great Britain on services between Britain and Spain. In 1979 sold to *Federal Commerce* of Canada for Canadian service and renamed the FEDERAL NOVA. In 1981 briefly renamed the CARIBBEAN SKY before being sold to *Linea Manuare* of Venezuela, renamed the MANUARE VII and used on services to the USA. In 1983 she was sold to new owners who chartered her to *Navigation Central* and renamed her the OYSTER BAY. Later that year she was chartered to *European Ferries*, renamed the VIKING TRADER and used on services between Portsmouth and France. In 1989 transferred to *Pandoro* and in 1996 renamed the LEOPARD. She was renamed the EUROPEAN NAVIGATOR in 1998. Use on the Liverpool - Dublin service until March 1999 when she was transferred to the Cairnryan - Larne route.

EUROPEAN PATHFINDER Built as the EUROPEAN CLEARWAY for *European Ferries* ro-ro freight services. She was built to a standard design rather than custom built. She was used on freight services between Dover and Calais and Dover and Zeebrugge. In 1992 she was moved to the Portsmouth - Le Havre route. In 1993 she was transferred to *Pandoro* to inaugurate a new Cherbourg - Rosslare service. In 1996 she was renamed the PANTHER. In early 1998 she was renamed the EUROPEAN PATHFINDER.

EUROPEAN PIONEER Built for *Stena Line* as the BISON and due to be chartered to *P&O* for *Pandoro* Irish Sea services. Before completion she was purchased by *P&O*. Between 1989 and 1993 she was operated by *B&I Line* of Ireland on a joint service with *Pandoro* between Dublin and Liverpool. An additional deck was added in 1995. In late 1997 she was renamed the EUROPEAN PIONEER. She is now used on the Fleetwood - Larne service.

EUROPEAN SEAFARER Ordered by *Stena Line* as the UNION TRADER but completed as the UNION MELBOURNE for the *Northern Coasters Ltd* of the UK and lengthened before entering service. Chartered to the *Union Steamship Company* of New Zealand and used on services to Australia. In 1980 she was sold to another *P&O* subsidiary and renamed the PUMA. In early 1998 she was renamed the EUROPEAN SEAFARER. She is now used on the Fleetwood - Larne service.

EUROPEAN TRADER Built for *European Ferries* ro-ro freight services; built to a standard design rather than custom built. In late 1991 she was transferred to the Portsmouth - Le Havre route and in 1994 to the Felixstowe - Zeebrugge service to supplement the service provided by the two passenger vessels. In 1996 she was transferred to the Cairnryan - Larne service. In March 1999 began also operating to Ardrossan.

P&O FERRYMASTERS

THE COMPANY *P&O Ferrymasters Ltd* is a British private sector company, a subsidiary of the *Peninsular and Oriental Steam Navigation Company*.

MANAGEMENT Managing Director: J Bradshaw, **Group Tenders and Contracts Manager:** D M Brinkley.

ADDRESS *Head Office:* 11-13 Lower Brook Street, IPSWICH IP4 1AJ, ***Port Office:*** PO Box South Bank 12, Teesport, MIDDLESBROUGH TS6 7RZ.

TELEPHONE *Head Office:* Administration: +44 (0)1473 581200, **Reservations:** +44 (0)1473

58120, **Fax:** +44 (0)1473 581222, **Port Office: Administration:** +44 (0)1642 394600, **Reservations:** +44 (0)1642 394600, **Fax:** +44 (0)1642 394666.
INTERNET Email: *Head Office:* elsa.cheshire@po-transeuropean.com *Port Office:* pofmmidd@aol.com

ROUTE OPERATED Middlesbrough *(dep: Mon, Thu)* - Göteborg (Sweden) *(dep: Tue, Fri)* - Helsingborg (Sweden) *(dep: Sat)* (up to 48 hrs; *(1)*), Middlesbrough *(dep: 12.00 Sat, 23.59 Tue)* - Göteborg (Sweden) *(dep: Sun pm or Mon am, 12.00 Thu)* - Helsingborg (Sweden) *(dep: 23.59 Thu)* (up to 48 hrs; *(2)*).

VESSELS

| 1 | ELK | 14374t | 78 | 18k | 12P | - | 140T | A | Ulsan, SK | GB |
| 2 | NORSE MERSEY | 16009t | 95 | 19.5k | 61P | - | 160T | A | Donanda, IT | IT |

ELK Built for *Stena Rederi* of Sweden and chartered to *P&O Ferrymasters*. Purchased by *P&O* in 1981; she is managed by *P&O Ship Management (Irish Sea) Ltd*, who manage the *P&O European Ferries (Irish Sea) Ltd* fleet. Lengthened in 1986.

NORSE MERSEY Built for Italian interests for charter. On delivery, chartered to *Norse Irish Ferries* and named the NORSE MERSEY. In July 1997 she was replaced by the MERSEY VIKING and was chartered to *P&O Ferrymasters*.

P&O NORTH SEA FERRIES

THE COMPANY, MANAGEMENT, ADDRESS AND TELEPHONE See Section 1.

ROUTES OPERATED Hull *(dep: 21.00)* - Rotterdam (Europoort) *(dep: 21.00)* (10 hrs; *(4,5)*; 1 per day), Middlesbrough *(dep: 19.00)* - Rotterdam *(dep: 19.00)* (16 hrs; *(7,13)*; 6 per week), Middlesbrough (Teesport) *(dep: 20.30)* - Zeebrugge *(dep: 20.30)* (16 hrs; *(8,9)*; 1 per day), Hull *(dep: 21.00)* - Zeebrugge *(dep: 21.00)* (13 hrs; *(6, see note)*; 4 per week), Felixstowe *(dep: 06.00, 11.30, 18.00, 22.30)* - Rotterdam (Europoort) *(dep: 06.30, 12.00, 19.00, 23.30)* (7 hrs 30 mins; *(1,2,10,11)*; 4 per day), Felixstowe *(dep: 11.00, 23.00)* - Zeebrugge *(dep: 11.00, 23.59)* (6 hrs; *(3,12)*; 2 per day. *Note:* the FINNBIRCH and FINNFOREST of *Finncarriers* (see *Finanglia Ferries*) currently operate a alternate weekly round-trip between Hull and Zeebrugge on charter to supplement the service provided by the NORCAPE.

VESSELS

1	EUROPEAN FREEWAY	21162t	77	16.5k	166P	-	163T	A2	Ulsan, SK	GB
2	EUROPEAN TIDEWAY	21162t	77	16.5k	166P	-	163T	A2	Ulsan, SK	GB
3	GABRIELE WEHR	7635t	78	15k	12P	-	80T	A	Bremerhaven, GY	GY
4	NORBANK	17464t	93	22k	114P	-	156T	A	Krimpen, NL	NL
5	NORBAY	17464t	94	22k	114P	-	156T	A	Krimpen, NL	GB
6	NORCAPE	14086t	79	18.7k	12P	-	138T	A	Tamano, JA	NL
7	NORCOVE	10279t	77	17.5k	8P	-	95T	A	Naantali, FI	SW
8	NORKING	17884t	80	19k	12P	-	155T	A	Rauma, FI	FI
9	NORQUEEN	17884t	80	19k	12P	-	155T	A	Rauma, FI	FI
10	PRIDE OF FLANDERS	16776t	78	17k	74P	-	81L	A2	Ulsan, SK	GB
11	PRIDE OF SUFFOLK	16776t	78	17k	74P	-	81L	A2	Ulsan, SK	GB
12	THOMAS WEHR	7628t	77	16k	12P	-	91T	A	Bremerhaven, GY	AN
13	TIDERO STAR	9698t	78	17k	10P	-	95T	R	Krimpen, NL	NO

EUROPEAN FREEWAY Built for *Stena Rederi* as the ALPHA ENTERPRISE and chartered to *Aghiris Navigation* of Cyprus. In 1979 she was renamed the SYRIA and chartered to *Hellas Ferries* for services between Greece and Syria. In 1981 she was lengthened by 33.6m. In 1982 she was chartered to *European Ferries* and used on freight services between Felixstowe and Rotterdam. In 1983 she was renamed the STENA TRANSPORTER and in 1986 the CERDIC FERRY. In 1992 she was renamed the EUROPEAN FREEWAY and, in 1994, purchased by *P&O European Ferries*.

EUROPEAN TIDEWAY Launched as the STENA RUNNER by *Stena Rederi* of Sweden. On completion, renamed the ALPHA PROGRESS and chartered to *Aghiris Navigation* of Greece. In 1979 renamed the HELLAS and operated by *Soutos-Hellas Ferry Services* on services between Greece and Syria. In 1982 she was lengthened by 33.6m. In 1982 she was chartered to *European Ferries* and used on freight services between Felixstowe and Rotterdam. The following year she was returned to *Hellas Ferries*. In 1985 she returned to *European Ferries* and the Rotterdam service. In 1986 she was renamed the DORIC FERRY. In 1992 she was renamed the EUROPEAN TIDEWAY and, in 1994, purchased by *P&O European Ferries*.

GABRIELE WEHR Built for *Wehr Transport* of Germany and chartered to several operators. In 1982, chartered to *Tor Lloyd* (later *Tor Line*) for North Sea service and renamed the TOR ANGLIA. This charter terminated in 1985 when she resumed her original name and, in early 1986, she was chartered to *North Sea Ferries* for their Hull - Zeebrugge service. This charter ended in summer 1987 when the lengthened NORLAND and NORSTAR entered service. Subsequent charters included *Kent Line* and *Brittany Ferries*. In 1989 she was chartered to *P&O European Ferries* for the Portsmouth - Le Havre freight service. Her charter was terminated following the transfer of the EUROPEAN TRADER to the route in late 1992 but in 1993 it was renewed, following the transfer of the EUROPEAN CLEARWAY (now the EUROPEAN PATHFINDER) to *Pandoro*. In 1996, she was transferred to the Felixstowe - Zeebrugge service.

NORBANK Built for *North Sea Ferries* for the Hull - Rotterdam service. She was owned by *Nedlloyd* and in 1996 was sold to *P&O* but retains Dutch crew and registry.

NORBAY Built for *North Sea Ferries* for the Hull - Rotterdam service. Owned by *P&O*.

NORCAPE Launched as the PUMA but, on completion chartered to *B&I Line* and renamed the TIPPERARY for their Dublin - Liverpool service. In 1989 sold to *North Sea Ferries*, renamed the NORCAPE and introduced onto the Ipswich - Rotterdam service. In 1995 that service ceased and she was moved to the Hull - Zeebrugge freight service. She retains Dutch crew and registry.

NORCOVE Built as the ROLITA for *Merivienti* of Italy. In 1979 chartered to *Finncarriers* of Finland, renamed the FINNFOREST and used on services between Finland and North West Europe. In 1982 sold to *EFFOA* of Finland and renamed the CANOPUS. In 1992 sold to Swedish interests and chartered to *Stora Line* for services from Sweden to NW Europe. She was renamed the CUPRIA. In 1995, chartered to *North Sea Ferries* to inaugurate a new service between Middlesbrough and Rotterdam and renamed the NORCOVE. She will be replaced on the route by the NORKING and NORQUEEN later in 1999.

NORKING, NORQUEEN Built as the BORE KING and the BORE QUEEN for *Bore Line* of Finland for Baltic services. In 1991 chartered to *North Sea Ferries* for their Middlesbrough - Zeebrugge service and renamed the NORKING and NORQUEEN respectively. During winter 1995/96 they were lengthened by 28.8 metres and re-engined. When newbuildings are delivered they will be transferred to the Middlesbrough - Rotterdam service.

PRIDE OF FLANDERS Built as the MERZARIO ESPANIA for *Stena Rederi* of Sweden and immediately chartered to *Merzario Line* for their service between Italy and Saudi Arabia. In the same year she was renamed the MERZARIO HISPANIA. In 1979 she was chartered to *European Ferries* for their ro-ro freight service between Felixstowe and Rotterdam and renamed the NORDIC FERRY. In 1982 she served in the Falkland Islands Task Force. In 1986 she was modified to carry 688 passengers and, with sister vessel the BALTIC FERRY (now PRIDE OF SUFFOLK), took over the Felixstowe - Zeebrugge passenger service. In 1992 she was renamed the PRIDE OF FLANDERS. In 1994, purchased by *P&O European Ferries*. In 1995 the Felixstowe - Zeebrugge passenger service ceased,

FERRIES OF THE BRITISH ISLES & NORTHERN EUROPE   135

Norbank *(Philippe Holthof)*

Maersk Anglia *(John Bryant)*

her additional passenger accommodation was removed, passenger capacity was reduced and she was transferred to the Felixstowe - Rotterdam freight service.

PRIDE OF SUFFOLK Built as the STENA TRANSPORTER, a ro-ro freight vessel for *Stena Rederi* of Sweden. In 1979 she was renamed the FINNROSE and chartered to *Finnlines*. She later served with *Atlanticargo* on their service between Europe and USA/Mexico. In 1980 she returned to *Stena Line* and resumed her original name. Later in 1980 she was chartered to *European Ferries* for their Felixstowe - Rotterdam freight-only service and renamed the BALTIC FERRY. In 1982 she served in the Falkland Islands Task Force. In 1986 she was modified in the same way as the PRIDE OF FLANDERS and moved to the Felixstowe - Zeebrugge service. In 1992 she was renamed the PRIDE OF SUFFOLK. In 1994 she was purchased by *P&O European Ferries*. In 1995 the Felixstowe - Zeebrugge passenger service ceased, her additional passenger accommodation was removed, passenger capacity was reduced and she was transferred to the Felixstowe - Rotterdam freight service.

THOMAS WEHR Built for *Wehr Transport* of Germany as THOMAS WEHR but on delivery chartered to *Wacro Line* and renamed the WACRO EXPRESS. In 1978 charter ended and she was renamed the THOMAS WEHR. Over the next few years she was chartered to several operators. In 1982 she was chartered to *Tor Lloyd* (later *Tor Line*) for North Sea service and renamed the TOR NEERLANDIA. In 1985 the charter was transferred to *DFDS* and she was renamed the DANA GERMANIA. This charter terminated in 1985 and she resumed her original name. In early 1986 she was chartered to *North Sea Ferries* for their Hull - Zeebrugge service. This charter ended in summer 1987. Subsequent charters included *Cobelfret* and *Elbe-Humber RoLine* and a twelve month period with *North Sea Ferries* again - this time on the Hull - Rotterdam and Middlesbrough - Zeebrugge routes. In 1993 she was renamed the MANA, then the SANTA MARIA and finally chartered to *TT-Line* and renamed the FULDATAL. 1994 she was chartered by *Horn Line* for service between Europe and the Caribbean and renamed the HORNLINK. Later that year she was chartered to *P&O European Ferries* for the Portsmouth - Le Havre freight service and resumed the name THOMAS WEHR. In late 1995 transferred to the Felixstowe - Zeebrugge freight service.

TIDERO STAR Built as the ANZERE for *Keller Shipping* of Switzerland and chartered to *Nautilus Line* for services between Europe and West Africa. In 1991 she was sold to *AS Tiderø* of Norway and renamed the TIDERO STAR. She was initially chartered to *Fred. Olsen Lines* and later to *Arimure Line* for service in the Far East. In 1994 chartered to *Fred. Olsen Lines* again. In early 1996 she was briefly chartered to *North Sea Ferries* for their Hull - Rotterdam service and then chartered to *Pandoro* and placed on the Liverpool - Dublin service. In early 1997, chartered to *P&O Ferrymasters*. Later in 1997 she was chartered to *P&O North Sea Ferries* and placed on the Middlesbrough - Rotterdam service. She will be replaced on the route by the NORKING and NORQUEEN later in 1999.

Under construction

14	NORSKY	c21000t	99	20k	12P	-	210T	A	Rauma, FI	NL
15	NORSTREAM	c21000t	99	20k	12P	-	210T	A	Rauma, FI	NL

NORSKY, NORSTREAM Under construction for *Bore Line* of Finland. They are to be chartered to *P&O North Sea Ferries* and will operate on the Middlesbrough - Zeebrugge service. The NORKING and NORQUEEN will be transferred to the Middlesbrough - Rotterdam service.

… **FERRIES OF THE BRITISH ISLES & NORTHERN EUROPE** … 137

P&O SCOTTISH FERRIES

THE COMPANY, MANAGEMENT AND ADDRESS See Section 1.

TELEPHONE Administration: +44 (0)1224 589111, **Reservations:** +44 (0)1224 589111, **Fax:** +44 (0)1224 574411.

INTERNET Website: http://www.poscottishferries.co.uk *(English)*

ROUTES OPERATED Aberdeen - Lerwick (14 hrs; *(1)*; up to 3 per week). There are no fixed sailing times. One southbound trip returns via Stromness or Kirkwall taking approx. 20 hours.

VESSEL

| 1 | ST ROGNVALD | 5297t | 70 | 16 k | 12P | - | 41L | A | Lübeck, GY | GB |

ST ROGNVALD Launched as the RHONETAL but renamed the NORCAPE on delivery and chartered to *North Sea Ferries* for their Hull - Rotterdam service; in 1972 she inaugurated their Hull - Zeebrugge service. In 1974 she returned to her owners and resumed the name RHONETAL. In 1975 sold to *Meridional D'Armements* of France for services to Corsica and renamed the RHONE. In 1987 sold to *Conatir* of Italy for Mediterranean services and renamed the MARINO TORRE. In 1989 taken on six months charter to *P&O Scottish Ferries*. In 1990 she was purchased by them and renamed the ST ROGNVALD. She initially operated alongside and then replaced the ST MAGNUS (1206t, 1970). Earlier calls at Leith, Hanstholm (Denmark) and Stavanger (Norway) have now been discontinued.

P&O STENA LINE

THE COMPANY AND ADDRESS See Section 1.

MANAGEMENT Freight Director: Brian Cork.

TELEPHONE Administration: See Section 1, **Reservations:** +44 (0)1304 863344, **Fax:** +44 (0)1304 863399, **Telex:** 96316.

ROUTES OPERATED Dover *(dep: 00.30, 04.30, 08.30, 12.30, 16.30, 20.30)* - Zeebrugge *(dep: 03.30, 07.30, 11.30, 15.30, 19.30, 23.30)* (4 hrs 30 mins; *(1,2,3)*; 6 per day).

VESSELS

1	EUROPEAN HIGHWAY	22986t	92	21k	200P	-	120L	BA2	Bremerhaven, GY	GB
2	EUROPEAN PATHWAY	22986t	92	21k	200P	-	120L	BA2	Bremerhaven, GY	GB
3	EUROPEAN SEAWAY	22986t	91	21k	200P	-	120L	BA2	Bremerhaven, GY	GB

EUROPEAN HIGHWAY, EUROPEAN PATHWAY, EUROPEAN SEAWAY Built for *P&O European Ferries* for the Dover - Zeebrugge freight service. In 1998 they were transferred to *P&O Stena Line*.

SEAFRANCE

THE COMPANY, MANAGEMENT, ADDRESS, TELEPHONE AND INTERNET See Section 1.

ROUTE OPERATED Calais *(dep: 02.30, 06.30, 14.30, 18.30, 22.30)* - Dover *(dep: 03.30, 07.30, 15.30, 19.30, 23.30)* (1 hr 30 mins; *(1)*; up to 5 per day). Service operates according to market demand; otherwise all traffic is conveyed on the multi-purpose ferries.

VESSEL

| 1 | SEAFRANCE NORD PAS-DE-CALAIS | 13727t | 87 | 21.5k | 80P | - | 114T | BA2 | Dunkerque, FR | FR |

SEAFRANCE NORD PAS-DE-CALAIS Built for *SNCF* for the Dunkerque (Ouest) - Dover train ferry service. Before being used on this service (which required the construction of a new berth at Dover

(Western Docks)) in May 1988, she operated road freight services from Calais to Dover Eastern Docks. The train ferry service continued to operate following the opening of the Channel Tunnel in 1994, to convey road vehicles and dangerous loads which were banned from the tunnel. However, it ceased in December 1995 and, after a refit, in February 1996 she was renamed the SEAFRANCE NORD PAS-DE-CALAIS and switched to the Calais - Dover service, primarily for road freight vehicles and drivers but also advertised as carrying up to 50 car passengers. Since the entry into service of a third multi-purpose ferry, she has operated on a freight-only basis.

SEATRUCK FERRIES

THE COMPANY *Seatruck Ferries Ltd* is a British private sector company, owned by *Crescent plc*.

MANAGEMENT Managing Director: Kevin Hobbs, **Commercial Director:** Ivan Brown.

ADDRESS *Warrenpoint (HQ):* Seatruck House, The Ferry Terminal, WARRENPOINT, County Down BT34 3JR. *Heysham:* North Quay, Heysham Port, Heysham, MORECAMBE, Lancs LA3 2UL.

TELEPHONE Administration: +44 (0)16937 54411, **Reservations:** *Warrenpoint:* +44 (0)16937 54400, *Heysham:* +44 (0)1524 853512, **Fax:** *Admin:* +44 (0)16937 54545, *Reservations - Warrenpoint:* +44 (0)16937 73737, *Reservations - Heysham:* +44 (0)1524 853549.

ROUTES OPERATED Heysham *(dep: 08.00 Tue-Sat, 20.00 Mon, 21.00 Tue-Sun)* - Warrenpoint *(dep: 09.00 Tue-Sat, 19.00 Mon, 20.00 Tue-Sat, 1700 Sun)* (8 hrs; *(1,2)*; 2 per day).

VESSELS

| 1 | MOONDANCE | 5881t | 78 | 15k | 12P | - | 70T | A | Bremerhaven, GY | BA |
| 2 | RIVERDANCE | 6041t | 77 | 15k | 12P | - | 70T | A | Bremerhaven, GY | BA |

MOONDANCE Built as the EMADALA for *Emadala Shipping* and chartered to *Gilnavi* of Italy for Mediterranean service. In 1987 she was purchased by *Gilnavi*. In 1990 sold to *Cenargo* of Great Britain and chartered to *Merchant Ferries* for their Heysham - Warrenpoint service and renamed the MERCHANT VICTOR. She was withdrawn from that service in 1993 and was chartered out to a number of operators. In 1997 she was chartered to *Seatruck Ferries* and renamed the MOONDANCE. In 1998 she was purchased by *Seatruck Ferries*.

RIVERDANCE Built as the MASHALA for *Mashala Shipping* and chartered to *Gilnavi* of Italy for Mediterranean services. After a long period out of service in the mid-nineteen eighties, in 1987 she was sold, renamed the HALLA and chartered for Caribbean service. In 1988 she was renamed the TIKAL. In 1989 she was sold to *Schiaffino Line* of France, renamed the SCHIAFFINO and put into service between Ramsgate and Oostende. In 1990 the company was taken over by *Sally Ferries* and in 1991 she was chartered to *Belfast Freight Ferries*. In 1993 she was renamed the SALLY EUROBRIDGE. In January 1994, she was chartered to *North Sea Ferries* to operate between Hull and Zeebrugge and renamed the EUROBRIDGE. In summer 1994 she returned to *Sally Ferries*, resumed the name SALLY EUROBRIDGE and became the second vessel on the Ramsgate - Vlissingen service; in the autumn the British terminal was switched to Dartford. In 1995 she was chartered to *Norfolk Line*, renamed the EUROBRIDGE and also sold by *Sally Ferries*. In 1996 she was chartered to *Seatruck Ferries* and renamed the RIVERDANCE. In 1997 she was purchased by *Seatruck Ferries*.

STENA LINE (NETHERLANDS)

THE COMPANY, MANAGEMENT, ADDRESS, TELEPHONE & INTERNET See Section 1.

ROUTE OPERATED Hoek van Holland *(dep: 12.30, 20.15, 23.15)* - Harwich *(dep: 07.45, 11.15, 23.00)* (7 hrs; *(1,2,3)*; 3 per day).

VESSELS

1	ROSEBAY	13700t	76	17k	165P	-	135T	A	Hamburg, GY	CY
2	STENA SEARIDER	20914t	69	17k	120P	-	198T	AS2	Helsinki, FI	IM
3	STENA SEATRADER	17991t	73	17.5k	221P	-	174T	AS2	Nakskov, DK	NL

ROSEBAY Built as the TRANSGERMANIA for *Poseidon Schiffahrt AG* of Germany interests for *Finncarriers- Poseidon* services between Finland and West Germany. In 1991 chartered to *Norse Irish Ferries* and used on their freight service between Liverpool and Belfast. In 1992 she was returned to *Finncarriers* and in 1993 sold to Cypriot interests for use in the Mediterranean and renamed the ROSEBAY. In 1994 chartered to *Stena Line* to inaugurate a new service between Harwich and Rotterdam (Frisohaven). In 1995 the service was switched to Hoek van Holland following the construction of a new linkspan. She also, during the summer, carried cars towing caravans, motor caravans and their passengers. In 1997 she was chartered to *Sally Freight* and renamed the EUROSTAR. Later in 1997 she was renamed the EUROCRUISER. In 1998 she returned on charter to *Stena Line* and resumed the name ROSEBAY. In 1999 she was temporarily transferred to the Irish Sea.

STENA SEARIDER Built as the FINNCARRIER for *Finnlines* of Finland for service between Finland, Denmark and Germany. In 1975 renamed the POLARIS. In 1984 sold to *Rederi AB Nordö* of Sweden to operate between Malmö (Sweden) and Travemünde (Germany) and renamed the SCANDINAVIA. In 1987 she was rebuilt to increase capacity from 122 trailers to 200. In 1989 the name of the company was changed to *Nordö Link* and she was renamed the SCANDINAVIA LINK. In 1990 she was sold to *Stena Line*, renamed the STENA SEARIDER and used on their Göteborg (Sweden) - Travemünde service. In 1991 she was chartered out for service in the Caribbean and renamed the SEARIDER. In 1992 she was chartered to *Norse Irish Ferries* and renamed the NORSE MERSEY. In 1995 she was replaced by a new vessel of the same name and returned to *Stena Line*, resumed the name STENA SEARIDER and resumed operating between Göteborg and Travemünde and Göteborg and Kiel. In May 1997, she was transferred to the Hoek van Holland - Harwich service. Passengers with caravans and motor-caravans are conveyed on some sailings.

STENA SEATRADER Built as the SVEALAND for *Lion Ferry AB* of Sweden and chartered to *Statens Järnvägar (Swedish State Railways)* for the train ferry service between Trelleborg (Sweden) and Sassnitz (East Germany). The charter ceased in 1980 and in 1982 she was sold to *Rederi AB Nordö* of Sweden. She was lengthened by 33.7 metres, renamed the SVEALAND AV MALMÖ and used on their lorry/rail wagon service between Malmö and Travemünde. In 1986 she was rebuilt with a higher superstructure and in 1987 she was renamed the SVEA LINK, the service being renamed *Nordö Link*. In 1990 she was sold to *Stena Line*, renamed the STENA SEATRADER and introduced onto the Hoek van Holland - Harwich service. Passengers with caravans and motor-caravans are conveyed on some sailings.

Roseanne *(John Hendy)*

Coutances *(Matthew Punter)*

STENA LINE (UK)

THE COMPANY, MANAGEMENT, ADDRESS AND TELEPHONE See Section 1.

ROUTES OPERATED Holyhead *(dep: 03.00, 16.00)* - Dublin *(dep: 10.00, 21.30)* (4 hrs; (STENA CHALLENGER - See Section 1); 2 per day), Stranraer *(dep: 02.30, 06.30, 12.00, 15.30, 21.30)* - Belfast *(dep: 02.00, 06.45, 10.45, 16.30, 19.45)* (3 hrs 15 mins; (STENA CALEDONIA, STENA GALLOWAY - See Section 1); 5 per day).

VESSELS

There are no vessels confined purely to freight operations. The vessels mentioned above operate primarily for freight but carry cars and passengers on certain day sailings at certain times of the year. Passengers are now conveyed on all Holyhead - Dublin sailings. The vessels are therefore listed in Section 1.

TRANSEUROPA LINES

THE COMPANY *TransEuropa Lines* is a Slovenian private sector company, owned by *Denval Ltd* of the UK. They operate the Ramsgate - Oostende service in a joint venture with *HR Services (Hogg Robinson Group)*, *Diaz Haulage* and the *Port of Oostende*. Agents in both Ramsgate and Oostende are *Ostend Cargo Handling Services Ltd (OCHS)* (also part of the *Hogg Robinson Group*). Operations started in November 1998, replacing those of *Sally Ferries*. A passenger service may restart in summer 1999 but at the time of going to press no announcement has been made.

MANAGEMENT *(OCHS)* **Managing Director:** G Bartlett, **Operations Director:** G Fordham.

ADDRESS *(OCHS)* **Belgium:** Slijkensesteenweg 18, 8400 OOSTENDE, Belgium, *UK:* Ferry Terminal, Ramsgate New Port, RAMSGATE, Kent CT11 8RP.

TELEPHONE *(OCHS)* **Admin (Belgium):** +32 (0)59 321010, **Reservations (UK):** +44 (0)1843 585151, **Fax:** *Admin (Belgium):* +32 (0)59 330882, **Reservations (UK):** +44 (0)1843 580894.

INTERNET *(OCHS)* **Email:** ochs@ochs.be **Website:** http://www.ochs.be

ROUTE OPERATED Ramsgate *(dep: 03.30, 05.30, 17.30)* - Oostende *(dep: 0100, 13.00, 17.00)* (4/5 hrs; *(1,2)*; 3 per day) (timetable liable to alteration when the PRIMROSE enters service).

VESSELS

1	EUROVOYAGER	12110t	78	22k	1500P	54C	68T	BA2	Hoboken, BE	CY
2	JUNIPER	5610t	76	15k	12P	280C	47T	A	Le Havre, FR	CY
3	PRIMROSE	‡6276t	76	22k	1200P	354C	68T	BA2	Hoboken, BE	CY

EUROVOYAGER Built as the PRINS ALBERT for *RMT* of Belgium for the Oostende - Dover service. During 1986 she had an additional vehicle deck added. In 1994 the British port became Ramsgate. Withdrawn after 28th February 1997 and laid up. In 1998 she was sold to *Denval Marine Consultants* of Great Britain, renamed the EUROVOYAGER and chartered to *Sally Line*. In July, she entered service with *Sally Freight*. In November the *Sally Freight* service ended and she immediately began operating for *TransEuropa Lines*.

JUNIPER Built as the CAP BENAT for *Chargeurs Réunis* of France and used on Mediterranean services. In 1986 she was sold to *Dexterson Shipping*, renamed the JUNIPER and placed on the charter market. She served with a number of companies including, *Norfolk Line*, *Irish Ferries* and *Commodore Ferries*. In 1995 she was placed on services between Italy, Slovenia, Montenegro and Albania services operated by associated company *TransEuropa Lines*. In November 1998 she was moved to the Ramsgate - Oostende service.

PRIMROSE Built as the PRINCESSE MARIE-CHRISTINE for *Regie voor Maritiem Transport* of

Belgium for the Oostende - Dover service. During 1985 she had an extra vehicle deck added, increasing vehicle capacity. Passenger capacity was increased by 200 by the conversion of an upper deck 'garage' into passenger accommodation. In January 1994 the British port became Ramsgate. In 1994 chartered briefly to *Sally Ferries* and operated between Ramsgate and Dunkerque. Since then a spare vessel and withdrawn in early 1997. In 1998 sold to *Denval Marine Consultants* of the UK and renamed the PRIMROSE. In 1999 she is expected to begin operating for *TransEuropa Lines* between Ramsgate and Oostende.

TRANSFENNICA

THE COMPANY *Transfennica Ltd* is a Finnish private sector company.

ADDRESS *Finland:* Eteläranta 12, FIN-00130 HELSINKI, Finland, *UK:* Convoys Wharf, Prince Street, Deptford, LONDON SE8 3JH.

TELEPHONE Administration & Reservations: *Finland:* +358 (0)9 13262, *UK:* +44 (0)181-691 2650, **Fax:** *Finland:* +358 (0)9 652377, *UK:* +44 (0)181-692 8107.

INTERNET Email: info@transfennica.com **Website:** http://www.transfennica.com

ROUTES OPERATED Kemi (Finland) *(dep: Mon)* - Oulu (Finland) *(dep: Tue)* - Antwerpen *(arr/dep: Sat)* - London (Deptford) *(arr: Sun/dep: Mon)* - Kemi *(arr: Fri)* - Oulu (Finland) *(arr: Sat)*, Kotka (Finland) *(dep: Thu)* - London (Deptford) *(arr: Tue)* (no return service advertised), Kotka *(dep: Mon)* - London (Tilbury) *(arr/dep: Sat)* - Kotka *(arr: Thu)*, Kotka *(dep: Fri)* - London (Tilbury) *(arr: Wed)* (no return service advertised), Rauma (Finland) *(dep: Thu)* - London (Tilbury) *(arr: Tue, dep: Wed)* - Rauma *(arr: Wed)*, Hanko (Finland) *(dep: Wed)* - London (Tilbury) *(arr: Mon)* (no return service advertised), Kotka *(dep: Thu)* - Blyth *(arr: Thu, dep: Fri)* - Kotka *(arr: Wed)*, Rauma - Warrenpoint (Northern Ireland) *(fortnightly)*.

Ships are run primarily for the carriage of forest products from Finland to UK and other North European countries.

VESSELS

1	ALTELAND	5599t	90	15.3k	0P	-	30T	AS	Emden, GY	GY
2	DEGERÖ	10215t	85	14.5k	0P	-	120T	AS	Rauma, FI	FI
3	HERALDEN	10570	97	20k	12P	-	116T	A2	Kristiansund, NO	FI
4	LINK STAR	5627t	89	15k	0P	-	22T	AS	Hamburg, GY	FI
5	LOVISA GORTHON	10165t	79	13k	0P	-	70T	A	Stockholm, SW	SW
6	MARTHA RUSS	5627t	90	15k	0P	-	22T	AS	Hamburg, GY	AN
7	MINI STAR	5627t	88	15k	0P	-	22T	AS	Hamburg, GY	FI
8	RAGNA GORTHON	10165t	79	13k	0P	-	66T	AS	Stockholm, SW	SW
9	SERENADEN	10570	98	20k	12P	-	116T	A2	Kristiansund, NO	FI
10	STIG GORTHON	10165t	79	13k	0P	-	66T	AS	Stockholm, SW	SW
11	TRANS BOTNIA	12251t	98	20k	0P	-	140T	A2	Rissa, NO	FI
12	TRANSGARD	10570	96	20k	12P	-	116T	A2	Kristiansund, NO	FI
13	UNITED CARRIER	12251t	98	20k	0P	-	140T	A2	Rissa, NO	FI
14	UNITED EXPRESS	12251t	97	20k	0P	-	140T	A2	Rissa, NO	FI
15	UNITED TRADER	12251t	98	20k	0P	-	140T	A2	Rissa, NO	FI

ALTELAND Launched as the ALTELAND but renamed the ORTVIKEN before entering service. Chartered to *SCA* of Sweden for a service between Sundsvall and Tilbury. In 1995 chartered to *Transfennica*. In 1996 renamed the ALTELAND.

DEGERÖ Chartered to *Transfennica*.

HERALDEN Built for *Engship* of Finland and chartered to *Transfennica*.

LINK STAR, MINI STAR Built for *Godby Shipping* of Finland and chartered to *Transfennica*.

LOVISA GORTHON, RAGNA GORTHON, STIG GORTHON Built for *B&N Gorthon Lines*. Rebuilt in 1993. Currently chartered to *Transfennica*.

MARTHA RUSS Built for *Ernst Russ* and chartered to *Transfennica*.

SERENADEN Built for *Engship* of Finland and chartered to *Transfennica*.

TRANS BOTNIA Built for *SeaTrans ASA* of Norway and chartered to *Transfennica*.

TRANSGARD Built for *Bror Husell Chartering* of Finland and chartered to *Transfennica*.

UNITED CARRIER Built for *Birka Line* of Finland and chartered to *Transfennica*.

UNITED EXPRESS Built for *United Shipping* of Finland and chartered to *Transfennica*.

UNITED TRADER Built for *Birka Line* of Finland and chartered to *Transfennica*.

TRUCKLINE FERRIES

THE COMPANY *Truckline Ferries* is *Brittany Ferries*' freight division.

MANAGEMENT Managing Director: Ian Carruthers, **Freight Director:** John Clarke.

ADDRESS New Harbour Road, POOLE, Dorset BH15 4AJ.

INTERNET Website: http://www.brittany-ferries.com *(English, French.)*

TELEPHONE Administration & Reservations: +44 (0)1202 675048, **Fax:** +44 (0)1202 679828, **Telex:** 41744, 41745.

ROUTES OPERATED Cherbourg *(Winter: dep: 09.30 Wed, Fri, Sun, 18.30 Tue, Thu, Sat, 23.45 Mon, Wed, Fri, Sun, Summer: 02.00 Mon, Sat, Sun, 09.30 Tue, Thu, 14.30 Fri, Sat, Sun, 18.30 Mon, Wed, 23.45 Tue, Thu)* - Poole *(Winter: dep: 16.00 Mon, Wed, Fri, Sun, 08.30, 23.45 Tue, Thu, Sat, Summer dep: 16.00 Tue, Thu, 08.30, 23.45 Mon, Wed, 07.30, 23.45 Fri, Sat, Sun)* (4 hrs 30 mins; *(1)*; 1/2 per day). **Note:** Operates with *Brittany Ferries* passenger vessel BARFLEUR to provide three or four sailings every 24 hrs.

VESSEL

| 1 | COUTANCES | 6507t | 78 | 17k | 58P | - | 64T | BA | Le Havre, FR | FR |

COUTANCES Built for *Truckline Ferries* for their Cherbourg - Poole service. In 1986 lengthened to increase vehicle capacity by 34%.

SECTION 4 - CHAIN, CABLE ETC FERRIES

In addition to the ferries listed above, there are a number of short chain ferries, cable ferries and ferries operated by unpowered floats:

BOURNEMOUTH-SWANAGE MOTOR ROAD AND FERRY COMPANY

Address *Company:* Shell Bay, Studland, SWANAGE, Dorset. **Tel:** +44 (0)1929 450203 (**Fax:** +44 (0)1929 450498), *Ferry:* Floating Bridge, Ferry Way, Sandbanks, POOLE, Dorset BH13 7QN. **Tel:** +44 (0)1929 450203.

Route: Sandbanks - Studland (Dorset).

1	BRAMBLE BUSH BAY	93	400P	48C	BA	Hessle, GB

BRAMBLE BUSH BAY chain ferry, built for the *Bournemouth-Swanage Motor Road and Ferry Company*.

CUMBRIA COUNTY COUNCIL

Address: Economy & Environment Department, Citadel Chambers, CARLISLE CA3 8SG. **Tel:** +44 (0)1228 606744, **Fax:** +44 (0)1228 606755.

Website: http://www.cumbria.gov.uk *(English (County Council web site - little about ferry))*

Route: Bowness-on-Windermere - Far Sawrey.

1	MALLARD	90	140P	18C	BA	Borth, Dyfed, GB

MALLARD Chain Ferry built for *Cumbria County Council*.

ISLE OF WIGHT COUNCIL (COWES FLOATING BRIDGE)

Address: Ferry Office, Medina Road, COWES, Isle of Wight PO31 7BX. **Tel:** +44 (0)1983 293041

Route: Cowes - East Cowes.

1	NO 5	76	-	15C	BA	East Cowes, GB

NO 5 Chain ferry built for *Isle of Wight County Council*, now *Isle of Wight Council*.

KING HARRY STEAM FERRY COMPANY

Address: Feock, TRURO, Cornwall TR3 6QJ. **Tel:** +44 (0)1872 862312.

Route: Across River Fal, King Harry Ferry (Cornwall).

1	KING HARRY FERRY	74	100P	28C	BA	Falmouth, GB

KING HARRY FERRY Chain ferry built for *King Harry Steam Ferry Company*.

PHILIP LTD

Address: Noss Works, DARTMOUTH, Devon TQ6 0EA. **Tel:** +44 (0)1803 833351.

Route: Dartmouth - Kingswear (Devon) across River Dart (higher route) (forms part of A379).

| 1 | HIGHER FERRY | 60 | 200P | 18C | BA | Dartmouth, GB |

HIGHER FERRY Diesel electric paddle propelled vessel guided by cross-river cables. Built by *Philip Ltd.*

REEDHAM FERRY

Address: Reedham Ferry, Ferry Inn, Reedham, NORWICH NR13 3HA. **Tel:** +44 (0)1493 700429, **Fax:** +44 (0)1493 700999.

Route: Acle - Reedham - Norton (across River Yare, Norfolk).

| 1 | REEDHAM FERRY | 84 | 12P | 3C | BA | Oulton Broad, GB |

REEDHAM FERRY Chain ferry built for *Reedham Ferry*. Maximum weight, 12 tons.

SOUTH HAMS DISTRICT COUNCIL

Address: Lower Ferry Office, The Square, Kingswear, DARTMOUTH, Devon TQ6 0AA. **Tel:** +44 (0)1803 752342, **Fax:** +44 (0)1803 752227.

Route: Dartmouth - Kingswear (Devon) across River Dart (lower route).

| 1 | THE TOM AVIS | 94 | 50P | 8C | BA | Fowey, GB |
| 2 | THE TOM CASEY | 89 | 50P | 8C | BA | Portland, GB |

THE TOM AVIS, THE TOM CASEY Floats propelled by tugs built for *South Hams District Council*.

C TOMS & SON LTD

Address: East Street, Polruan, FOWEY, Cornwall PL23 1PB. **Tel:** +44 (0)1726 870232.

Route: Fowey - Bodinnick (Cornwall).

| 1 | NO 3 | 63 | 47P | 6C | BA | Fowey, GB |
| 2 | NO 4 | 75 | 48P | 8C | BA | Fowey, GB |

NO 3, NO 4 (Floats propelled by motor launches) built by *C Toms & Son Ltd* in their own yard.

Under construction

| 3 | NEWBUILDING | 99 | 50P | 15C | BA | Fowey, GB |

NEWBUILDING New craft being built by *C Toms & Sons*. It will be self propelled and steered rather than a float. Due to enter service in summer 1999.

TORPOINT FERRY

Address: 2 Ferry Street, TORPOINT, Cornwall PL11 2AX. **Tel:** +44 (0)1752 812233.

Route: Devonport (Devon) - Torpoint (Cornwall) across the Tamar. Pre-booking is not possible and the above number cannot be used for that purpose.

1	LYNHER	61	350P	48C	BA	Southampton, GB
2	PLYM	68	350P	54C	BA	Bristol, GB
3	TAMAR	60	350P	48C	BA	Southampton, GB

LYNHER, PLYM, TAMAR Chain ferries built for the *Torpoint Ferry*. The three ferries operate in parallel on their own 'track'.

WATERFORD CASTLE HOTEL

Address: The Island, WATERFORD, Irish Republic. **Tel:** +353 (0)51 78203.

Website: http://www.waterfordcastle.com *(English (mainly about hotel; little about ferry))*

Route: Grantstown - Little Island (in River Suir, County Waterford).

1	LITTLE ISLAND FERRY	68	24P	6C	BA	Cork, IR

LITTLE ISLAND FERRY Chain ferry built for *Waterford Castle Hotel*.

SECTION 5 - MAJOR PASSENGER FERRIES

There are a surprisingly large number of passenger only ferries operating in the British Isles, mainly operated by launches and small motor boats. There are, however, a few 'major' operators who operate only passenger vessels (of rather larger dimensions) and have not therefore been mentioned previously.

Alizés COTES DES ISLES, (199t, 1976, 140 passengers, (ex BRITTANIA 1997, ex FJORDDROTT 1990) (Westermoen W86 catamaran), **Routes Operated:** Carteret (France) - Gorey (Jersey), Portbail (France) - Gorey.

Channel Hoppers VARANGERFJORD (417t, 1990, 167 passengers) (Fjellstrand 38m catamaran). **Route operated:** Portsmouth - St Helier (Jersey) - St Anne (Alderney). **Tel:** +44(0) 1705 291900, **Fax:** +44 (0) 1705 825873, **Email:** info@channelhoppers.com **Website:** http://www.channelhoppers.com

Clyde Marine Motoring FENCER (18t, 1976, 33 passengers), KENILWORTH (44t, 1936, 127 passengers (ex HOTSPUR II (Southampton - Hythe ferry) 1979)), ROVER (48t, 1964, 120 passengers), THE SECOND SNARK (45t, 1938, 120 passengers). **Route operated:** Gourock - Kilcreggan - Helensburgh (generally the KENILWORTH is used on the ferry services and other vessels on excursions). **Tel:** +44 (0)1475 721281, **Fax:** +44 (0)1475 888023.

Dart Pleasure Craft EDGCOMBE BELLE (357, 1957, 150 passengers), KINGSWEAR BELLE (43t, 1972, 257 passengers). **Route operated:** Dartmouth - Kingswear. Note: Pleasure craft owned by this operator are also used for the ferry service on some occasions. **Tel:** +44 (0)1803 834488, **Fax:** +44 (0)1803 835248, **Email:** sales@ riverlink.co.uk, **Website:** http://www.riverlink.co.uk

Doolin Ferry Company/O'Brien Shipping DONEMARK (70t, 1978, 65 pass), HAPPY HOOKER (77t, 1989, 96 passengers), ROSE OF ARAN (113t, 1976, 66 passengers), TRANQUILITY (43t, 1988, 48 passengers). **Route operated:** Doolin - Inishere, Doolin - Inishmaan, Doolin - Inishmore. OILEAN ARANN (416t, 1992, 190 passengers). **Route operated:** Galway - Inishere, Galway - Inishmaan, Galway - Inishmore. **Tel:** +353 (0)65 7074455, **Fax:** +353 (0)65 7074417, **Email:** doolinferries@tinet.ie.

Gosport Ferry GOSPORT QUEEN (159t, 1966, 250 passengers), PORTSMOUTH QUEEN (159t, 1966, 250 passengers), SOLENT ENTERPRISE (274t, 1971, 250 passengers (ex GAY ENTERPRISE 1979) (mainly used on excursion work)). **Route operated:** Gosport - Portsmouth. **Tel:** +44 (0)1705 524551.

Hovertravel COURIER (73t, 1986, 84 passengers) (BHC AP1-88/100 hovercraft) (ex BENIDORM 1993, ex COURIER 1990), DOUBLE O SEVEN (73t, 1989, 98 passengers) (BHC AP1-88/100 hovercraft), FREEDOM 90 (73t, 1990, 98 passengers) (BHC AP1-88 hovercraft), IDUN VIKING (73t, 1983, 98 passengers) (BHC AP1-88/100 hovercraft), LIV VIKING (73t, 1985, 82 passengers) (BHC AP1-88/100 hovercraft), REGJA VIKING (73t, 1985, 82 passengers) (BHC AP1-88/100 hovercraft).

Varangerfjord *(Philippe Holthof)*

Great Expections *(John Hendy)*

Route operated: Southsea - Ryde. **Tel:** +44 (0)1983 811000, **Fax:** +44 (0)1983 562216, **Email:** info@hovertravel.co.uk, **Website:** http://www.hovertravel.co.uk *(English)*.

Island Ferries ARAN EXPRESS (117t, 1984, 180 passengers), ARAN FLYER (170t, 1988, 208 passengers), ARAN SEABIRD (164t, 1976, 181 passengers), ISLAND DISCOVERY (107t, 1991, 130 passengers), SEA SPRINTER (16t, 1993, 36 passengers). **Routes operated:** Rossaveal (Co Galway) - Aran Islands. **Tel:** +353 (0)91 572273, 561767, 568903, **Fax:** +353 (0)91 562069, 568538, **Email:** island@iol.ie, **Internet Website:** http://www.iol.ie/~island/ *(English)*.

Lundy Company OLDENBURG (288t, 1958, 267 passengers). **Routes operated:** Bideford - Lundy Island, Ilfracombe - Lundy Island, Clovelly - Lundy Island, Watchet - Lundy Island, Porthcawl - Lundy Island, Porthcawl - Ilfracombe. **Tel:** +44 (0)1237 470422, **Fax:** +44 (0)1237 477779, **Email:** LundySO@aol.com.

Mersey Ferries MOUNTWOOD (464t, 1960, 750 passengers), OVERCHURCH (468t, 1962, 860 passengers), WOODCHURCH (464t, 1960, 750 passengers). **Routes operated:** Liverpool - Birkenhead (Woodside), Liverpool - Wallasey (Seacombe). **Tel:** +44 (0)151 630 1030, **Fax:** +44 (0)151 639 0609, **Website:** http://www.merseyworld.com/ferries *(English)*.

Nexus (trading name of Tyne & Wear PTE) PRIDE OF THE TYNE (222t, 1993, 350 passengers), SHIELDSMAN (93t, 1976, 350 passengers). **Route operated:** North Shields - South Shields. Also cruises South Shields - Newcastle. **Tel:** +44 (0)454 8183, **Fax:** +44 (0)427 9510.

Strathclyde Passenger Transport (trading name of Strathclyde PTE) RENFREW ROSE (65t, 1984, 50 passengers), YOKER SWAN (65t, 1984, 50 passengers). **Route operated:** Renfrew - Yoker. Note: although this a passenger only service, the vessels are built as small front loading car ferries and are able to convey one vehicle if necessary. This facility is sometimes used for the conveyance of ambulances. **Tel:** +44 (0)141 333 3159.

Waverley Excursions BALMORAL (735t, 1949, 800 passengers), WAVERLEY (693t, 1947, 950 passengers). **Routes operated:** Excursions all round British Isles. However, regular cruises in the Clyde and Bristol Channel provide a service which can be used for transport rather than an excursion and therefore both vessels are, in a sense, ferries. **Tel:** +44 (0)141 221 8152, **Fax:** +44 (0)141 248 2150.

White Horse Fast Ferries MARTIN CHUZZELWIT (25.6t, 1995, 60 passengers (tri-maran)), WILKINS MICAWBER (25.6t, 1996, 60 passengers), PHILIP PIRRIP (25.6t, 1999, 60 passengers (tri-maran)), EBENEZER SCROOGE (4.3t, 1992, 12 passengers), **Under Construction:** ABEL MAGWITCH (25.6t, 1999, 60 passengers (tri-maran)), NEWBUILDING 2 (25.6t, 1999, 60 passengers (tri-maran)), NEWBUILDING 3 (25.6t, 1999, 60 passengers (tri-maran)). **Routes operated:** Gravesend (Kent) - Tilbury (Essex), *from 1st June 1999:* Waterloo (London) - Canary Wharf, *from 1st January 2000:* Greenwich - Greenwich Millennium Dome. **Tel:** +44 (0)1474 566220, **Fax:** +44 (0)1474 553383, **Email:** fastferries@whitehorse.co.uk, **Website:** http://www.whitehorse.co.uk/fastferries *(English)*.

White Horse Ferries GREAT EXPECTATIONS (66t, 1992, 95 passengers) (catamaran), HOTSPUR IV (50t, 1946, 243 passengers). **Route operated:** Southampton - Hythe (Hants). ***Head Office:*** **Tel:**. +44 (0)1793 618566, **Fax:** +44 (0)1793 488428, ***Local Office:*** **Tel:** +44 (0)1703 840722, **Fax:** +44 (0)1703 846611, **Email:** post@hytheferry.co.uk, **Website:** http://www.hytheferry.co.uk *(English)*.

SECTION 6 - NORTHERN EUROPE
ÅNEDIN LINE

THE COMPANY *Ånedin Line* is the trading name of *Rederi AB Allandia*, a Swedish company.

MANAGEMENT Managing Director: Björn Ericson, **Marketing Manager:** Torsten Sundberg.

ADDRESS PO Box 1151, S-11181 STOCKHOLM, Sweden.

TELEPHONE Administration: +46 (0)8-456 2200, **Reservations:** +46 (0)8-456 2200, **Fax:** +46 (0)8-10 07 41.

ROUTE OPERATED Cruises from Stockholm to Mariehamn (Åland) (22 hrs; *(1)*; 1 per day)

CONVENTIONAL FERRY

1	BALTIC STAR	3564t	53	15k	400P	0C	0L	-	Stockholm, SW	PA

BALTIC STAR Built as the BIRGER JARL for *Stockholms Rederi AB Svea* of Sweden to operate between Stockholm and Turku and Stockholm and Helsinki. She was a crane loading car ferry with capacity for 25 cars, since removed. In 1973 she was sold to *Jacob Line*, to operate between Pietarsaari (Finland) and Skellefteå (Sweden); she was renamed the BORE NORD. In 1974 she started a service from Turku to Visby (Gotland) but this was short lived and, for a time, she served as an accommodation vessel at Stavanger. In 1977 she was sold to *Mini Carriers* of Finland who renamed her the MINISEA and announced plans for a new Finland - Sweden service. These plans did not materialise and in 1978 she was acquired by the *Caribbean Shipping Company* of Panama, chartered to *Rederi AB Allandia*, renamed the BALTIC STAR and started operating 24 hour cruises. In 1997, following changes to Swedish customs regulations, these became 22 hour cruises.

BASTØ FOSEN

THE COMPANY *Bastø Fosen* is a Norwegian private sector company, a subsidiary of *Fosen Trafikklag* of Trondhiem.

MANAGEMENT Managing Director: Olav Brein, **Operations Manager:** Jan F Jonas.

ADDRESS PO Box 94, 3191 HORTEN, Norway.

TELEPHONE Administration: +47 33 03 17 40, **Reservations:** not applicable, **Fax:** +47 33 03 17 49.

INTERNET Email: ferge@basto-fosen.no **Website:** http://www.basto-fosen.no *(Norwegian)*

ROUTE OPERATED Moss - Horten (across Oslofjord, Norway) (30 mins; *(1,2,3)*; up to every 45 mins).

CONVENTIONAL FERRIES

1	BASTØ I	5505t	97	14k	550P	220C	18L	BA	Fevaag, NO	NO
2	BASTØ II	5505t	97	14k	550P	220C	18L	BA	Fevaag, NO	NO

BASTØ I, BASTØ II Built for *Bastø Fosen*.

BIRKA CRUISES

THE COMPANY *Birka Cruises* is an Åland Islands company.

MANAGEMENT Managing Director: Michael Larkner.

ADDRESS Box 15131, Södermalmstorg 2, S-104 65 STOCKHOLM, Sweden.

TELEPHONE Administration: +46 (0)8-714 5510, **Reservations:** +46 (0)8-714 5520, **Fax:** +46 (0)8-714 9830.

INTERNET Email: marknad@birkaline.com **Website:** http://www.birkacruises.com *(from September 1999)*

ROUTES OPERATED Cruises from Stockholm to Mariehamn (Åland) (22 hrs; *(1)*; 1 per day). Note: although primarily a cruise service, conventional passengers can be conveyed. Also weekend cruises to Gotland, Bornholm and Gdynia (Poland).

CRUISE SHIP

1	BIRKA PRINCESS	22660t	86	18k	1500P	0C	0L	-	Helsinki, FI	FI

BIRKA PRINCESS Built for *Birka Cruises*. As built, she had capacity for 10 cars, loaded via a side door. During winter 1998/99 she was the subject of a major refit to modernise her and increase passenger capacity and the vehicle facility was removed.

BORNHOLMSTRAFIKKEN

THE COMPANY *BornholmsTrafikken* is a Danish state owned company.

MANAGEMENT Managing Director: K P Dinesen, **Sales and Marketing Manager:** Eddie Ørpe.

ADDRESS Havnen, DK-3700 RØNNE, Denmark.

TELEPHONE Administration: +45 56 95 18 66, **Reservations:** +45 56 95 18 66, **Fax:** +45 56 91 07 66.

INTERNET Email: info@bornholmferries.dk **Website:** http://www.bornholmferries.dk *(Danish, German)*

ROUTES OPERATED København - Rønne (Bornholm, Denmark) (7 hrs; *(1,2,3)*; 1/2 per day), Ystad (Sweden) - Rønne (2 hrs 30 mins; *(1,2,3)*; 2-4 per day), Rønne - Fährhafen Sassnitz (Germany) (3 hrs 30 mins; *(1,2,3)*; up to 6 per week), Rønne - Swinoujscie (Poland) (6 hrs; *(2)*).

CONVENTIONAL FERRIES

1	JENS KOFOED	12131t	79	19.5k	1500P	262C	44T	BA	Aalborg, DK	DK
2	PEDER OLSEN	8586t	74	19.0k	1150P	222C	33T	BA	Bremerhaven, GY	DK
3	POVL ANKER	12131t	78	19.5k	1500P	262C	44T	BA	Aalborg, DK	DK

JENS KOFOED, POVL ANKER Built for *BornholmsTrafikken*. Used primarily on the København - Rønne and Ystad - Rønne services.

PEDER OLSEN Launched as KATTEGAT II for *Jydsk Færgefart* of Denmark. Before delivery, she was renamed the KALLE III and used on their service between Juelsminde (Jylland) and Kalundborg (Sjælland). In 1981 the other service of this company - between Grenaa (Jylland) and Hundested (Sjælland) - was taken over by *DFDS* and operations transferred to a *DFDS* subsidiary called *Grenaa - Hundested Linien*. The Juelsminde - Kalundborg service was not taken over by *DFDS* and operations were transferred to a new company called *Juelsminde-Kalundborg Linien*, the ownership of KALLE III passing to *Dansk Investeringsfond*, a financial institution. In 1983 she was chartered to *Rederi AB Sally*, modified in Bremerhaven to make her suitable for Channel operations (eg stabilisers, large duty free supermarket), renamed THE VIKING and, in July, introduced onto the Ramsgate - Dunkerque service. She was subsequently re-registered in Finland. In 1989 she was transferred to associated company *Vaasanlaivat* of Finland for their service between Vaasa (Finland) and Umeå (Sweden) and renamed the WASA PRINCE. In 1991 the charter ended and she was renamed the PRINCE. She was then chartered by *BornholmsTrafikken*, renamed the PEDER OLSEN and is used primarily on the Rønne - Ystad, Rønne - Sassnitz and Rønne - Swinoujscie services. She

Christian IV *(Miles Cowsill)*

Prins Richard *(Richard Mayes)*

will be withdrawn at the end of 1999.

Under construction

| 4 | NEWBUILDING | - | 99 | 40k | 1000P | 186C | - | BA | Fremantle, AL | DK |

NEWBUILDING Austal Auto-Express 86 catamaran under construction for *BornholmsTrafikken*. To be delivered in December 1999 and replace the PEDER OLSEN on services from Rønne to Ystad in 2000.

COLOR LINE

THE COMPANY *Color Line ASA* is a Norwegian private sector stock-listed limited company. The company merged with *Larvik Line* of Norway (which owned *Scandi Line*) in 1996. *Larvik Line's* operations were incorporated into *Color Line* in 1997; *Scandi Line* continued as a separate subsidiary until 1999, when it was also incorporated into *Color Line*.

MANAGEMENT Managing Director: Trygve Sigerset, **Marketing Manager:** Elisabeth Anspach.

ADDRESS *Commercial:* Postboks 1422 Vika, 0115 OSLO, Norway, *Technical Management:* Color Line Marine AS, PO Box 2090, N-3210 SANDEFJORD, Norway.

TELEPHONE Administration: +47 22 94 44 00, **Reservations:** +47 22 94 44 44, **Fax:** +47 22 83 07 76.

INTERNET Website: http://www.colorline.no *(Norwegian, English)*

ROUTES OPERATED Conventional Ferries: Oslo - Kiel (Germany) (19 hrs 30 mins; *(4,6)*; 1 per day), Oslo - Hirtshals (Denmark) (8 hrs 30 mins; *(3)*; 1 per day), Moss (Norway) - Hirtshals (Denmark) (7 hrs; *(8)*; 1 per day (3 per week in winter)), Kristiansand (Norway) - Hirtshals (4 hrs 30 mins; *(2,8)*; 2 per day), Larvik (Norway) - Moss (Norway) - Frederikshavn (Denmark) (6 hrs 15 mins; *(5)*; 1 or 2 per day), Sandefjord (Norway) - Strömstad (Sweden) (2 hrs 30 mins; *(1,7)*; 6 per day) (under the name *Color Scandi Line*). **Fast Ferries (under the name 'Color Line Express'):** *Summer only:* Kristiansand - Hirtshals (2 hrs 25 mins; *(9)*; 3 per day).

CONVENTIONAL FERRIES

1	BOHUS	8772t	71	19.5k	1480P	280C	40T	BA	Aalborg, DK	NO
2	CHRISTIAN IV	21699t	82	21k	2000P	530C	64T	BA2	Bremerhaven, GY	NO
3	COLOR FESTIVAL	34417t	85	22k	2000P	440C	88T	BA2	Helsinki, FI	NO
4	KRONPRINS HARALD	31914t	87	21.5k	1432P	700C	100T	BA	Turku, FI	NO
5	PETER WESSEL	29706t	81	21k	2200P	650C	80T	BA2	Landskrona, SW	NO
6	PRINSESSE RAGNHILD	38438t	81	19.5k	1875P	770C	78T	BA	Kiel, GY	NO
7	SANDEFJORD	5678t	65	17.8k	1100P	145C	30T	BA	Lübeck, GY	NO
8	SKAGEN	12333t	75	19.5k	1238P	400C	22T	BA	Aalborg, DK	NO

BOHUS Built as the PRINSESSAN DESIREE for *Rederi AB Göteborg-Frederikshavn Linjen* of Sweden (trading as *Sessan Linjen*) for their service between Göteborg and Frederikshavn. In 1981 the company was taken over by *Stena Line* and she became surplus to requirements. During 1981 she had a number of charters including *B&I Line* of Ireland and *Sealink* UK. In 1982 she was chartered to *Sally Line* to operate as second vessel on the Ramsgate - Dunkerque service between June and September. She bore the name VIKING 2 in large letters on her hull although she was never officially renamed and continued to bear the name PRINSESSAN DESIREE on her bow and stern. In September 1982 she returned to *Stena Line* and in 1983 she was transferred to subsidiary company *Varberg-Grenaa Line* for their service between Varberg (Sweden) and Grenaa (Denmark) and renamed the EUROPAFÄRJAN. In 1985 she was renamed the EUROPAFÄRJAN II. In 1986, following a reorganisation within the *Stena Line* Group, ownership was transferred to subsidiary company *Lion Ferry AB* and she was named the LION PRINCESS. In 1993 she was sold to *Scandi Line* and renamed the BOHUS. In 1999 *Scandi Line* operations were integrated into *Color Line*.

CHRISTIAN IV Built as the OLAU BRITANNIA for *Olau Line* of Germany for their service between Vlissingen (Netherlands) and Sheerness (England). In 1989 sold to *Nordström & Thulin* of Sweden for delivery in spring 1990. She was subsequently resold to *Fred. Olsen Lines* of Norway and, on delivery, renamed the BAYARD and used on their service between Kristiansand and Hirtshals. In December 1990 she was acquired by *Color Line* and in 1991 renamed the CHRISTIAN IV.

COLOR FESTIVAL Built as the SVEA for *Johnson Line* for the *Silja Line* Stockholm - Mariehamn - Turku service. During winter 1991/92 she was extensively rebuilt and in 1991 renamed the SILJA KARNEVAL; ownership was transferred to *Silja Line*. In 1993 she was sold to *Color Line* and renamed the COLOR FESTIVAL. She is used on the Oslo - Hirtshals service.

KRONPRINS HARALD Built for *Jahre Line* of Norway for the Oslo - Kiel service. In 1991 ownership was transferred to *Color Line*.

PETER WESSEL Built for *Rederi AB Gotland* of Sweden. A sister vessel of the VISBY (see *Destination Gotland*), it was intended that she should be named the GOTLAND. However, she was delivered as the WASA STAR and chartered to *Vaasanlaivat* of Finland and used on their Vaasa - Sundsvall service. In 1982 she was chartered to *Karageorgis Line* of Greece for service between Patras (Greece) and Ancona (Italy). This charter was abruptly terminated in 1983 following a dispute over payment of charter dues. She returned the Baltic and was laid up until February 1984 when she was sold to *Larvik Line*. She was renamed the PETER WESSEL. In 1988 she was lengthened to increase capacity. In 1996 acquired by *Color Line*. She remains on the Larvik - Moss - Frederikshavn route.

PRINSESSE RAGNHILD Built for *Jahre Line* of Norway for the Oslo - Kiel service. In 1991 ownership transferred to *Color Line*. In 1992 rebuilt in Spain with an additional midships section and additional decks.

SANDEFJORD Built as the VIKING III for *Otto Thoresen* of Norway for the *Thoresen Car Ferries* Southampton (England) - Cherbourg and Southampton - Le Havre services. During the winter, until 1970/71, she was chartered to *Lion Ferry* of Sweden for their Harwich - Bremerhaven service. In 1967 the service was acquired by *European Ferries* of Great Britain, trading as *Townsend Thoresen*. She was chartered to this organisation and retained Norwegian registry. During winter 1971/72 and 1972/73 she was chartered to *Larvik Line*. She became surplus to requirements following the delivery of the 'Super Vikings' in 1975 and was the subject of a number of short term charters until 1982 when she was sold to *Da-No Linjen* of Norway, renamed the TERJE VIGEN and used on their Fredrikstad (Norway) - Frederikshavn (Denmark) service. In 1986 she was sold to *KG Line* to operate between Kaskinen (Finland) and Gävle (Sweden) and renamed the SCANDINAVIA. In 1990 she was sold *Johnson Line* and used on *Jakob Line* service, being renamed the FENNO STAR. In 1991 she was sold to *Scandi Line* and renamed the SANDEFJORD but served briefly as the FENNO STAR on the *Corona Line* service between Karlskrona and Gdynia before being introduced onto the Sandefjord - Strömstad service in 1992. In 1999 *Scandi Line* operations were integrated into *Color Line*.

SKAGEN Built as the BORGEN for *Fred. Olsen Lines* of Norway for Norway - Denmark services. In December 1990 acquired by *Color Line* and in 1991 renamed the SKAGEN. Until 1997 she operated mainly between Hirtshals and Kristiansand. She now also operates between Hirtshals and Moss. Although built with rail freight capacity, this is no longer conveyed.

FAST FERRY

9	SILVIA ANA L		7895t	96	38k	1250P	238C	4L	A	San Fernando, SP	BA

SILVIA ANA L Bazan Alhambra monohull vessel built for *Buquebus* of Argentina. Initially operated between Buenos Aires (Argentina) and Piriapolis (Uruguay). In 1997 chartered to *Color Line* to operate between Kristiansand and Hirtshals. During winter 1997/98 she again operated in South America but returned to *Color Line* in spring 1998. This was repeated during winter 1998/99 and spring 1999.

DESTINATION GOTLAND

THE COMPANY *Destination Gotland AB* is a Swedish private sector company owned by *Rederi AB Gotland*. It took over the operations of services to Gotland from 1st January 1998 on a six year concession. *Silja Line* involvement in the company ceased at the end of 1998.

MANAGEMENT Managing Director: Jan-Eric Nilsson, **Marketing Manager:** Per-Erling Evensen.

ADDRESS PO Box 1234, 621 23 VISBY, Gotland, Sweden.

TELEPHONE Administration: +46 (0)498-20 18 00, **Reservations:** +46 (0)498-20 10 20, **Fax:** +46 (0)498-20 18 90.

INTERNET Email: per-erling.evensen@destinationgotland.se **Website:** http://www.destinationgotland.se *(Swedish, English)*

ROUTES OPERATED Conventional Ferries: *All year:* Visby (Gotland) - Nynäshamn (Swedish mainland) (5 hrs 30 mins; *(1,2)*; 1/2 per day), Visby - Oskarshamn (Swedish mainland) (4 hrs 30 mins; *(1,2)*; 1/2 per day). **Fast Ferry:** Visby (Gotland) - Nynäshamn (2 hrs 50 mins; *(3)*; 2 per day).

CONVENTIONAL FERRIES

1	THJELVAR	16829t	81	19k	1500P	440C	76L	BA2	Helsinki, FI	SW
2	VISBY	23775t	80	20k	1800P	510C	45L	BA2	Landskrona, SW	SW

THJELVAR Built as the TRAVEMÜNDE for *Gedser-Travemünde Ruten* of Denmark for their service between Gedser (Denmark) and Travemünde (Germany). In 1986 the company's trading name was changed to *GT Linien* and in 1987, following the take-over by *Sea-Link AB* of Sweden, it was further changed to *GT Link*. The vessel's name was changed to the TRAVEMÜNDE LINK. In 1988 she was purchased by *Rederi AB Gotland* of Sweden, although remaining in service with *GT Link*. Later in 1988 she was chartered to *Sally Ferries* and entered service in December on the Ramsgate - Dunkerque service. She was renamed the SALLY STAR. In 1997 she was transferred to *Silja Line*, to operate between Vaasa and Umeå during the summer period and operated under the marketing name WASA EXPRESS (although not renamed). She returned to *Rederi AB Gotland* in autumn 1997, renamed the THJELVAR and entered service with *Destination Gotland* in January 1998.

VISBY Built as the VISBY for *Rederi AB Gotland* of Sweden for their services between the island of Gotland and the Swedish mainland. In 1987, the franchise to operate these services was lost by the company and awarded to *Nordström & Thulin* of Sweden. A subsidiary called *N&T Gotlandslinjen AB* was formed to operate the service. The VISBY was chartered to this company and managed by *Johnson Line*, remaining owned by *Rederi AB Gotland*. In early 1990 she was chartered to *Sealink* and renamed the FELICITY. After modifications at Tilbury, she was, in March 1990, introduced onto the Fishguard - Rosslare route. Later in 1990 she was renamed the STENA FELICITY. In summer 1997 she was returned to *Rederi AB Gotland* for rebuilding, prior to her entering service with *Destination Gotland* in January 1998. She was renamed the VISBY.

FAST FERRY

3	GOTLAND	4000t	99	35k	700P	140C	-	A	Nantes, FR	SW

GOTLAND Alstom Leroux Corsair 11500 monohull vessel built for *Rederi AB Gotland* and chartered to *Destination Gotland*. Unlike previous fast ferries used on the route, it is planned to operate her all year round.

DFDS SEAWAYS

THE COMPANY *DFDS Seaways* is the trading name of the passenger division of *DFDS A/S (Det Forenede Dampskibs Selskab - The United Steamship Company)*, a Danish private sector company.

MANAGEMENT Managing Director: Thorleif Blok.

ADDRESS Sankt Annæ Plads 30, DK-1295 KØBENHAVN K, Denmark.

TELEPHONE Administration: +45 33 42 33 42, **Reservations:** +45 33 42 30 00, **Fax:** +45 33 42 33 41, **Telex:** 19435.

INTERNET Website: http://www.scansea.com *(English, Danish, Norwegian, Swedish, German, Dutch)*

ROUTE OPERATED København - Helsingborg (Sweden) - Oslo (Norway) (16 hrs; *(1,2)*; 1 per day). See Section 1 for services operating to Britain.

CONVENTIONAL FERRIES

1	CROWN OF SCANDINAVIA	35498t	94	19.5k	2136P	450C	80T	BA2	Split, CR	DK
2	QUEEN OF SCANDINAVIA	33575t	81	21k	1624P	430C	86T	BA	Turku, FI	DK

CROWN OF SCANDINAVIA Launched for *Euroway* for their Lübeck - Travemünde - Malmö service. However, political problems led to serious delays and, before delivery, the service had ceased. She was purchased by *DFDS*, renamed the CROWN OF SCANDINAVIA and introduced onto the København - Oslo service.

QUEEN OF SCANDINAVIA Built as the FINLANDIA for *EFFOA* of Sweden for *Silja Line* services between Helsinki and Stockholm. In 1990 she was sold to *DFDS*, renamed the QUEEN OF SCANDINAVIA and introduced onto the København - Helsingborg - Oslo service.

REDERIJ DOEKSEN

THE COMPANY *Rederij G Doeksen & Zonen bv* is a Dutch public sector company. Ferries are operated by subsidiary *Terschellinger Stoomboot Maatschappij*, trading as *Rederij Doeksen*.

MANAGEMENT Managing Director: H Oosterbeek, **Marketing Manager:** C Dekker.

ADDRESS Willem Barentskade 21, Postbus 40, 8880 AA WEST TERSCHELLING, Netherlands.

TELEPHONE Administration: +31 (0)562 442141, **Reservations:** +31 (0)562 446111, **Fax:** +31 (0)562 443241.

ROUTES OPERATED Harlingen (Netherlands) - Terschelling (Frisian Islands) (2 hrs; *(1,2)*; up to 4 per day), Harlingen (Netherlands) - Vlieland (Frisian Islands) (1 hrs 45 mins; *(3)*; 3 per day).

CONVENTIONAL FERRIES

1	FRIESLAND	3583t	89	14k	1750P	122C	12L	BA	Krimpen, NL	NL
2	MIDSLAND	1812t	74	15.5k	1200P	55C	6L	BA	Emden, GY	NL
3	OOST-VLIELAND	1350t	70	15k	1100P	45C	4L	BA	Emden, GY	NL

FRIESLAND Built for *Rederij Doeksen*. Used on the Harlingen - Terschelling route.

MIDSLAND Built as the RHEINLAND for *AG Ems* of Germany. In 1993 purchased by *Rederij Doeksen* and renamed the MIDSLAND. Used mainly on the Harlingen - Terschelling route but also used on the Harlingen - Vlieland service. She is now a reserve vessel.

OOST-VLIELAND Built as the OSTFRIESLAND for *AG Ems* of Germany. In 1981 purchased by *Rederij Doeksen* and renamed the SCHELLINGERLAND. In 1994 renamed the OOST VLIELAND. Now mainly used on the Harlingen - Vlieland service.

Rederij Doeksen also operate the Harding 35m passenger only catamaran KOEGELWIECK (439t, 1992, 317 passengers) between Harlingen and Terschelling, Harlingen and Vlieland and Terschelling and Vlieland.

EASY LINE

THE COMPANY *Easy Line A/S* is a Danish company, jointly owned by *Eidsiva Rederi ASA* of Norway and *DIFKO A/S* of Denmark.

MANAGEMENT Managing Director: Tom Bringsværd.

ADDRESS 1 Sverigesvej, Postbox 109, DK-4970 RØDBY, Denmark.

TELEPHONE Administration & Reservations: +45 54 60 50 50, **Fax:** +45 54 60 57 57.

INTERNET Email: info@easy-line.dk **Website:** http://www.easy-line.dk *(Danish)*

ROUTE OPERATED Gedser (Denmark) - Rostock (Germany) **(**2 hrs 10 mins; *(1,2)*; 6 per day).

CONVENTIONAL FERRIES

1	ANJA 11	4101t	88	13k	253P	170C	24T	BA	Sunderland, GB	DK
2	GITTE 3	4296t	87	12.7k	300P	170C	24T	BA	Sunderland, GB	DK

ANJA 11 Built as the SUPERFLEX KILO for *Vognmandsruten* of Denmark. In 1989 sold to *Mercandia* and renamed the MERCANDIA I. In 1990 she began operating on the *Kattegatbroen* Juelsminde - Kalundborg service. In 1996 this service ceased but it has not proved possible to use her on the *Sundbroen* Helsingør - Helsingborg service. In 1997 chartered to *Litorina Line* to inaugurate a new service between Öland and Gotland. In 1998, sold to *Eidsiva Rederi* and renamed the ANJA 11. She inaugurated a new service between Gedser and Rostock. Note: she actually carries the name 'ANJA #11' but the '#' character does not form part of her registered name.

GITTE 3 Built as the SUPERFLEX DELTA for *Vognmandsruten* to establish a new service between Korsør (Fyn) and Nyborg (Sjælland). In 1990 this company was taken over by *DIFKO* and she was renamed the DIFKO STOREBÆLT. In 1998, following the opening of the Great Belt fixed link, the service ceased and she was laid up. In 1999 she was chartered to *Easy Line* and renamed the GITTE 3

ECKERÖ LINE

THE COMPANY *Eckerö Line Ab Oy* is a Finnish company, 100% owned by *Eckerö Linjen* of Åland, Finland. Until January 1998, the company was called *Eestin-Linjat*.

MANAGEMENT Managing Director: Jarl Danielsson, **Marketing Director:** Håkan Nordström.

ADDRESS Hietalahdenranta 13, FIN-00180 HELSINKI, Finland.

TELEPHONE Administration: +358 (0)9 22885421, **Reservations:** +358 (0)9 2288544, **Fax:** +358 (0)9 22885222.

INTERNET Email: info@eckeroline.fi **Website:** http://www.eckeroline.fi *(Swedish, Finnish, English, German)*

ROUTE OPERATED Helsinki - Tallinn (Estonia) (3 hrs 30 mins; *(1)*; 1 per day).

CONVENTIONAL FERRY

1	NORDLANDIA	21473t	81	21k	2048P	530C	64T	BA	Bremerhaven, GY	FI

NORDLANDIA Built as the OLAU HOLLANDIA for *Olau Line* of Germany for the service between Vlissingen (Netherlands) and Sheerness (England). In 1989 she was replaced by a new vessel of the same name and she was sold to *Nordström & Thulin*. She was renamed the NORD GOTLANDIA and introduced onto *Gotlandslinjen* services between Gotland and the Swedish mainland. In 1997 she was purchased by *Eckerö Linjen* of Åland for delivery in early 1998, following the ending of *Nordström & Thulin's* concession to operate the Gotland services. She was renamed the NORDLANDIA and placed on the *Eckerö Line* Helsinki - Tallinn service, operating day trips.

Eckerö Line also utilise the ALANDIA of associated company *Eckerö Linjen*.

ECKERÖ LINJEN

THE COMPANY *Eckerö Linjen* is an Åland Islands company.

MANAGEMENT Managing Director: Jarl Danielsson, **Marketing Director:** Christer Lindman.

ADDRESS Torggatan 2, Box 158, FIN-22100 MARIEHAMN, Åland.

TELEPHONE Administration: +358 (0)18 28000, **Reservations:** +358 (0)18 28300, **Fax:** +358 (0)18 28380.

ROUTE OPERATED Eckerö (Åland) - Grisslehamn (Sweden) (2 hrs; *(1,2)*; 5 per day).

INTERNET Website: http://www.eckerolinjen.fi *(Finnish)*

CONVENTIONAL FERRIES

1	ALANDIA	6754t	72	17k	1200P	225C	34T	BA	Papenburg, GY	FI
2	ROSLAGEN	6652t	72	18.7k	1200P	225C	34T	BA	Papenburg, GY	FI

ALANDIA Built as the DIANA for *Rederi AB Slite* of Sweden for *Viking Line* services. In 1979 she was sold to *Wasa Line* of Finland and renamed the BOTNIA EXPRESS. In 1982 she was sold to *Sally Line* of Finland; later that year she was sold to *Suomen Yritysraheitis Oy* and chartered back. In 1992 she was sold to *Eckerö Linjen* and renamed the ALANDIA. She is also used by subsidiary company *Eckerö Line*.

ROSLAGEN Built as the VIKING 3 for *Rederi AB Sally* and used on *Viking Line* Baltic services. In 1976 she was sold to *Vaasanlaivat* of Finland for their service between Vaasa (Finland) and Umeå/Sundsvall (Sweden) and renamed the WASA EXPRESS. In 1982 *Vaasanlaivat* was taken over by *Rederi AB Sally* and in April 1983 she resumed her original name, was transferred to *Sally Line* and used on the Ramsgate - Dunkerque service. She remained in the Channel during winter 1983/4 on freight-only services. However, in early 1984 she returned to *Vaasanlaivat* and resumed the name WASA EXPRESS. In 1988 she was sold to *Eckerö Linjen* and renamed the ROSLAGEN. During winter 1992/3 she operated between Helsinki and Tallinn for *Estonia New Line* and returned to *Eckerö Linjen* in the spring.

ELBE-FERRY

THE COMPANY *Elbe-Ferry GmbH & Co KG* is a subsidiary of *E H Harms GmbH*, a German private sector company.

MANAGEMENT Managing Director: F P Harms, **Administration & Marketing Manager:** Klaus H Birke.

ADDRESS Am Fährhafen, 27472 CUXHAVEN, Germany.

TELEPHONE Administration & Reservations: +49 4721 79790, **Fax:** +49 4721 797920.

ROUTE OPERATED Cuxhaven - Brunsbüttel (across mouth of River Elbe) (1 hr 30 mins; *(1,2,3)*; hourly). (Operations start 1st June 1999).

Mercandia IV *(Philippe Holthof)*

CONVENTIONAL FERRIES

1	HINRICH KOPF	5148t	64	16k	1125P	124C	23T	BA	Aalborg, DK	GY
2	JOCHEN STEFFEN	5293t	60	17k	800P	157C	23T	BA	Aalborg, DK	GY
3	WILHELM KAISEN	2402t	67	12k	450P	55C	15L	BA	Århus, DK	GY

HINRICH KOPF Built as the PRINSESSE ELISABETH for *DSB* for the Århus - Kalundborg service. In 1986 transferred to the Helsingør - Helsingborg service. In 1998, sold to *E H Harms GmbH* of Bremen, renamed the HINRICH KOPF and inaugurated a new service between Cuxhaven and Brunsbüttel.

JOCHEN STEFFEN Built as the PRINSESSE ANNE-MARIE for *DSB* for the Århus - Kalundborg service. In 1986 transferred to the Helsingør - Helsingborg service, generally as a relief vessel. Following the withdrawal of the REGULA and URSULA she became a regular vessel with a Swedish crew. Withdrawn in 1997. In 1998, sold to *E H Harms GmbH* of Bremen, renamed the JOCHEN STEFFEN and inaugurated a new service between Cuxhaven and Brunsbüttel.

WILHELM KAISEN Built as the NAJADEN, a vehicle/train ferry for *DSB* for the Helsingør - Helsingborg service. In 1987 converted to a vehicle ferry and transferred to the Fynshav - Bøjden service. In 1997, transferred to subsidiary *SFDS A/S*. In 1998 she was sold to *E H Harms GmbH* of Bremen, renamed the WILHELM KAISEN and inaugurated a new service between Cuxhaven and Brunsbüttel.

… FERRIES OF THE BRITISH ISLES & NORTHERN EUROPE …

AG EMS

THE COMPANY *AG Ems* is a German public sector company.

MANAGEMENT Managing Director & Chief Executive: B W Brons, **Marine Superintendent:** J Alberts, **Marketing Manager & Assistant Manager:** P Eesmann.

ADDRESS Am Aussenhafen, Postfach 1154, 26691 EMDEN, Germany.

TELEPHONE Administration & Reservations: +49 (0)4921 89070 or +49 (0)4921 890722, **Fax:** +49 (0)4921 890742.

INTERNET Email: info@ag-ems.de **Website:** http://www.ag-ems.de *(German)*

ROUTES OPERATED Emden (Germany) - Borkum (German Frisian Islands) (2 hrs; *(1,2,3)*; up to 4 per day), Eemshaven (Netherlands) - Borkum (55 mins; *(1,2,3)*; up to 4 per day).

CONVENTIONAL FERRIES

1	MÜNSTERLAND	1859t	86	15.5k	1200P	70C	10L	BA	Leer, GY	GY
2	OSTFRIESLAND	1859t	85	15.5k	1200P	70C	10L	BA	Leer, GY	GY
3	WESTFALEN	1812t	72	15.5k	1200P	65C	10L	BA	Emden, GY	GY

MÜNSTERLAND, OSTFRIESLAND, WESTFALEN Built for *AG Ems*. The WESTFALEN was rebuilt in 1994.

Services also operated by 33k Fjellstrand 38m passenger only catamaran NORDLICHT (435t, 1989) and the 11.5k 358 passenger only ferry WAPPEN VON BORKUM (287t, 1976, rebuilt 1995) (previously PRINCESS ISABELLA).

ESTLINE

THE COMPANY *EstLine AB* is a Swedish private sector company owned by the *Estonian Shipping Company (ESCO Ltd)* of Estonia.

MANAGEMENT Managing Director: Anders Wehtje, **Marketing Manager:** Bo Östenius.

ADDRESS Frihamnen, Magasin 2, Box 27304, S-10254 STOCKHOLM, Sweden.

TELEPHONE Administration: +46 (0)8-666 6000, **Reservations:** +46 (0)8-667 0001, **Fax:** *Admin:* +46 (0)8-666 6025, *Reservations:* +46 (0)8-666 6052.

INTERNET Email: passenger@estline.se **Website:** http://www.estline.com (*Estonian, Finnish, Swedish, English*)

ROUTE OPERATED Stockholm - Tallinn (Estonia) (14 hrs; *(1,2,3)*; 1 per day).

CONVENTIONAL FERRIES

1	BALTIC KRISTINA	12281t	73	19k	578P	344C	44T	BA	Turku, FI	ES
2	NEPTUNIA	8547t	77	17k	412P	-	62T	BA	Korneuburg, AU	ES
3	REGINA BALTICA	18345t	80	21.3k	1450P	500C	78T	BA	Helsinki, FI	ES

BALTIC KRISTINA Built as the BORE 1 for *Ångfartygs AB Bore* of Finland for *Silja Line* services between Turku and Stockholm. In 1980, *Bore Line* left the *Silja Line* consortium and disposed of its passenger ships. She was acquired by *EFFOA* of Finland and continued to operate on *Silja Line* service, being renamed the SKANDIA. In 1983 she was sold to *Stena Line* and renamed the STENA BALTICA. She was then resold to *Latvia Shipping* of the USSR, substantially rebuilt, renamed the ILLICH and introduced onto a Stockholm - Leningrad (now Sankt-Peterburg) service trading as *ScanSov Line*. In 1986 operations were transferred to *Baltic Shipping Company*. In 1992 she inaugurated a new service between Stockholm and Riga but continued to also serve Sankt-Peterburg.

In 1995 the Swedish terminal was changed to Nynäshamn. In late 1995 arrested and laid up in Stockholm; her current ownership is unknown. In 1997, services were planned to restart between Kiel and Sankt-Peterburg under the auspices of a German company called *Baltic Line*, with the vessel renamed the ANASTASIA V. However, this did not materialize and she was sold to *Windward Line* of Barbados and renamed the WINDWARD PRIDE. In 1997, she was chartered to *ESCO*, and renamed the BALTIC KRISTINA. In late 1997 she sailed for *EstLine* between Stockholm and Tallinn in a freight-only role. Following a major refurbishment, she entered service with *EstLine* in May 1998, allowing a daily full passenger service to be operated.

NEPTUNIA Built as the STENA TOPPER, a ro-ro freight vessel for *Stena Line AB* of Sweden. Built in sections which were welded together at Galatz in Romania. Purchased by *James Fisher* of Barrow in 1978 and renamed the DARNIA. Chartered to *Sealink UK* for use on the Stranraer – Larne route. In 1982 passenger capacity was increased from 92 to 412 in order to operate on passenger/car ferry services. In 1991 she was sold to *Nordström & Thulin*, renamed the NORD NEPTUNUS and used generally on a freight-only role on their *Gotlandslinjen* service between Sweden and Gotland. She also operated for associated company *EstLine* and has been chartered to *TT-Line*. Later in 1997 she was purchased by *ESCO*, renamed the NEPTUNIA and placed on the Stockholm - Tallinn route as a ro-pax vessel. When all three vessels are operating, she general operates in tandem with the BALTIC KRISTINA.

REGINA BALTICA Built as the VIKING SONG for *Rederi AB Sally* of Finland and used on the *Viking Line* service between Stockholm and Helsinki. In 1985 replaced by the MARIELLA of *SF Line* and sold to *Fred. Olsen Lines*. She was named BRAEMAR and used on services between Norway and Britain as well as Norway and Denmark. Services to Britain ceased in June 1990 and she continued to operate between Norway and Denmark. She was withdrawn in 1991 and sold to *Rigorous Shipping* of Cyprus (a subsidiary of *Fred. Olsen Lines*). She was chartered to the *Baltic Shipping Company* of Russia, renamed the ANNA KARENINA and inaugurated a service between Kiel and Sankt-Peterburg (St Petersburg). In 1992 a Nynäshamn call was introduced. In 1996 the service ceased and she was returned to her owners and renamed the ANNA K. Later in 1996 she was sold to *Empremare Shipping Co Ltd* of Cyprus (a company jointly owned by *Nordström & Thulin* and *Estonian Shipping Company*), chartered to *EstLine* and renamed the REGINA BALTICA.

EUROSEABRIDGE

THE COMPANY *Euroseabridge GmbH* is a subsidiary of *Scandlines AS* of Denmark and *Reederei F Laeisz GmbH* of Germany.

MANAGEMENT Managing Directors: M Westernberger, H Ahlers **Marketing Manager:** P Jenssen.

ADDRESS Postfach 401404, D-18125 ROSTOCK, Germany.

TELEPHONE Administration: +49 (0)381 4584400, **Reservations:** +49 (0)381 4584440, **Fax:** +49 (0)381 4584402.

INTERNET Email: esb@euroseabridge.de   info@euroseabridge.de   **Website:** http://www.euroseabridge.de *(German)*

ROUTE OPERATED Travemünde (Germany) - Klaìpeda (Lithuania) (28 hrs; *(1,2)*; 4 per week), Sassnitz (Germany) - Klaìpeda (Lithuania) (18 hrs; *(3)*; 3 per week) (Sassnitz service is joint with *Lisco* of Lithuania - *Euroseabridge* ro-pax vessel 3 times per week, *Lisco* ro-ro KLAIPEDA 3 times per week)

CONVENTIONAL FERRIES

1	GREIFSWALD	21890t	88	15.5k	120P	100C	100L	A2	Wismar, GE	LB
2	KAHLEBERG	10271t	83	15.5k	75P	-	50T	AS	Wismar, GE	LB
3	PETERSBURG	25353t	86	15k	140P	100C	100L	A2	Wismar, GE	LB

GREIFSWALD Built as a train ferry for *DSR* of the former East Germany to operate on the service between Mukran and Klaìpeda (Lithuania). In 1994 she was rebuilt to introduce road vehicle and additional passenger capacity. In 1996 she was transferred to the new Travemünde - Klaìpeda service. During winter 1998/99 she was chartered to *Stena Line* to operate between Göteborg and Kiel.

KAHLEBERG Built for *DSR* of the former East Germany. In 1991 chartered to *TT Line* for *TR Line* service between Rostock and Trelleborg. In 1997 she returned to *DSR* to operate for *Euroseabridge*.

PETERSBURG Built as the MUKRAN for *DSR* of the former East Germany. In 1995 she was rebuilt to introduce road vehicle and additional passenger capacity and was renamed the PETERSBURG. She inaugurated the Travemünde service in 1995 but is now used on the Sassnitz - Klaìpeda service. This service is operated jointly with the *Lisco* vessel KLAIPEDA, a sister vessel which has not been converted to ro-pax format.

FAABORG-GELTING LINIEN

THE COMPANY *Faaborg-Gelting Linien* is the trading name of *Nordisk Færgefart*, a Danish private sector company and now a wholly owned subsidiary of are *Förde Reederei Seetouristik* of Germany.

MANAGEMENT Managing Director: Esben Jensen, **Marketing Manager:** Axel Jörgensen.

ADDRESS Odensevej 95, DK-5600 FAABORG, Denmark.

TELEPHONE Administration: +45 62 61 15 33, **Reservations:** +45 62 61 15 00, **Fax:** +45 62 61 15 42.

INTERNET Email: info@faaborg-gelting.dk **Website:** http://www.faaborg-gelting.dk *(Danish)*

ROUTE OPERATED Faaborg (Fyn, Denmark) - Gelting (Germany) (2 hrs; *(1)*; 2-3 per day). The service is currently scheduled to cease at the end of June 1999 but may continue if the abolition of duty-free is deferred.

CONVENTIONAL FERRY

1	GELTING SYD	6672t	74	19.5k	800P	145C	34T	BA	Papenburg, GY	DK

GELTING SYD Built as the STELLA SCARLETT for *Stockholms Rederi AB Svea* of Sweden and used on the *SL (Skandinavisk Linjetrafik)* (later *Scandinavian Ferry Lines*) service between Landskrona (Sweden) and København (Tuborg Havn) (Denmark). In 1980 the Swedish terminal became Malmö. The service ceased in 1981 and she was sold to *Nordisk Færgefart*, renamed the GELTING SYD and took over the Faaborg - Gelting service.

FERRY SERVISS

THE COMPANY *Ferry Serviss* is the trading name of *LS Reederia*, a Latvian company.

ADDRESS Ferry Serviss, Passenger Terminal (South), Exportaeila 3, RIGA, Latvia.

TELEPHONE Administration: *Latvia:* +371 750 8050, **Reservations: *Sweden:*** +46 (0)8-456 2250, **Fax: *Latvia:*** +371 732 6191.

INTERNET Website: http://www.russ.lv

ROUTE OPERATED Riga (Latvia) - Stockholm (18 hrs; *(1)*; 3 per week).

CONVENTIONAL PASSENGER FERRY

1p	RUSS	12797t	86	20k	412P	0C	0L	-	Stocznra, PO	RU

RUSS Built as the KONSTANTIN CHERNENKO for *Far Eastern Shipping* of the Soviet Union and later of Russia. She was engaged in cruising. In 1988 renamed the RUSS. In 1996 chartered to *LS Redereja* of Latvia to start a service from Riga to Stockholm (trading as *LS Line*). Permission to convey passengers from Sweden was obtained in April 1997. The company has now changed its name to *Ferry Serviss*.

FINNLINES (FINNCARRIERS)

THE COMPANIES *Finnlines Ltd* is a Finnish private sector company. *Finncarriers Oy Ab* is a subsidiary operating ro-ro and ro-pax services.

MANAGEMENT Managing Director: Asser Ahleskog, **Marketing Director:** Simo Airas.

ADDRESS *Finncarriers*: PO Box 197, Porkkalankatu 7, FIN-00181 HELSINKI, Finland.

TELEPHONE Administration & Reservations: +358 (0)10 34350, **Fax:** +358 (0)10 3435200.

INTERNET Email: info@finncarriers.fi **Websites:** http://www. finncarriers.fi http://www. finnlines.fi

ROUTES OPERATED All year: Helsinki - Lübeck (36 hrs; *(3,4,5,6,)*; 1 per day), Helsinki - Travemünde (32 hrs; *(1,2)*; 4 per week). **Note:** frequencies refer to services which convey passengers.

CONVENTIONAL FERRIES

1	FINNCLIPPER	30500t	99	22k	440P	-	206T	BA	Puerto Real, SP	SW
2	FINNEAGLE	30500t	99	22k	440P	-	206T	BA	Puerto Real, SP	SW
3	FINNHANSA	32531t	94	21.3k	112P	-	250T	A2	Gdansk, PO	FI
4	FINNPARTNER	32534t	94	21.3k	112P	-	250T	A2	Gdansk, PO	FI
5	FINNTRADER	32534t	95	21.3k	112P	-	250T	A2	Gdansk, PO	FI
6	TRANSEUROPA	32534t	95	21.3k	90P	-	250T	A2	Gdansk, PO	GY

FINNCLIPPER, FINNEAGLE 'Ro-pax' vessels ordered by *Stena Ro-Ro* of Sweden. In 1998 they were sold, before delivery, to *Finnlines*. Due to enter service in spring and early summer 1999.

FINNHANSA, FINNPARTNER, FINNTRADER 'Ro-pax' vessels built for *Finnlines Oy* of Finland to provide a daily service conveying both freight and a limited number of cars and passengers on a previously freight-only route.

TRANSEUROPA 'Ro-pax' vessel build for *Poseidon Schiffahrt* of Germany to operate on a joint service between Lübeck and Helsinki. In 1997 *Poseidon Schiffahrt* was acquired by *Finnlines*.

FJORD LINE

THE COMPANY *Fjord Line* is 100% owned by *Bergen-Nordhordland Rutelag AS (BNR)*, a Norwegian company.

MANAGEMENT Managing Director: Oddvar Vigestad, **Marketing Manager:** Linda F. Vikenes.

ADDRESS Skoltegrunnskaien, PO Box 6020, N-5020 BERGEN, Norway.

TELEPHONE Administration: +47 55 54 87 00, **Reservations:** +47 55 54 88 00, **Fax:** +47 55 54 86 01.

INTERNET Email: fjordline@flordline.com **Website:** http://www.fjordline.no *(Danish, English)*

ROUTE OPERATED Bergen - Egersund (Norway) - Hanstholm (Denmark) (15 hrs 30 mins; *(1)*; 3 per week), Egersund - Hanstholm (6 hrs 45 mins; *(1)*; 7 per week in summer). Also UK route - see Section 1.

CONVENTIONAL FERRY

1	BERGEN	16794t	93	20k	882P	160C	40L	BA	Rissa, NO	NO

BERGEN Built for *Rutelaget Askøy-Bergen* and used on *Fjord Line* service.

HH-FERRIES

THE COMPANY *HH-Ferries* is a Danish/Swedish private sector company. They lease the service and charter the ships from *Mercandia* of Denmark.

MANAGEMENT Managing Director: Lars Meijer, **Marketing Manager:** Jon Cavalli-Björkman.

ADDRESS Oceangatan 2, S-252 25 HELSINGBORG, Sweden.

TELEPHONE Administration: +46 (0)42-26 80 00, **Reservations: *Denmark:*** +45 49 26 01 55, ***Sweden:*** +46 (0)42-19 8000, **Fax: *Denmark:*** +45 49 26 01 56, ***Sweden:*** +46 (0)42-28 10 70.

INTERNET Email: admin@hhferries.se **Website:** http://www.hhferries.se *(Swedish, Danish, English)*

ROUTE OPERATED Helsingør - Helsingborg (20 mins; *(1,2)*; every 30 minutes).

CONVENTIONAL FERRIES

1	MERCANDIA IV	4296t	88	13k	420P	170C	24T	BA	Sunderland, GB	DK
2	MERCANDIA VIII	4296t	87	13k	420P	170C	24T	BA	Sunderland, GB	DK

MERCANDIA IV Built as the SUPERFLEX NOVEMBER for *Vognmandsruten* of Denmark. In 1989 sold to *Mercandia* and renamed the MERCANDIA IV. In 1990 she began operating on their *Kattegatbroen* Juelsminde - Kalundborg service. In 1996 she was transferred to their *Sundbroen* Helsingør - Helsingborg service. In 1997 the service and vessel were leased to *HH-Ferries*. She has been equipped to carry dangerous cargo.

MERCANDIA VIII Built as the SUPERFLEX BRAVO for *Vognmandsruten* of Denmark and used on their services between Nyborg and Korsør and København (Tuborg Havn) and Landskrona (Sweden). In 1991 she was chartered by *Scarlett Line* to operate on the København and Landskrona route. In 1993 she was renamed the SVEA SCARLETT but later in the year the service ceased and she was laid up. In 1996 she was purchased by *Mercandia*, renamed the MERCANDIA VIII and placed on their *Sundbroen* Helsingør - Helsingborg service. In 1997 the service and vessel was leased to *HH-Ferries*.

HH-Ferries also look after the DIFKO FYN (see *DIFKO Frærger A/S*, Section 7) which is laid up at Helsingborg. She is available for them to charter if one of their own vessels is unavailable.

HURTIGRUTEN

SERVICE The *'Hurtigruten'* is the *'Norwegian Coastal Express Service'*. It is part cruise, part passenger ferry, part cargo line and part car ferry (although this is a fairly minor part of the operation). The service operated by a consortium of two operators - *Ofotens og Vesteraalen Dampskipsselskab* and *Troms Fylkes Dampskipsselskab*.

ADDRESS *Ofotens og Vesteraalen Dampskipsselskab:* Postboks 43, 8501 NARVIK, Norway, *Troms Fylkes Dampskipsselskab:* 9005 TROMSØ, Norway.

TELEPHONE Administration: *Ofotens og Vesteraalen D/S:* +47 76 96 76 00, *Troms Fylkes D/S:* +47 77 64 81 00, *Reservations (UK):* +44 (0)171 371 4011, **Fax:** *Ofotens og Vesteraalen D/S:* +47 76 96 76 01, *Troms Fylkes D/S:* +47 77 64 81 80, *Reservations (UK):* +44 (0)171 371 4070.

INTERNET Email: booking@ovds.no booking@tfds.no **Website:** http://www.monet.no/hr/ *(English, Norwegian, German, Dutch, Spanish, Finnish, French, Italian and Swedish)*

ROUTE OPERATED Bergen - Kirkenes with many intermediate calls. Daily departures throughout the year. The round trip takes just under 11 days.

CONVENTIONAL FERRIES

1	HARALD JARL	2621t	60	16k	410P	4C	-	C	Trondheim, NO	NO
2	KONG HARALD	11204t	93	18k	691P	50C	-	SC	Stralsund, GY	NO
3	LOFOTEN	2621t	64	16k	410P	4C	-	C	Oslo, NO	NO
4	MIDNATSOL	6167t	82	18k	550P	40C	-	SC	Ulsteinvik, NO	NO
5	NARVIK	6257t	82	18k	550P	40C	-	SC	Trondheim, NO	NO
6	NORDKAPP	11386t	96	18k	691P	50C	-	SC	Ulsteinvik, NO	NO
7	NORDLYS	11200t	94	18k	691P	50C	-	SC	Stralsund, GY	NO
8	NORDNORGE	11386t	97	18k	691P	50C	-	SC	Ulsteinvik, NO	NO
9	POLARLYS	1200t	96	18k	691P	50C	-	SC	Ulsteinvik, NO	NO
10	RICHARD WITH	11205t	93	18k	691P	50C	-	SC	Stralsund, GY	NO
11	VESTERÅLEN	6261t	83	18k	550P	40C	-	SC	Harstad, NO	NO

HARALD JARL Built for *Nordenfjeldske D/S*. In 1988 she was sold to *Troms Fylkes Dampskibsselskap*.

KONG HARALD Built for *Troms Fylkes D/S*.

LOFOTEN Built for *Vesteraalens D/S*. In 1984 she was sold to *Finnmark Fylkesrederi og Ruteselskap*. In 1996 she was sold to *Ofotens og Vesteraalen D/S*.

MIDNATSOL Built for *Troms Fylkes D/S*.

NARVIK Built for Built for *Ofoten D/S*. Since 1984 owned by *Ofotens og Vesteraalen D/S*.

NORDKAPP Built for *Ofotens og Vesteraalen D/S*.

NORDLYS Built for *Troms Fylkes D/S*.

NORDNORGE Built for *Ofotens og Vesteraalen D/S*.

POLARLYS Built for *Troms Fylkes D/S*.

RICHARD WITH Built for *Ofotens og Vesteraalen D/S*.

VESTERÅLEN Built for *Vesteraalens D/S*. Since 1984 owned by *Ofotens og Vesteraalen D/S*.

LANGELAND-KIEL LINJEN

THE COMPANY *Langeland-Kiel Linjen* is the trading name of *Langeland-Kiel Linien A/S*, a Danish private sector company, now 50% owned by *Nordisk Færgefart A/S* (operators of *Faaborg-Gelting Linien*) and 50% owned by *A/S Rudkøbing-Vemmenæs Færgerute*. The service ceased at the end of 1998 but resumed on 1st March 1999. At present, no service is advertised beyond the end of June 1999.

MANAGEMENT Managing Director: Erik Lund-Nielsen, **Sales and Marketing Manager:** Henrik Ph. Hoegstrup.

ADDRESS Færgevej 2, DK-5935 BAGENKOP, Denmark.

TELEPHONE Administration & Reservations: +45 62 56 14 00, **Fax:** +45 62 56 19 59.

INTERNET Email: info@faaborg-gelting.dk **Website:** http://www.langeland-kiel.dk *(Danish, German)*

ROUTE OPERATED Bagenkop (Langeland, Denmark) - Kiel (Germany) (2 hrs 30 mins; *(1)*; up to 2 per day).

CONVENTIONAL FERRY

1	APOLLO	6840t	70	17.5k	1200P	250C	34T	BA	Papenburg, GY	GY

APOLLO Built as the APOLLO for *Rederi AB Slite* of Sweden, a partner in the *Viking Line* consortium. In 1975 sold to *Olau Line* and renamed the OLAU KENT. In 1978, when the company was sold to *TT-Line*, she remained in the ownership of Ole Lauritzen although remaining in service with *Olau Line*. In late 1980, she was 'arrested' in Vlissingen in respect of non-payment of debts relating to her owner's unsuccessful *Dunkerque-Ramsgate Ferries* venture. In 1981 she was sold to *Nordisk Færgefart* of Denmark, renamed the GELTING NORD and used on their service between Faaborg (Denmark) and Gelting (Germany). In 1982 she inaugurated a new service between Hundested (Denmark) and Sandefjord (Norway). In 1984 this service ceased and she was taken by *Brittany Ferries* on long term charter, renamed the BENODET and used on the Plymouth - Roscoff service. In 1985 transferred to *Channel Island Ferries*, renamed the CORBIERE and used on their Portsmouth - Channel Islands service. In 1989 she was transferred to *Brittany Ferries'* subsidiary *Truckline Ferries* for their service between Poole and Cherbourg. At the end of the 1991 season the charter was terminated and she was sold to *Eckerö Linjen* of Åland. She inaugurated services for *Estonia New Line* between Helsinki and Tallinn. Initially she operated as LINDA I, although she was never formally renamed (she continued to carry the CORBIERE on her bows), but this name was subsequently abandoned. In 1994 she operated with *Tallink* but in 1995 the service became separately operated again - this time with *Eckerö Linjen* subsidiary *Eestin-Linjat*. In 1995 she resumed her original name of APOLLO. She was operated on day trips from Helsinki to Tallinn. She was withdrawn in early 1998 and was laid up until 1999 when she was chartered to *Langeland-Kiel Linjen*. She may be renamed the LANGELAND IV.

LISCO

THE COMPANY *Lisco* is the trading name of the *Lithuanian Shipping Company*, a Lithuanian state owned company. Passenger and cargo services are marketed by *Krantas Shipping*.

ADDRESS 24 J. Janonio Str, KLAÌPEDA LT-5813, Lithuania.

TELEPHONE *Lisco (Klaìpeda):* **Administration:** +370 (0)6 393103, **Fax:** +370 (0)6 393140, **Telex:** 278126 lisco lt, *Krantas (Klaìpeda):* **Reservations:** +370 (0)6 365444, **Fax:** +370 (0)6 365443, **Telex:** 278350 KRANT LT, *Krantas: (Stockholm):* **Reservations:** +46 (0)8-673 3200, **Fax:** +46 (0)8-673 6303.

INTERNET Email: *Lisco:* lisco@klaipeda.omnitel.net *Krantas:* krantaspass@klaipeda.omnitel.net

Website: *Lisco:* http://www.lisco.lt *(English, German) Krantas:* http://www1.omnitel.net/krantas *(English)*

ROUTES OPERATED Klaìpeda (Lithuania) - Stockholm (18 hrs; *(2)*; 2 per week), Klaìpeda - Kiel (33 hrs; *(1,3)*; up to 5 per week), Klaìpeda - Sassnitz (Germany) (18 hrs; *(Euroseabridge vessel)*; 3 per week) (Joint service with *Euroseabridge* of Germany - *Euroseabridge* ro-pax vessel 3 times per week, *Lisco* ro-ro 3 times per week).

CONVENTIONAL FERRIES

1	KAUNAS	25606t	89	19k	200P	460C	90T	A2	Wismar, GE	LT
2	PALANGA	11630t	79	20k	102P	-	80T	A	Le Havre, FR	LT
3	VILNIUS	21800t	87	19k	120P	460C	90T	A2	Wismar, GE	LT

KAUNUS, VILNIUS Built as train ferries for the Soviet Union and used by *Lisco* to operate between Klaìpeda and Mukran in the former East Germany. This was part of a series of vessels built to link the USSR and DDR, avoiding Poland. In 1992, they became the property of *Lisco* and in 1994 were modified to increase passenger capacity in order to offer a limited passenger facilities and placed on the Klaìpeda - Kiel service.

PALANGA Built as the MONTE STELLO for *SNCM* of France for Mediterranean service; rebuilt in 1992 to increase passenger capacity. In 1996 sold to *Lisco*, renamed the PALANGA and, in 1997, placed on the Klaìpeda - Stockholm service.

MOLS-LINIEN

THE COMPANY *Mols-Linien A/S* is a Danish private sector company; previously a subsidiary of *J Lauritzen A/S*, it was, in 1988 sold to *DIFKO No LXII (Dansk Investeringsfond)*. Since 1994 shares in the company have been traded on the stock exchange. In January 1999 a 40% share in the company was acquired by *Scandlines A/S*. Their *Scandlines Cat-Link* Århus - Kalundborg service became part of *Mols-Linien* in February 1999 and the service was switched from Kalundborg to Odden in April 1999.

MANAGEMENT Managing Director: Preben Wolff, **Marketing Manager:** Christian Hingelberg.

ADDRESS Færgehavnen, DK-8400 EBELTOFT, Denmark.

TELEPHONE Administration: +45 89 52 52 00, **Reservations:** +45 89 52 52 52, **Fax:** *Admin:* +45 89 52 52 90, **Reservations:** +45 89 52 52 92.

INTERNET Email: Mols-Linien@Mols-Linien.dk **Website:** http://www.Mols-Linien.dk *(Danish)*

ROUTES OPERATED Conventional Ferries: Ebeltoft (Jylland) - Odden (Sjælland) (1 hr 40 mins; *(1,2)*; 10 per day), **Fast Ferries:** Århus - Odde (1 hr; *(3,5)*; every 1/2 hr), Ebeltoft (Jylland) - Odden (45 mins; *(4,6)*; hourly).

CONVENTIONAL FERRIES

1	MAREN MOLS	14221t	96	19k	600P	344C	100T	BA2	Frederikshavn, DK	DK
2	METTE MOLS	14221t	96	19k	600P	344C	100T	BA2	Frederikshavn, DK	DK

MAREN MOLS, METTE MOLS 'Ro-pax' vessels built for *Mols-Linien*.

FAST FERRIES

3	MADS MOLS	5619t	98	43k	800P	220C	-	A	Hobart, AL	DK
4	MAI MOLS	3971t	96	44.4k	450P	120C	-	BS	Aalborg, DK	DK
5	MAX MOLS	5617t	98	43k	800P	220C	-	A	Hobart, AL	BA
6	MIE MOLS	3971t	96	44.4k	450P	120C	-	BS	Aalborg, DK	DK

Stena Saga *(Philippe Holthof)*

Silja Festival *(Philippe Holthof)*

MADS MOLS InCat 91 metre catamarans, built speculatively. In spring 1998, following *InCat's* acquisition of a 50% share in *Scandlines Cat-Link A/S*, she was chartered to that company and named the CAT-LINK V. She is the current holder of the Hales Trophy for fastest crossing of the Atlantic during her delivery voyage between the USA and Falmouth, UK. In 1999 the charter was transferred to *Mols-Linien* and she was renamed the MADS MOLS.

MAI MOLS Danyard SeaJet 250 catamaran built for *Mols-Linien*.

MAX MOLS InCat 91 metre catamarans, built speculatively. In 1998 she was sold to. In spring 1998, following *InCat's* acquisition of a 50% share in *Scandlines Cat-Link A/S*, she was sold to that company and named the CAT-LINK IV. In 1999 purchased by *Mols-Linien* and renamed the MAX MOLS.

MIE MOLS Danyard SeaJet 250 catamaran built for *Mols-Linien*.

REEDEREI NORDEN-FRISIA

THE COMPANY *Aktiengesellschaft Reederei Norden-Frisia* is a German public sector company.

MANAGEMENT President/CEO: Dr Stegmann, **Managing Director/CFO:** Prok. Graw.

ADDRESS Postfach 1262, 26534 NORDERNEY, Germany.

TELEPHONE Administration: +49 (0)4932 9130, **Fax:** +49 (0)4932 91310.

INTERNET Email: info@reederei-frisia.de **Website:** http://www.reederei-frisia.de *(German)*

ROUTES OPERATED *Car Ferries:* Norddeich (Germany) - Norderney (German Frisian Islands) (1 hr; *(1,3,5)*; up to 15 per day), Norddeich - Juist (German Frisian Islands) (1 hr 20 mins; *(2,4,6)*; up to 15 per day), **Passenger only fast ferry (summer only - from 1 June 1999):** Norderney - Helgoland (1hr 15 mins; *(new fast ferry)*), Cuxhaven - Helgoland (1 hr; *(new fast ferry)*).

CONVENTIONAL FERRIES

1	FRISIA I	1020t	70	12.3k	1500P	55C	-	-	Papenburg, GY	GY
2	FRISIA II	1058t	78	12k	1340P	55C	-	-	Papenburg, GY	GY
3	FRISIA V	1007t	65	11k	1442P	55C	-	-	Papenburg, GY	GY
4	FRISIA VI	768t	68	12k	1096P	35C	-	-	Papenburg, GY	GY
5	FRISIA VIII	1058t	62	12.5k	1340P	55C	-	-	Papenburg, GY	GY
6	FRISIA IX	571t	80	10k	785P	9C	-	-	Oldersum, GY	GY

FRISIA I, FRISIA II, FRISIA V, FRISIA VI, FRISIA VIII, FRISIA IX Built for *Reederei Norden-Frisia*. Passenger figures relate to the summer seasons. Capacity is reduced during the winter.

Reederei Norden-Frisia also operate two passenger only vessels - the FRISIA III (710t, 1960) and the FRISIA X (187t, 1972). A new 250t, 40k, 450 passenger high-speed catamaran, the HSC NO 1, will be delivered during summer 1999; she will operate to Helgoland.

NORDIC JET LINE

THE COMPANY *Nordic Jet Line* is the trading name of *Express Ferries International Ltd*, an international company, registered in Guernsey. Main shareholders are *Förde Reederei Seeturistik* of Germany, *Finnmark Fylkesrederi og Ruteselskap* of Norway and *Kværner Fjellstrand* (shipbuilders) of Norway.

MANAGEMENT Managing Director: Michael Granrot, **Deputy Managing Director:** Götz Becker.

ADDRESS Kanavaterminaali K5, 00160 Helsinki, Finland.

TELEPHONE *Finland:* **Administration:** +358 (0)9 68177150, **Reservations:** +358 (0)9 681770,

Fax: +358 (0)9 6817111, **Estonia: Administration:** +372 (0)6 137200, **Reservations:** +372 (0)6 137000, **Fax:** +372 (0)6 137222.

INTERNET Email: info@njl.fi **Website:** http://www.njl.fi *(English, Finnish, Swedish, Estonian, German)*

ROUTE OPERATED Helsinki (Finland) - Tallinn (Estonia) (1 hrs 30 mins; *(1,2)*; up to 6 per day (3 per day until June 1999) (all year except during winter ice period).

FAST FERRIES

1	BALTIC JET	2273t	99	36k	430P	52C	-	A	Omastrand, NO	NO
2	NORDIC JET	2273t	98	36k	430P	52C	-	A	Omastrand, NO	NO

BALTIC JET, NORDIC JET Kværner Fjellstrand JumboCat 60m catamarans built for *Nordic Jet Line*. The BALTIC JET enters service in May 1999. Alternative traffic mix is 38 cars and 2 buses.

POLFERRIES

THE COMPANY *Polferries* is the trading name of *Polska Zegluga Baltycka (Polish Baltic Shipping Company)*, a Polish state owned company.

MANAGEMENT General Director & President of the Board: Stanislaw Balazy, **Sales & Marketing Director:** Radoslaw Staniewski.

ADDRESS ul Portowa 41, PL 78-100 KOLOBRZEG, Poland.

TELEPHONE Administration: +48 (0)94 3525211, **Reservations: *Swinoujscie:*** +48 (0)91 3216140, ***Gdansk:*** +48 (0)58 3436978, **Fax: *Admin:*** +48 (0)94 3526612, ***Reservations (Swinoujscie):*** +48 (0)91 3216168, ***Reservations (Gdansk):*** +48 (0)58 3430975.

INTERNET Email: info@polferries.com.pl **Website:** http://www.polferries.com.pl *(Polish, English)*

ROUTES OPERATED Conventional Ferries: Swinoujscie - Malmö (9 hrs 30 mins; *(2)*; 2 per day), Swinoujscie - København (9 hrs 45 mins; *(4)*; 5 per week), Swinoujscie - Rønne (6 hrs; *(4)*; 1 per week), Gdansk - Nynäshamn (Sweden) (19 hrs; *(1,3)*; 6 per week), Gdansk - Oxelösund (Sweden) (18 hrs 30 mins; *(1,3)*; 1 per week). **Fast Ferry:** Swinoujscie - Malmö (4 hrs; *(5)*; up to 2 per day).

CONVENTIONAL FERRIES

1	NIEBOROW	8697t	73	22k	920P	225C	36T	BA	Rendsburg, GY	PO
2	POMERANIA	12087t	78	18.2k	1000P	146C	38T	BA	Szczecin, PO	PO
3	ROGALIN	10241t	72	21k	920P	225C	22T	BA	Nantes, FR	PO
4	SILESIA	10553t	79	19k	984P	277C	38T	BA	Szczecin, PO	PO

NIEBOROW Built for *Prinzenlinien* of Germany as PRINZ HAMLET for the Harwich - Hamburg service. In 1981 *Prinzenlinien* was acquired by *DFDS*. In 1987 she was renamed the PRINS HAMLET, re-registered in Denmark and transferred to the seasonal Newcastle - Esbjerg and Newcastle - Göteborg summer services. During winter 1987/88 she operated for *B&I Line* of Ireland between Rosslare and Pembroke Dock. At the end of the 1988 summer season she was acquired by a *Stena Line* subsidiary, chartered to *Polferries* and renamed the NIEBOROW. In 1999 she will be used on the Gdansk - Nynäshamn and Gdansk - Oxelösund services.

POMERANIA Built for *Polferries*. In 1978 and 1979 she briefly operated between Felixstowe and Swinoujscie via København. In recent years she was the regular vessel on the Gdansk - Helsinki service before that service was withdrawn. She was rebuilt in 1997. In 1999 she will operate on the København - Malmö service.

ROGALIN Built as the AALLOTAR for the *EFFOA* of Finland. Used on overnight *Silja Line* services (joint with *Svea Line* of Sweden and *Bore Line* of Finland) between Stockholm and Helsinki. Later used on the Stockholm - Mariehamn - Turku service. In 1978 she was sold to *Polferries*. She was renamed the ROGALIN and operated on various services between Poland, West Germany and Scandinavia. In 1983 she was chartered to *Farskip* of Iceland from the end of May until September, renamed the EDDA and inaugurated a service between Reykjavik (Iceland), Newcastle and Bremerhaven (Germany). In September of that year she returned to *Polferries* and resumed the name ROGALIN. This service was not repeated in 1984 and she continued to operate for *Polferries* until chartered (with crew) by *Swansea Cork Ferries* in 1987. She was renamed the CELTIC PRIDE and inaugurated a new Swansea - Cork service. This service also operated during summer 1988 but during winter 1987/88 and after the 1988 summer season she was returned to *Polferries* and resumed the name ROGALIN, operating on Baltic services. She did not serve with *Swansea Cork Ferries* in 1989 or 1990 but in 1991 she was taken on charter (again with crew) and was again renamed the CELTIC PRIDE. This charter terminated at the end of 1992 and she returned to the Baltic and resumed the name ROGALIN. She is now used on the Gdansk - Nynäshamn and Gdansk - Oxelösund services.

SILESIA Built for *Polferries*. Rebuilt during winter 1997/98, although not as extensively as the POMERANIA. In 1999 she will normally operate on the Swinoujscie - Malmö routes.

FAST FERRY

| 5 | BOOMERANG | 5419t | 97 | 37k | 700P | 175C | - | A | Fremantle, AL | BA |

BOOMERANG Austal Ships Auto Express 82 catamaran built for *Polferries* and used on the Swinoujscie - Malmö route.

PROVINCIALE STOOMBOOTDIENSTEN IN ZEELAND

THE COMPANY *Provinciale Stoombootdiensten in Zeeland* is a Dutch public sector company.

MANAGEMENT Managing Director: D F Vos.

ADDRESS Prins Hendrikweg 10, 4382 NS VLISSINGEN, Netherlands (***Correspondence:*** Postbus 171, 4380 AD VLISSINGEN, Netherlands).

TELEPHONE Administration: +31 (0)118 460900, **Reservations:** not applicable, **Fax:** +31 (0)118 468096.

INTERNET Email: psdiz@world.access

ROUTES OPERATED Vlissingen - Breskens (20 mins; *(1,2)*; half hourly), Perkpolder - Kruiningen (20 mins; *(3,5)*; half hourly).

CONVENTIONAL FERRIES

1	KONINGIN BEATRIX	7910t	93	17k	1000P	210C	22L	BA2	Vlissingen, NL	NL
2	PRINS JOHAN FRISO	7865t	97	16.5k	1000P	210C	22L	BA2	Vlissingen, NL	NL
3	PRINS WILLEM-ALEXANDER	7038t	70	16.5k	1000P	234C	22L	BA2	Hardinxveld, NL	NL
4	PRINSES CHRISTINA	6831t	68	16.5k	1000P	234C	22L	BA2	Hardinxveld, NL	NL
5	PRINSES JULIANA	8166t	86	14.5k	1000P	210C	22L	BA2	Hardinxveld, NL	NL

KONINGIN BEATRIX Built for *bv Veerboot Westerschelde* (a subsidiary of *De Schelde Shipyards*) and chartered to *PSD*. Purchased by *PSD* in 1997. Used on the Vlissingen - Breskens service.

PRINS JOHAN FRISO Built for *PSD*. Used on the Vlissingen - Breskens service.

PRINS WILLEM-ALEXANDER Built for *PSD*. Used on the Perkpolder - Kruiningen service.

PRINSES CHRISTINA Built for *PSD*. Used on the Perkpolder - Kruiningen service until autumn 1997 when she became a spare vessel.

PRINSES JULIANA Built for *PSD*. Initially used on the Vlissingen - Breskens service. In 1997 she was replaced by the PRINS JOHAN FRISO and, in the autumn, transferred to the Perkpolder - Kruiningen service.

RÖMÖ-SYLT LINIE

THE COMPANY *Römö-Sylt Linie GmbH* is a German company, a subsidiary of *FRS (Förde Reederei Seeturistik)* of Flensburg.

MANAGEMENT Managing Director: R Bunzel, **Marketing Manager:** H Wietz.

ADDRESS *Germany:* Buttgraben, D-25992 LIST, Germany. *Denmark:* Kilebryggen, DK-6792 RØMØ, Denmark.

TELEPHONE Administration (Germany): +49 (0)4651 870475, **Reservations (Denmark):** +45 73 75 53 03, **Fax:** *Admin:* +49 (0)4651 871446, *Reservations:* +45 73 75 53 05.

INTERNET Email: romo-sylt@post12.tele.dk **Website:** http://www.romo-sylt.dk *(Danish, German)*

ROUTE OPERATED List (Sylt, Germany) - Havneby (Rømø, Denmark) (45 mins; *(1,2)*; variable; half hourly at peaks). Note: the island of Rømø is linked to the Danish mainland by a road causeway; the island of Sylt is linked to the German mainland by a rail-only causeway on which cars are conveyed on shuttle wagons.

CONVENTIONAL FERRIES

1	VIKINGLAND	1963t	74	11k	420P	60C	8L	BA	Husum, GY	GY
2	WESTERLAND	1509t	71	11k	400P	40C	5L	BA	Husum, GY	GY

VIKINGLAND, WESTERLAND Built for *Römö-Sylt Linie*.

SCANDLINES (DENMARK & GERMANY)

THE COMPANY *Scandlines AG* is a German company, 50% owned by *Deutsche Bahn AG (German Railways)* (which is owned by the Federal Government) and 50% owned by the Kingdom of Denmark. In 1998 it took over *DFO (Deutsche Fährgesellschaft Ostsee mbH)* of Germany (renamed *Scandlines Deutschland GmbH*) and *Scandlines A/S* of Denmark (renamed *Scandlines Danmark A/S*).

Scandlines A/S was formerly *DSB Rederi A/S* and before that the Ferries Division of *DSB (Danish State Railways)*. DFO was formed in 1993 by the merging of the ferry departments of *Deutsche Bundesbahn (German Federal Railways)* (which operated in the former West Germany) and *Deutsche Reichsbahn (German State Railways)* (which operated in the former East Germany).

Swedish state operator *Scandlines AB* also trades under this name but remains a separate company. Danish domestic routes are operated by subsidiary company *SFDS A/S*, but are marketed as part of the *Scandlines* network.

MANAGEMENT Chairman: Dr Eberhard Sinnecker, **Managing Director:** Ole Rendbæk, **Head of Passenger Services:** Geir Jansen.

ADDRESS *Denmark:* Dampfærgevej 10, DK-2100 KØBENHAVN Ø, Denmark. *Germany:* Hochhaus am Fährhafen, D-18119 ROSTOCK-WARNEMÜNDE, Germany.

TELEPHONE *Denmark:* Administration: +45 35 29 02 00, **Reservations:** +45 33 15 15 15, **Fax:** +45 35 29 02 01. *Germany:* Administration: +49 (0)381 5435680, **Reservations:** +49 (0)180 5343441, +49 (0)180 5343443, **Fax:** +49 (0)180 5343442, +49 (0)180 5343444.

Vana Tallinn *(Philippe Holthof)*

Gabriella *(Philippe Holthof)*

FERRIES OF THE BRITISH ISLES & NORTHERN EUROPE

INTERNET Email: info@scandlines.de

Websites: http://www.scandlines.de *(German, English)* http://www.scandlines.dk *(Danish)*

ROUTES OPERATED Conventional Ferries: Helsingør (Sjælland, Denmark) - Helsingborg (Sweden) (25 mins; *(9,30)*; every 20 mins) (joint with *Scandlines* of Sweden), Rødby (Lolland, Denmark) - Puttgarden (Germany) (45 mins; *(4, 20,21,25)*; half hourly) (train/vehicle ferry), Gedser (Falster, Denmark) - Rostock (Germany) (2 hrs; *(13)*; 4 per day), Rostock (Germany) - Trelleborg (Sweden) (5 hrs 30 mins (7 hrs night); *(15)*; 3 per day) (joint with *Scandlines AB* of Sweden), Sassnitz (Germany) - Trelleborg (3 hrs 30 mins; *(24)*; 5 per day) (joint with *Scandlines AB* of Sweden), Sassnitz - Rønne (Bornholm, Denmark) (3 hrs 45 mins; *(23)*; 1 per day (summer), weekends only (winter)), Rønne - Ystad (Sweden) (2 hrs 30 mins; *(23)*; 1 per day (summer), weekends only (winter)).

Fast Ferry: Gedser (Falster, Denmark) - Rostock (Germany) (1 hrs 10 mins; *(32)*; 4-6 per day).

Danish domestic services operated by subsidiary *Sydfyenske Dampskibsselskab (SFDS)* and form part of *Scandlines* network: Fynshav (Als) - Bøjden (Fyn) (50 mins; *(28)*; two hourly), Esbjerg (Jylland) - Nordby (Fanø) (20 mins; *(7,16)*; half hourly), Spodsbjerg (Langeland) - Tårs (Lolland) (45 mins; *8,17,26)*; hourly).

CONVENTIONAL FERRIES

#	Name	Tonnage	Year	Speed	Pass	Cars	Other	Type	Port	Flag
1•	ARVEPRINS KNUD	8548t	63	17k	1500P	341C	30T	BA	Helsingør, DK	DK
2•	ASK	11160t	82	18k	610P	291C	76T	AS	Venezia, IT	DK
3•	DANMARK	10350t	68	0k	1325P	211C	342r	BA2	Helsingør, DK	DK
4	DEUTCHSLAND	15550t	97	18.5k	900P	305C	480r	BA	Krimpen, NL	GY
5•	DRONNING INGRID	16071t	80	19.5k	2280P	-	494r	BA	Helsingør, DK	DK
6	DRONNING MARGRETHE II	10850t	73	16.5k	1500P	211C	344r	BA	Nakskov, DK	DK
7	FENJA	751t	98	11k	400P	38C	4L	BA	Svendborg, DK	DK
8	FRIGG SYDFYEN	1676t	84	12k	338P	50C	8L	BA	Svendborg, DK	DK
9	HAMLET	10067t	97	13k	1000P	240C	36L	BA2	Rauma, FI	DK
10•	HOLGER DANSKE	2779t	76	14.5k	600P	55C	14T	BA	Aalborg, DK	DK
11	KARL CARSTENS	12830t	86	18.1k	1500P	333C	405r	BA2	Kiel, GY	GY
12•	KRAKA	9986t	82	15k	540P	275C	74T	BA	Frederikshavn, DK	DK
13	KRONPRINS FREDERIK	16071t	81	19.5k	2280P	-	494r	BA	Nakskov, DK	DK
14•	LODBROG	10404t	82	15k	600P	273C	74T	BAQ	Frederikshavn, DK	DK
15	MECKLENBURG-VORPOMMERN	36185t	96	18k	887P	440C	945r	A2	Bremerhaven, GY	GY
16	MENJA	751t	98	11k	400P	38C	4L	BA	Svendborg, DK	DK
17	ODIN SYDFYEN	1698t	82	12k	338P	50C	8L	BA	Svendborg, DK	DK
18•	PRINS HENRIK	10850t	74	17k	1500P	211C	344r	BA2	Nakskov, DK	DK
19•	PRINS JOACHIM	16071t	80	18k	2280P	-	494r	BA	Nakskov, DK	DK
20	PRINS RICHARD	14621t	97	16.5k	900P	286C	118r	BA	Frederikshavn, DK	DK
21	PRINSESSE BENEDIKTE	14621t	97	16.5k	900P	286C	118r	BA	Frederikshavn, DK	DK
22•	ROMSØ	9401t	73	18k	1500P	338C	26T	BA	Helsingør, DK	DK
23	RÜGEN	12289t	72	20.5k	1468P	220C	480r	A2	Rostock, GE	GY
24	SASSNITZ	21154t	89	17k	800P	100C	711r	A2	Frederikshavn, DK	GY
25	SCHLESWIG-HOLSTEIN	15550t	97	18.5k	900P	294C	480r	BA	Krimpen, NL	GY
26	SPODSBJERG	1478t	72	12k	300P	48C	9L	BA	Nakskov, DK	DK
27•	SPROGØ	6590t	62	17k	1200P	172C	252r	BA	Helsingør, DK	DK
28	THOR SYDFYEN	1479t	78	12k	300P	50C	9L	BA	Århus, DK	DK
29•	TRANEKÆR	1273t	73	15k	235P	45C	-	BS	Eid, NO	DK
30	TYCHO BRAHE	10845t	91	13.5k	1250P	240C	259r	BA	Tomrefjord, NO	DK
31•	URD	11030t	81	17k	610P	291C	76T	AS	Venezia, IT	DK

ARVEPRINS KNUD Vehicle ferry built for *DSB*. Used on the Knudshoved - Halsskov service. Withdrawn in June 1998. Laid up.

ASK Built as the LUCKY RIDER, a ro-ro freight ferry, for *Delpa Maritime* of Greece. In 1985 she was acquired by *Stena Line* and renamed the STENA DRIVER. Later that year she was acquired by *Sealink British Ferries* and renamed the SEAFREIGHT FREEWAY to operate freight-only services between Dover and Dunkerque. In 1988 she was sold to *SOMAT* of Bulgaria for use on *Medlink* services in the Mediterranean and renamed the SERDICA. In 1990 she was sold and renamed the NORTHERN HUNTER. In 1991 she was sold to *Blæsbjerg* of Denmark, renamed the ARKA MARINE and chartered to *DSB*. She was the converted into a passenger/vehicle ferry, renamed the ASK and introduced onto the Århus - Kalundborg service. Purchased by *Scandlines* in 1997. Withdrawn at the end of 1998. Currently undergoing rebuilding and likely to operate in a freight-only role.

DANMARK Train/vehicle ferry built for *DSB* for the Rødby - Puttgarden service. Withdrawn in 1997. There is a project to remove the engines and place her in a berth at Puttgarden as a duty-paid supermarket but this has not yet come to fruition.

DEUTSCHLAND Train/vehicle ferry built for *DFO* for the Puttgarden - Rødby service.

DRONNING INGRID Train/vehicle ferry built for *DSB* for the Nyborg - Korsør service. Withdrawn in 1997. Laid up. In 1999 to be converted to hospital ship, taking aid to Africa.

DRONNING MARGRETHE II Train/vehicle ferry built for *DSB* for the Nyborg - Korsør service. In 1981 transferred to the Rødby - Puttgarden service. An additional vehicle deck was added in 1982. Withdrawn in 1997. In 1998 became a back-up freight-only vessel on the Rødby - Puttgarden and Gedser - Rostock routes.

FENJA Built for *SFDS A/S* for the Esbjerg - Nordby service.

FRIGG SYDFYEN Vehicle ferry built for *Sydfyenske Dampskibsselskab (SFDS)* of Denmark for the service between Spodsbjerg and Tårs. In 1996, this company was taken over by *DSB Rederi*.

HAMLET Vehicle ferry built for *Scandlines* for the Helsingør - Helsingborg service.

HOLGER DANSKE Built as a train/vehicle ferry for *DSB* for the Helsingør - Helsingborg service. In 1991 transferred to the Kalundborg - Samsø route (no rail facilities). In 1997 transferred to subsidiary *SFDS*. In 1997, transferred to subsidiary *SFDS A/S*. Withdrawn by the end of November 1998 when the service passed *Samsø Linien*. Laid up.

KARL CARSTENS Train/vehicle ferry built for *DB* and used on the Puttgarden - Rødby service. Withdrawn at the end of 1997. Initially used as a reserve vessel but now laid up.

KRAKA Built as the MERCANDIAN PRESIDENT, a ro-ro freight ferry, for *Mercandia* of Denmark. Used on various freight services. In 1988 chartered to *DSB*, converted into a passenger/vehicle ferry, renamed the KRAKA and introduced onto the Knudshoved - Halsskov service. In 1997 she was purchased by *Scandlines*. Withdrawn in June 1998. Laid up.

KRONPRINS FREDERIK Train/vehicle ferry built for *DSB* for the Nyborg - Korsør service. Withdrawn in 1997. After modification, she was transferred to the Gedser - Rostock route (no rail facilities).

LODBROG Built as the MERCANDIAN GOVERNOR, a ro-ro freight ferry, for *Mercandia* of Denmark. Between 1984 and 1985 she was renamed the GOVERNOR. She was used on various freight services. In 1988 chartered to *DSB*, converted into a passenger/car ferry, renamed the LODBROG and introduced onto the Rødby - Puttgarden service to provide additional road vehicle capacity. In 1997 she was transferred to the Halsskov - Knudshoved route and later purchased by *Scandlines*. Withdrawn in June 1998. Laid up.

MECKLENBURG-VORPOMMERN Train/vehicle ferry built for *DFO* for the Rostock - Trelleborg service.

MENJA Built for *SFDS A/S* for the Esbjerg - Nordby service.

ODIN SYDFYEN Vehicle ferry built for *Sydfyenske Dampskibsselskab (SFDS)* of Denmark for the service between Spodsbjerg and Tårs. In 1996, this company was taken over by *DSB Rederi*.

PRINS HENRIK Vehicle ferry built for *DSB* for the Nyborg - Korsør service. In 1981 transferred to the Rødby - Puttgarden service. An additional vehicle deck was added in 1981. Withdrawn in 1997. Laid up.

PRINS JOACHIM Train/vehicle ferry, built for *DSB* for the Nyborg - Korsør service. Withdrawn in 1997. Laid up.

PRINS RICHARD, PRINSESSE BENEDIKTE Train/vehicle ferries, built for *DSB Rederi* for the Rødby - Puttgarden service.

ROMSØ Vehicle ferry built for *DSB* for the Knudshoved - Halsskov service. Withdrawn in 1998. Laid up.

RÜGEN Train/vehicle ferry built for *Deutsche Reichsbahn* of the former East Germany for services between Trelleborg and Sassnitz. In 1993 ownership was transferred to *DFO*. Since 1989 she has been used on the Sassnitz - Rønne service. In 1998 she also operated between Ystad and Rønne.

SASSNITZ Train/vehicle ferry built for *Deutsche Reichsbahn*. In 1993 ownership transferred to *DFO*. Used on the Sassnitz - Trelleborg service.

SCHLESWIG-HOLSTEIN Train/vehicle ferry built for *DFO* for the Puttgarden - Rødby service.

SPODSBJERG Vehicle ferries built for *Sydfyenske Dampskibsselskab (SFDS)* of Denmark for the service between Spodsbjerg and Tårs. In 1996, this company was taken over by *DSB Rederi*.

SPROGØ Train/vehicle ferry built for *DSB* for the Nyborg - Korsør and Knudshoved - Halsskov services. Withdrawn in June 1998. Laid up.

THOR SYDFYEN Vehicle ferries built for *Sydfyenske Dampskibsselskab (SFDS)* of Denmark for the service between Spodsbjerg and Tårs. In 1996, this company was taken over by *DSB Rederi*. In 1998 she was transferred to the Fynshav - Bøjden route.

TRANEKÆR Built as the STAVANGER for *Det Stavangerske Dampskibsselskab* of Norway and used on services in South Western Norway. In 1982 she was sold to *Finnmark Fylkesrederi og R/S* of Norway, renamed the PORSANGERFJORD and operated in the far north of Norway. In 1992 she was sold to *Langelandfærgen A/S* of Denmark, renamed the LUNDEBORG and reopened the Korsør - Lohals service, which had ceased at the end of 1990. In 1994, the service ceased again and she was laid up. In 1996, *DSB Rederi* re-started the route using the same vessel. She was renamed the TRANEKÆR. In 1997, transferred to subsidiary *SFDS A/S*. Withdrawn at the end of 1998 following the ending of the service and laid up.

TYCHO BRAHE Train/vehicle ferry, built for *DSB* for the Helsingør - Helsingborg service.

URD Built as the EASY RIDER, a ro-ro freight ferry, for *Delpa Maritime* of Greece and used on Mediterranean services. In 1985 she was acquired by *Sealink British Ferries* and renamed the SEAFREIGHT HIGHWAY to operate freight-only service between Dover and Dunkerque. In 1988 she was sold to *SOMAT* of Bulgaria for use on *Medlink* services in the Mediterranean and renamed the BOYANA. In 1990 she was sold to *Blæsbjerg* of Denmark, renamed the AKTIV MARINE and chartered to *DSB*. In 1991 she was converted into a passenger/vehicle ferry, renamed the URD and introduced onto the Århus - Kalundborg service. Purchased by *Scandlines* in 1997. Withdrawn at the end of March 1999 and laid up.

Note: At the time of going to press, most of the laid up vessels were at Nakskov.

FAST FERRY

| 32 | BERLIN EXPRESS | 4675t | 95 | 35k | 600P | 160C | 12T | BA | Bergen, NO | DK |

BERLIN EXPRESS Mjellam & Karlsen Jet Ship monohull vessel. Built at the KATTEGAT for *Driftsselskabet Grenaa - Hundested* for service between Grenaa (Jylland) and Hundested (Sjælland). In 1996 the company went into liquidation and she was chartered to *DSB* to operate between Gedser and Rostock.

SCANDLINES (SWEDEN)

THE COMPANY *Scandlines AB* (formerly *SweFerry*) is a Swedish state owned company. Danish/German state operator *Scandlines AG* also trades under the *Scandlines* name.

MANAGEMENT Managing Director: Åke Svensson.

ADDRESS Knutpunkten 43, S-252 78 HELSINGBORG, Sweden.

TELEPHONE Administration: +46 (0)42-18 62 00, **Reservations:** *Helsingborg:* +46 (0)42-18 61 00, *Limhamn:* +46 (0)40-36 20 20, *Trelleborg:* +46 (0)410-621 00, **Fax:** *Admin:* +46 (0)42-18 60 49, **Reservations - Helsingborg:** +46 (0)42-18 74 10, **Reservations - Limhamn:** +46 (0)40-16 13 87, **Reservations - Trelleborg:** +46 (0)410-620 29, **Telex:** 725 02 ferry s.

INTERNET Email: man@mbox303.swipnet.se **Website:** http://www.scandlines.se *(Swedish)*

ROUTES OPERATED Conventional Ferries: Helsingør (Denmark) - Helsingborg (Sweden) (25 mins; *(1)*; every 20 mins) (joint with *Scandlines AG*), Limhamn (Sweden) - Dragør (Denmark) (55 mins; *(3)*; 18 per day) (joint with *Scandlines AG*) (service ceases in autumn 1999), Trelleborg (Sweden) - Rostock (Germany) (6 hrs; *(4)*; 4 per day) (joint with *Scandlines AG*), Trelleborg - Sassnitz (Germany) (3 hrs 30 mins; *(5)*; 3 per day) (joint with *Scandlines AG*), Trelleborg (Sweden) - Travemünde (Germany) (8 hrs; *(2)*; 1 per day - freight-only), **Fast Ferry:** Limhamn (Sweden) - Dragør (Denmark) (25 mins; *(6)*; 18 per day) (service ceases in autumn 1999).

CONVENTIONAL FERRIES

1	AURORA AF HELSINGBORG	10918t	92	14.9k	1250P	240C	260r	BA	Tomrefjord, NO	SW
2	GÖTALAND	18060t	73	18.5k	400P	118C	811r	AS2	Nakskov, DK	SW
3	SCANIA	3474t	72	14k	800P	70C	16T	BA	Aalborg, DK	SW
4	SKÅNE	42500t	98	21k	600P	-	1120r	AS2	Cadiz, SP	SW
5	TRELLEBORG	20028t	82	21k	900P	108C	755r	A2	Landskrona, SW	SW

AURORA AF HELSINGBORG Train/vehicle ferry built for *SweFerry* for *ScandLines* joint service. Owned by *Aurora 93 Trust* of the USA and chartered to *Scandlines*.

GÖTALAND Train/vehicle ferry built for *Statens Järnvägar (Swedish State Railways)* for freight services between Trelleborg and Sassnitz. In 1990 transferred to *SweFerry*. In 1992 modified to increase passenger capacity in order to run in passenger service. She is was on the Trelleborg - Rostock service until autumn 1998 when she was replaced by the SKÅNE. She then inaugurated a new freight-only Trelleborg - Travemünde service.

SCANIA Vehicle ferry built for *Svenska Rederi-AB Öresund* of Sweden and used on the Limhamn - Dragør service. In 1980 sold to *Scandinavian Ferry Lines*. In 1990 transferred to *SweFerry*. Since introduction of fast ferry the FELIX, mainly used for freight and coaches.

SKÅNE Train/vehicle ferry built for an American trust and chartered to *Scandlines*. She is used on the Trelleborg - Rostock service.

TRELLEBORG Train/vehicle ferry built for *Svelast* of Sweden (an *SJ* subsidiary). In 1990 ownership transferred to *SweFerry*. She is used on the Trelleborg - Sassnitz service.

FAST FERRY

6	FELIX	5307t	96	36k	616P	150C	-	BA	Hamilton, AL	SW

FELIX Austal Ships Auto Express 82 catamaran built for the Limhamn - Dragør service. Built as the FELIX; shortly after delivery she was renamed the FELIX I. In 1997 she was renamed the FELIX.

SEACAT

THE COMPANY *SeaCat AB* is an operation of *Sea Containers*.

MANAGEMENT General Manager: John Smith.

ADDRESS Fiskhamngatan 2, Box 4040, S-400 40 GÖTEBORG, Sweden.

TELEPHONE Administration: +46 (0)31-775 4200, **Reservations:** +46 (0)31-720 0800, **Fax:** +46 (0)31-12 6090.

INTERNET Website: http://www.seacat.se *(English, Swedish)*

ROUTE OPERATED Göteborg (Sweden) - Frederikshavn (Denmark) (1 hr 45 mins; *(1)*; up to 3 per day).

FAST FERRY

1	SUPERSEACAT ONE	4463t	97	37.8k	782P	175C	-	A	La Spézia, IT	IT

SUPERSEACAT ONE Fincantieri MDV1200 monohull vessel. Built for *Sea Containers*.

SEAWIND LINE

THE COMPANY *SeaWind Line* is a Swedish private sector company owned by *Silja Service Oy*.

MANAGEMENT Managing Director: Sören Lindman, **Marketing Manager:** Ole Engblom.

ADDRESS Linnankatu 84, FIN-20100 TURKU, Finland.

TELEPHONE Administration: +358 (0)2 210 28 00, **Reservations:** +358 (0)2 210 28 00, **Fax:** +358 (0)2 210 28 10.

INTERNET Website: http://www.seawind.fi *(English, Swedish, Finnish)*

ROUTE OPERATED Stockholm (Sweden) - Turku (Finland) **Until late 1999:** (10 hrs 45 mins; *(1)*; 1 per day).

From late 1999: (10 hrs 45 mins; *(1,2)*; 2 per day).

CONVENTIONAL FERRIES

1	SEA WIND	15879t	71	18k	260P	60C	600r	BAS	Helsingør, DK	SW
2	STAR WIND	13788t	77	18k	300P	100C	598r	A	Bergen, NO	SW

SEA WIND Train/vehicle ferry built as the SVEALAND for *Stockholms Rederi AB Svea* and used on the *Trave Line* Helsingborg (Sweden) - København (Tuborg Havn) - Travemünde freight service. Later she operated between Travemünde and Malmö, first for *Saga Line* and then for *TT-Saga Line*. In 1984 she was rebuilt to increase capacity and renamed the SAGA WIND. In 1989 she was acquired by *SeaWind Line*, renamed the SEA WIND and inaugurated a combined rail freight, trailer and lower priced passenger service between Stockholm and Turku.

STAR WIND Train/vehicle ferry built as the ROSTOCK for *Deutsche Reichsbahn* of the former East Germany. Used on freight services between Trelleborg and Sassnitz. In 1992 modified to increase passenger capacity in order to run in passenger service. In 1993 ownership transferred to *DFO* and in 1994 she opened a new service from Rostock to Trelleborg. In 1997 she was used when winds preclude the use of the new MECKLENBURG-VORPOMMERN. Following modifications to this vessel in late 1997, the ROSTOCK continued to operate to provide additional capacity until the delivery of the SKÅNE of *Scandlines AB*, after which she was laid up. In 1999 she was sold to *SeaWind Line*; due to enter service in May after modification in freight-only mode. In autumn 1999 she will be lengthened, the number of cabins increased and the passenger accommodation bought up to Scandinavian standard. When she returns to traffic, she will inaugurate an all year round two vessel service.

SILJA LINE

THE COMPANY *Silja Line* is a subsidiary of *Neptun Maritime Oyj* (formerly *Silja Oy Ab*), an international (Finnish/Swedish) company based in Finland. In 1993 the services of *Jakob Line* and *Vaasanlaivat* were integrated into *Silja Line*. In 1998 the headquarter functions were concentrated in Finland, with marketing organisations in Sweden, Estonian and Germany.

MANAGEMENT President: Jukka Suominen, **Managing Director Passenger services:** Riitta Vermas, **Managing Director Cargo:** Sören Lindman, **Marketing Managers:** *Finland:* Jaana Kaartinen, *Sweden:* Camilla Laaksonen.

ADDRESS POB 880, Mannerheimintie 2, FIN-00101 HELSINKI, Finland.

TELEPHONE Administration: *Finland:* +358 (0)9 18041, **Reservations:** *Finland:* +358 (0)9 1804 422, *Sweden:* +46 (0)8-222 140, **Fax:** *Finland*: +358 (0)9 1804 279, *Sweden:* +46 (0)8-667 8681.

INTERNET Website: http://www.silja.com *(English, Finnish and Swedish)*

ROUTES OPERATED *All year:* Helsinki (Finland) - Mariehamn (Åland) - Stockholm (Sweden)(16 hrs; *(4,5)*; 1 per day), Turku (Finland) - Mariehamn (Åland) (day)/Långnäs (Åland) (night) - Stockholm (Sweden) (11 hrs; *(2,3)*; 2 per day), Helsinki - Tallinn (Estonia) (3 hrs 30 mins (4 hrs 30 mins in ice period); *(1 (Winter only), 6)*; 1/2 per day), *Summer only:* Helsinki - Tallinn - Rostock (Germany) (24 hrs (Helsinki - Tallinn, 2 hr 30 min, Tallinn - Rostock, 19 hrs)); *(1)*; 3 per week).

CONVENTIONAL FERRIES

1	FINNJET	32940t	77	31k	1790P	374C	50T	BA	Helsinki, FI	FI
2	SILJA EUROPA	59912t	93	21.5k	3000P	400C	78T	BA	Papenburg, GY	FI
3	SILJA FESTIVAL	34414t	85	22k	2000P	400C	88T	BA2	Helsinki, FI	SW
4	SILJA SERENADE	58376t	90	21k	2641P	450C	78T	BA	Turku, FI	FI
5	SILJA SYMPHONY	58377t	91	21k	2641P	450C	78T	BA	Turku, FI	SW
6	WASA QUEEN	16546t	75	22k	1200P	240C	38T	BA	Nantes, FR	FI

FINNJET Built for *Finnlines* to operate between Helsinki and Travemünde, replacing several more conventional ferries with intermediate calls. Her exceptionally fast speed was achieved by the use of jet turbine engines. During winter 1981/82 she was equipped with diesel engines for use during periods when traffic did not justify so many crossings per week. Later the trading name was changed to *Finnjet Line*. In 1986 the company was acquired by *EFFOA* and the trading name changed to *Finnjet Silja Line*. In winter 1997/98 she operated between Helsinki and Tallinn (Muuga Harbour). In summer 1998 operated a weekly Travemünde - Tallinn - Helsinki - Travemünde triangular service in addition to two weekly Travemünde - Helsinki round trips. In autumn 1998 she resumed operating between Helsinki and Tallinn and in summer 1999 she will operate Helsinki - Tallinn - Rostock.

SILJA EUROPA Ordered by *Rederi AB Slite* of Sweden for *Viking Line* service between Stockholm and Helsinki and due to be called EUROPA. In 1993, shortly before delivery was due, the order was cancelled. A charter agreement with her builders was then signed by *Silja Line* and she was introduced onto the Stockholm - Helsinki route as SILJA EUROPA. In early 1995 she was transferred to the Stockholm - Turku service.

SILJA FESTIVAL Built as the WELLAMO for *EFFOA* for the *Silja Line* Stockholm - Mariehamn - Turku service. In 1990, following the sale of the FINLANDIA to *DFDS*, she was transferred to the Stockholm

- Helsinki service until the SILJA SERENADE was delivered later in the year. During winter 1991/92 she was extensively rebuilt and in 1991 renamed the SILJA FESTIVAL; ownership was transferred to *Silja Line*. In 1993 she was transferred to the Malmö - Travemünde service of *Euroway*, which was at this time managed by *Silja Line*. This service ceased in 1994 and she was transferred to the Vaasa - Sundsvall service. In 1994 and 1995 she operated on this route during the peak summer period and on the Helsinki - Tallinn route during the rest of the year. The Vaasa - Sundsvall service did not operate in summer 1996 and she continued to operate between Helsinki and Tallinn. In 1997 she was transferred to the Stockholm - Turku route replacing the SILJA SCANDINAVIA (see the GABRIELLA, *Viking Line*).

SILJA SERENADE, SILJA SYMPHONY Built for *Silja Line* for the Stockholm - Helsinki service. In 1993, SILJA SERENADE was transferred to the Stockholm - Turku service but in early 1995 she was transferred back to the Helsinki route.

WASA QUEEN Built as the BORE STAR for *Bore Line* of Finland for *Silja Line* services between Finland and Sweden (Helsinki - Stockholm, Turku - Stockholm). She also performed a number of cruises. In 1981 *Bore Line* left the *Silja Line* consortium and she was sold to the *Finland Steamship Company* (*EFFOA*) and renamed the SILJA STAR. In January 1986 she was sold to *Sea Containers* to inaugurate, in May 1986, a new service between Venice and Istanbul connecting with the Orient Express rail service, also operated by a subsidiary of *Sea Containers*. She was re-named the ORIENT EXPRESS. During winter 1986/7 she was chartered to *Club Sea Inc* of the USA to operate Caribbean cruises and renamed the CLUB SEA but this charter was terminated prematurely and she was laid up for a time. In 1989 she was renamed the EUROSUN and chartered to *Europe Cruise Lines* for Mediterranean and Canary Island Cruises. In 1991 she was chartered to *Damens Service Far East*, renamed the ORIENT SUN and operated cruises from Singapore. In 1992 she 'returned home' as WASA QUEEN for *EffJohn* subsidiary *Wasa Line* and received Finnish registration. She was used on the Vaasa - Umeå service during the summer period when the FENNIA moved to the Pietarsaari - Skellefteå route but at other times she operated mainly on the Helsinki - Tallinn service. Since 1997, she has remained permanently on the Helsinki - Travemünde service, operating either day trips or two return trips per day.

STENA LINE

THE COMPANY *Stena Line* is a Swedish private sector company. Services of subsidiary company *Lion Ferry* were absorbed in January 1998.

MANAGEMENT Managing Director: Bo Severed. **Marketing Manager:** Gunnar Blomdahl.

ADDRESS Första Långgatan 26, S-405 19 GÖTEBORG, Sweden.

TELEPHONE Administration: +46 (0)31-85 8000, **Reservations:** +46 (0)31-701 0000, **Fax:** +46 (0)31-24 1038, **Telex:** 21914 StenaL S.

INTERNET Email: info@stenaline.com **Website:** http://www.stenaline.com *(English, Swedish)*

ROUTES OPERATED Conventional Ferries: Göteborg (Sweden) - Frederikshavn (Denmark) (3 hrs 15 mins; *(1,3,4,8)*; 7 per day), Göteborg - Kiel (Germany) (14 hrs; *(3,8)*; 1 per day), Frederikshavn - Oslo (Norway) (8 hrs 45 mins; *(7)*; 1 per day), Varberg (Sweden) - Grenaa (Denmark) (4 hrs; *(5)*; 2 per day), Karlskrona (Sweden) - Gdynia (Poland) (10 hrs 30 mins; *(2)*; 1 per day). **Fast Ferry:** Göteborg - Frederikshavn (2 hrs; *(9)*; 4 per day).

CONVENTIONAL FERRIES

1	STENA DANICA	28727t	83	19.5k	2274P	555C	136T	BA2	Dunkerque, FR	SW
2	STENA EUROPE	24828t	81	19k	2076P	456C	140T	BA2	Göteborg, SW	PO
3	STENA GERMANICA	38772t	87	20k	2400P	550C	140T	BA2	Gdynia, PO	SW
4	STENA JUTLANDICA	29691t	96	21.5k	1500P	550C	175T	BA	Krimpen, NL	SW

5	STENA NAUTICA	19763t	86	19.4k	2000P	330C	48T	BA	Nakskov, DK	SW
6•	STENA PRINCE	8909t	69	19.5k	1400P	255C	40T	BA	Aalborg, DK	SW
7	STENA SAGA	33750t	81	22k	2000P	510C	86T	BA	Turku, FI	SW
8	STENA SCANDINAVICA	38756t	88	20k	2400P	5500C	140T	BA2	Gdynia, PO	SW

STENA DANICA Built for *Stena Line* for the Göteborg - Frederikshavn service. Sister vessel STENA JUTLANDICA was transferred to the Dover - Calais service in July 1996 and renamed the STENA EMPEREUR. This vessel is listed in Section 1.

STENA EUROPE Built as the KRONPRINSESSAN VICTORIA for *Göteborg - Frederikshavn-Linjen* of Sweden (trading as *Sessan Linjen*) for their Göteborg - Frederikshavn service. Shortly after delivery, the company was taken over by *Stena Line* and services were marketed as *Stena-Sessan Line* for a period. In 1982 she was converted to an overnight ferry by the conversion of one vehicle deck to two additional decks of cabins and she was switched to the Göteborg - Kiel route (with, during the summer, daytime runs from Göteborg to Frederikshavn and Kiel to Korsør (Denmark)). In 1989 she was transferred to the Oslo - Frederikshavn route and renamed the STENA SAGA. In 1994, transferred to *Stena Line bv*, renamed the STENA EUROPE and operated between Hoek van Holland and Harwich. She was withdrawn in June 1997, transferred to the *Lion Ferry* Karlskrona - Gdynia service and renamed the LION EUROPE. In 1998 she was transferred back to *Stena Line* (remaining on the same service) and renamed the STENA EUROPE.

STENA GERMANICA, STENA SCANDINAVICA Built for *Stena Line* for the Göteborg - Kiel service. Names were swapped during construction in order that the STENA GERMANICA should enter service first. There were originally intended to be four vessels. Only two were delivered to *Stena Line*. The third (due to be called the STENA BALTICA) was sold by the builders as an unfinished hull to *Fred. Olsen Lines* of Norway and then resold to *ANEK* of Greece who had her completed at Perama and delivered as EL VENIZELOS for service between Greece and Italy. The fourth hull (due to be called the STENA POLONICA) was never completed. During the summer period, the vessel arriving in Göteborg overnight from Kiel operates a round trip to Frederikshavn before departing for Kiel the following evening. During winter 1998/99 they were modified to increase freight capacity and reduce the number of cabins.

STENA JUTLANDICA Train/vehicle 'ro-pax' vessel built for *Stena Line* to operate between Göteborg and Frederikshavn. She was launched as the STENA JUTLANDICA III and renamed on entry into service. During winter she operates in 'freight-only' mode.

STENA NAUTICA Built as the NIELS KLIM for *DSB (Danish State Railways)* for their service between Århus (Jylland) and Kalundborg (Sjælland). In 1990 she was purchased by *Stena Rederi* of Sweden and renamed the STENA NAUTICA. In 1992 she was chartered to *B&I Line*, renamed the ISLE OF INNISFREE and introduced onto the Rosslare - Pembroke Dock service, replacing the MUNSTER (8093t, 1970). In 1993 she was transferred to the Dublin - Holyhead service. In early 1995 she was chartered to *Lion Ferry*. She was renamed the LION KING. In 1996 she was replaced by a new LION KING and renamed the STENA NAUTICA. During summer 1996 she was chartered to *Trasmediterranea* of Spain but returned to *Stena Rederi* in the autumn and remained laid up during 1997. In December 1997 she was chartered to *Stena Line* and placed on the Halmstad - Grenaa route. This route ended on 31 January 1999 and she was transferred to the Varberg - Grenaa route.

STENA PRINCE Built as the PRINSESSAN CHRISTINA for *Göteborg - Frederikshavn-Linjen* of Sweden (trading as *Sessan Linjen*) for their service between Göteborg and Frederikshavn. In 1979 she was purchased by *JCE Safe Rederi* (a subsidiary of *Consafe Offshore* (an oil industry supply company)) and chartered back to *Sessan Linjen*. In 1981 she was delivered to *JCE Safe Rederi* and renamed the SAFE CHRISTINA. She was intended to be used as an accommodation vessel but in August 1981 she was chartered to *Sally Line* for service between Ramsgate (England) and Dunkerque (France) and continued to operate until October when the service was suspended for the winter. In 1982 *JCS Safe*

TT-Line - the direct way to Sweden.

TT-Line

TT-Line, Mattentwiete 8, D-20457 Hamburg,
Tel:. 040/3601-442, Fax 040/3601-407, http://www.TTLine.de

Peter Pan *(Mike Louagie)*

Rederi formed *Vinga Line* and operated the vessel on the Göteborg - Frederikshavn route in competition with *Stena Line*. However, after ten days they agreed to sell the vessel back to *Stena Line* and the service ended. She was re-introduced onto *Stena Line*'s Göteborg - Frederikshavn service and reverted to the name PRINSESSAN CHRISTINA. In 1983 she inaugurated a new service between Frederikshavn and Moss (Norway) and was renamed the STENA NORDICA. In 1985 she was transferred to the Grenaa - Helsingborg (Sweden) service, following *Stena Line*'s acquisition of the service, replacing EUROPAFÄRJAN IV (4391t, 1967) and renamed the EUROPAFÄRJAN I. In 1986, following a reorganisation within the *Stena Group*, ownership was transferred to subsidiary company *Lion Ferry AB* and she was renamed the LION PRINCE. In 1998 she was transferred back to *Stena Line* and renamed the STENA PRINCE. She operated between Varberg and Grenaa until February 1999 when she was replaced by the STENA NAUTICA and withdrawn.

STENA SAGA Built as the SILVIA REGINA for *Stockholms Rederi AB Svea* of Sweden. She was registered with subsidiary company *Svea Line* of Turku, Finland and was used on *Silja Line* services between Stockholm and Helsinki. In 1981 she was sold to *Johnson Line* and in 1984 sold to a Finnish Bank and chartered back. In 1990 she was purchased by *Stena Line* of Sweden for delivery in 1991. In 1991 she was renamed the STENA BRITANNICA and took up service on the Hoek van Holland - Harwich service for Dutch subsidiary *Stena Line bv*, operating with a British crew. In 1994 she was transferred to the Oslo - Frederikshavn route and renamed the STENA SAGA.

FAST FERRY

| 9 | STENA CARISMA | 8631t | 97 | 40k | 900P | 210C | - | A | Kristiansand, NO | SW |

STENA CARISMA Westamarin HSS 900 craft built for *Stena Line* for the Göteborg - Frederikshavn service. Work on a sister vessel, approximately 30% completed, was ceased.

TALLINK

THE COMPANY *Tallink* is the trading name of *Hansatee As*, an Estonian company owned by the *As Infortar* (51.4%), *Union Bank of Estonia* (16.7%), management and employees (14%) and others (17.9%). Services are marketed outside Estonia by *Tallink Finland Oy*, a wholly owned Finnish company.

MANAGEMENT Director, Tallink Finland Oy: Keijo Mehtonen.

ADDRESS PO Box 195, 00181 HELSINKI, Finland.

TELEPHONE Administration: +358 (0)9 228211, **Reservations:** +358 (0)9 22821211, **Fax:** +358 (0)9 228 21242.

INTERNET Website: http://www.tallink.ee *(Finnish, Estonian, English)*

ROUTE OPERATED **Conventional Ferries:** Helsinki - Tallinn (Estonia) (3 hrs 30 mins; *(1,2,3,4)*; up to 4 per day), **Fast Ferry:** Helsinki - Tallinn (1 hrs 30 mins; *(5)*; up to 3 per day)

CONVENTIONAL FERRIES

1	FANTAASIA	16630t	79	21.3k	1700P	549C	60T	BA2	Turku, FI	ES
2	GEORG OTS	12549t	80	20k	1200P	110C	26T	BA	Gdansk, PO	ES
3	MELOODIA	17955t	79	21k	1500P	480C	58T	BA2	Papenburg, GY	ES
4	VANA TALLINN	10002t	74	18k	1500P	300C	48L	BAS	Helsingør, DK	ES

FANTAASIA Built as the TURELLA for *SF Line* of Finland for the *Viking Line* Stockholm - Mariehamn - Turku service and later moved to the Kapellskär - Mariehamn - Naantali service. In 1988 she was sold to *Stena Line*, renamed the STENA NORDICA and placed onto the Frederikshavn - Moss (night) and Frederikshavn - Göteborg (day) service. In 1996 the Frederikshavn - Moss service ceased and she was transferred to subsidiary *Lion Ferry* and renamed the LION KING. She operated between

Halmstad and Grenaa. In December 1997 she was sold to *Tallink Line Ltd* of Cyprus and renamed the FANTAASIA. In February 1998, after substantial modification, she was placed on the *Tallink* service.

GEORG OTS Built for *Estonian Shipping Company*. Chartered to *Tallink*.

MELOODIA Built as DIANA II for *Rederi AB Slite* for *Viking Line* services between Stockholm and Turku, Mariehamn, Kapellskär and Naantali. In 1992 sold to a *Nordbanken* and chartered to *TT-Line* of Germany (trading as *TR-Line*) for service between Trelleborg and Rostock. In 1994 sold and chartered to *EstLine* and renamed the MARE BALTICUM. During winter 1994/95 she was completely renovated. In 1996, following the delivery of the REGINA BALTICA, she was chartered to *Tallink* and renamed the MELOODIA.

VANA TALLINN Built as the DANA REGINA for *DFDS* and used on their Esbjerg - Harwich service until 1983 when she was moved to the København - Oslo route. In 1990 she was sold to *Nordström & Thulin* of Sweden, renamed the NORD ESTONIA and used on the *EstLine* Stockholm - Tallinn service. In 1992 she was chartered to *Larvik Line* to operate as a second vessel between Larvik and Frederikshavn and renamed the THOR HEYERDAHL. In 1994 she was sold to *Inreko Ships Ltd*, chartered to *Tallink* and renamed the VANA TALLINN. In November 1996 she was withdrawn and in December 1996 she was chartered to a new company called *TH Ferries* and resumed sailings between Helsinki and Tallinn. In January 1998 she was sold to *Hansatee* subsidiary *Vana Tallinn Line Ltd* of Cyprus and placed on *Tallink* service. *TH Ferries* then ceased operations.

FAST FERRY

5	TALLINK AUTOEXPRESS	4859t	95	32k	586P	150C	-	BA	Fremantle, AL	ES

TALLINK AUTOEXPRESS Austal Ships Auto Express 79 catamaran ordered by *Sea Containers* and launched as the AUTO EXPRESS 96. On completion she was renamed the SUPERSEACAT FRANCE. However, due to a dispute between *Sea Containers* and the builders, delivery was not taken and it was announced that she was to be sold to *Stena Rederi* of Sweden, renamed the STENA LYNX IV and chartered to *Stena Line (UK)*, inaugurating a Newhaven - Dieppe service in February 1996. This did not happen and she was instead sold to *DSB Rederi* (now *Scandlines Danmark A/S*) and, in summer 1996, she was chartered to *Cat-Link* and renamed the CAT-LINK III. Following delivery of the CAT-LINK IV and CAT-LINK V, she was laid up. In 1999 she was sold to *Tallink* and renamed the TALLINK AUTOEXPRESS.

Tallink also operate the TALLINK EXPRESS I (432t, 1989, 271 passengers (ex SLEIPNER, 1997)), a Fjellstrand 38m passenger-only catamaran.

TESO

THE COMPANY *TESO* is a Dutch public sector company. Its full name is *Texels Eigen Stoomboot Onderneming*.

MANAGEMENT Managing Director: R Wortel.

ADDRESS Pontweg 1, 1797 SN DEN HOORN, Texel, Netherlands.

TELEPHONE Administration: +31 (0)222 369600, **Reservations:** n/a, **Fax:** +31 (0)222 369659.

INTERNET Email: teso.nl@wxs.nl **Website:** http://www.teso.nl *(Dutch, English, German, French)*

ROUTES OPERATED Den Helder (Netherlands) - Texel (Dutch Frisian Islands) (20 minutes; *(1,2)*; hourly).

CONVENTIONAL FERRIES

1	MOLENGAT		6170t	80	13k	1200P	126C	19L	BA2	Heusden, NL	NL

| 2 | SCHULPENGAT | 8311t | 90 | 13.6k | 1320P | 156C | 25L | BA2 | Heusden, NL | NL |

MOLENGAT, SCHULPENGAT Built for *TESO*.

TT-LINE

THE COMPANY *TT-Line GmbH & Co* is a German private sector company.

MANAGEMENT Managing Director: Hans Heinrich Conzen & Dr Heinrich von Oertzen, **Sales Manager:** Jörg Althaus.

ADDRESS Mattenwiete 8, D-20457 HAMBURG, Germany.

TELEPHONE Administration: *Hamburg:* +49 (0)40 3601 372, *Rostock:* +49 (0)381 6707911, **Reservations:** *Hamburg:* +49 (0)40 3601 442, *Rostock:* +49 (0)381 670790, **Fax:** *Hamburg:* +49 (0)40 3601 407, *Rostock:* +49 (0)381 6707980.

INTERNET Website: http://www.TTLine.de *(German)*

ROUTES OPERATED Passenger Ferries: Travemünde (Germany) - Trelleborg (Sweden) (7 hrs 30 mins; *(2,3)*; up to 3 per day), **Ro-pax Ferries:** Travemünde (Germany) - Trelleborg (Sweden) (7 hrs 30 mins; *(1,4)*; 2 per day), Rostock (Germany) - Trelleborg (Sweden) (6 hrs; *(5,6)*; 3 per day), **Fast Ferry:** Rostock (Germany) - Trelleborg (Sweden) (2 hrs 45 mins; *(7)*; up to 3 per day).

CONVENTIONAL FERRIES

1	NILS DACKE	26790t	95	21k	308P	-	200T	BA	Rauma, FI	BA
2	NILS HOLGERSSON	30740t	89	20k	1040P	280C	110T	BAS	Bremerhaven, GY	GY
3	PETER PAN	30740t	88	18k	1040P	280C	110T	BAS	Bremerhaven, GY	BA
4	ROBIN HOOD	26800t	95	21k	308P	-	200T	BA	Rauma, FI	GY
5	SAGA STAR	17672t	81	19k	250P	-	116T	BA	Kalmar, SW	BA
6	TT-TRAVELLER	18332t	92	18k	120P	-	150T	BA2	Fevaag, NO	SW

NILS DACKE, ROBIN HOOD Built for *TT-Line*. Primarily a freight vessel but accompanied cars - especially camper vans and cars towing caravans - are conveyed.

NILS HOLGERSSON Built as the ROBIN HOOD, a 'ro-pax' vessel. During winter 1992/93 rebuilt to transform her into a passenger/car ferry and renamed the NILS HOLGERSSON, replacing a similarly named vessel (31395t, 1987) which had been sold to *Brittany Ferries* and renamed the VAL DE LOIRE.

PETER PAN Built as the NILS DACKE, a 'ro-pax' vessel. During summer 1993 rebuilt to transform her into a passenger/car ferry and renamed the PETER PAN, replacing a similarly named vessel (31356t, 1986) which had been sold to *Tasmanian Transport Commission (TT Line)* of Australia and renamed SPIRIT OF TASMANIA.

SAGA STAR Built as the SAGA STAR for *TT-Saga-Line* and, from 1982, used on freight services between Travemünde and Trelleborg/Malmö. In 1989 sold to *Cie Meridonale* of France, renamed the GIROLATA and used on *SNCM* (later *CMR*) services in the Mediterranean. In 1993 she was chartered back to *TT-Line*, resumed her original name and was used on the Travemünde - Trelleborg service. Following delivery of the ROBIN HOOD and the NILS DACKE in 1995, she was transferred to the Rostock - Trelleborg route. In July 1997 she was purchased by *TT-Line* and in 1998 passenger facilities were completely renovated to full ro-pax format.

TT-TRAVELLER Built for *Stena Rederi*. Sister to the STENA CHALLENGER but with a lower passenger capacity. After a short period with *Stena Line* on the Hoek van Holland - Harwich service, she was chartered to *Sealink Stena Line* for their Southampton - Cherbourg route, initially for 28 weeks. At the end of the 1992 summer season she was chartered to *TT-Line* to operate between Travemünde and Trelleborg and was renamed the TT-TRAVELLER. In late 1995, she returned to *Stena Line*, resumed the name STENA TRAVELLER and inaugurated a new service between Holyhead and Dublin. In autumn 1996 she was replaced by the STENA CHALLENGER. In early 1997 she was again chartered to *TT-Line* and renamed the TT-TRAVELLER. She operates on the Rostock - Trelleborg route.

FAST FERRY

7	DELPHIN	5333t	96	37.5k	600P	175C	-	A	Fremantle, AL	BA

DELPHIN Austal Ships Auto Express 82 catamaran built for *TT-Line* to operate between Rostock and Trelleborg.

UNITY LINE

THE COMPANY *Unity Line* is a Polish company, jointly owned by *Polish Steamship Company* and *Euroafrica Shipping Lines*.

MANAGEMENT Chairman of the Board: Ms Hanna Hanc, **Managing Director:** Pawel Porzycki.

ADDRESS Poland, 70-419 SZCZECIN, Plac Rodla 8.

TELEPHONE Administration: +48 (0)91 3595 795, **Reservations:** +48 (0)91 3595 692, **Fax: Admin:** +48 (0)91 3595 885, **Reservations:** +48 (0)91 3595 673.

INTERNET Email: unity@dialcom.com.pl **Website:** http://www.unityline.pl *(Polish, English)*

ROUTE OPERATED Swinoujscie (Poland) - Ystad (Sweden) (6 hrs 30 mins (day), 9 hrs (night); *(1)*; 1 per day).

CONVENTIONAL FERRY

1	POLONIA	29875t	95	17.2k	920P	860C	740r	BA	Tomrefjord, NO	BA

POLONIA Train/vehicle ferry built for *Polonia Line Ltd* and chartered to *Unity Line*. Maximum trailer capacity (with no rail wagons conveyed) is approx 130.

VIKING LINE

THE COMPANY *Viking Line AB* is an Åland (Finland) company (previously *SF Line*, trading (with *Rederi AB Slite* of Sweden) as *Viking Line*). Services are marketed by subsidiary company *Viking Line Marketing AB OY* of Finland and Sweden; this dates from the time that *Viking Line* was a consortium of three operators.

MANAGEMENT Managing Director *(Viking Line AB)*: Nils-Erik Eklund, **Managing Director *(Viking Line Marketing AB OY)*:** Boris Ekman.

ADDRESS *Viking Line AB*: Norragatan 4, FIN-22100 MARIEHAMN, Åland, ***Viking Line Marketing AB OY*:** PO Box 35, FIN-22101 MARIEHAMN, Åland.

TELEPHONE Administration: +358 (0)18 26011, **Reservations:** +358 (0)9 12351, **Fax:** +358 (0)9 1235292.

INTERNET Email: susanne.nyholm@vikingline.se

Website: http://www.vikingline.fi *(Finnish, Swedish)* http://www.vikingline.se *(Swedish)*

ROUTES OPERATED *All year:* Stockholm (Sweden) - Mariehamn (Åland) - Helsinki (Finland) (14 hrs; *(4,6)*; 1 per day), Stockholm - Mariehamn (day)/Långnäs (Åland) (night) - Turku (Finland) (9 hrs 10 mins; *(2,5)*; 2 per day), cruises from Helsinki to Tallinn (Muuga Harbour) (Estonia) (20 hrs - 21 hrs round trip; *(3)*; 1 per day) (freight vehicles are conveyed on this service but not private cars; only 1 hrs 30 minutes is spent in port), ***Summer only:*** Kapellskär (Sweden) - Mariehamn (Åland) (2 hrs

15 mins; *(1)*; up to 3 per day), Kapellskär (Sweden) - Mariehamn (Åland) - Turku (Finland) (8 hrs 45 mins; *(7)*; 1 per day) (peak period only), **Except summer peak period:** Cruises from Stockholm to Mariehamn (21 hrs - 24 hrs round trip (most 22 hrs 30 mins); *(7)*; 1 per day).

CONVENTIONAL FERRIES

1	ÅLANDSFÄRJAN	6172t	72	17k	1004P	200C	18T	BA	Helsingør, DK	SW
2	AMORELLA	34384t	88	21.5k	2420P	550C	53T	BA2	Split, YU	FI
3	CINDERELLA	46398t	89	21.5k	2700P	480C	60T	BA	Turku, FI	FI
4	GABRIELLA	35492t	92	21.5k	2400P	400C	65T	BA2	Split, CR	FI
5	ISABELLA	34937t	89	21.5k	2200P	410C	30T	BA2	Split, YU	FI
6	MARIELLA	37799t	85	22k	2700P	480C	60T	BA	Turku, FI	FI
7	ROSELLA	16850t	80	21.3k	1700P	350C	43T	BA2	Turku, FI	FI

ÅLANDSFÄRJAN Built as the KATTEGAT for *Jydsk Færgefart* on Denmark for the Grenaa - Hundested service. She was used on this route until 1978 when the service became a single ship operation. She was then sold to *P&O Ferries*, renamed the N F TIGER and introduced as the second vessel on the Dover - Boulogne service. Sold to *European Ferries* in 1985 and withdrawn in June 1986. In 1986 sold to *Finlandshammen AB*, Sweden, renamed the ÅLANDSFÄRJAN and used on *Viking Line* summer service between Kapellskär and Mariehamn.

AMORELLA Built for *SF Line* for the Stockholm - Mariehamn - Turku service.

CINDERELLA Built for *SF Line*. Until 1993 provided additional capacity between Stockholm and Helsinki and undertook weekend cruises from Helsinki. In 1993 she replaced the OLYMPIA (a sister vessel of the MARIELLA) as the main Stockholm - Helsinki vessel after the OLYMPIA had been chartered to *P&O European Ferries* and renamed the PRIDE OF BILBAO. In 1995 switched to operating 20 hour cruises from Helsinki to Estonia in the off peak and the Stockholm - Mariehamn - Turku service during the peak summer period (end of May to end of August). During 1997 she remained cruising throughout the year.

GABRIELLA Built as the FRANS SUELL for *Sea-Link AB* of Sweden to operate for subsidiary company *Euroway AB*, who established a service between Lübeck, Travemünde and Malmö. In 1994 this service ceased and she was chartered to *Silja Line*, renamed the SILJA SCANDINAVIA and transferred to the Stockholm - Turku service. In 1997 she was sold to *Viking Line* to operate between Stockholm and Helsinki. She was renamed the GABRIELLA.

ISABELLA Built for *SF Line*. Used on the Stockholm - Naantali service until 1992 until she was switched to operating 24 hour cruises from Helsinki and in 1995 she was transferred to the Stockholm - Helsinki route. During 1996 she additionally operated short cruises to Muuga in Estonia during the 'layover' period in Helsinki. In 1997 she was transferred to the Stockholm - Turku route.

MARIELLA Built for *SF Line*. Used on the Stockholm - Helsinki service. During 1996 additionally operated short cruises to Muuga in Estonia during the 'layover' period in Helsinki but this has now ceased.

ROSELLA Built for *SF Line*. Used mainly on the Stockholm - Turku and Kapellskär - Naantali services until 1997. She now operates 21-24 hour cruises from Stockholm to Mariehamn under the marketing name 'The Dancing Queen', except in the peak summer period when she operates between Kapellskär and Turku.

WAGENBORG PASSAGIERDIENSTEN

THE COMPANY *Wagenborg Passagierdiensten BV* is a Dutch public sector company.

MANAGEMENT Managing Director: G van Langen.

ADDRESS Postbus 70, 9163 ZM Nes, AMELAND, Netherlands.

TELEPHONE Administration & Reservations: +31 (0)519 546111, **Fax:** +31 (0)519 542905.

ROUTES OPERATED Holwerd (Netherlands) - Ameland (Frisian Islands) (45 minutes; *(2,3)*; up to 10 per day), Lauwersoog (Netherlands) - Schiermonnikoog (Frisian Islands) (45 minutes; *(4)*; up to 6 per day).

CONVENTIONAL FERRIES

1	BRAKZAND	450t	67	10.5k	1000P	20C	-	A	Hoogezand, NL	NL
2	OERD	1121t	85	12.2k	1000P	46C	9L	BA	Hoogezand, NL	NL
3	SIER	2286t	95	11.2k	1440P	72C	22L	BA	Wartena, NL	NL
4	ROTTUM	1121t	85	12.2k	1140P	46C	9L	BA	Hoogezand, NL	NL

BRAKZAND, OERD, SIER Built for *Wagenborg Passagiersdiensten BV*. The BRAKZAND is now a spare vessel.

ROTTUM Built for *Wagenborg Passagiersdiensten BV* as the SIER and used on the Holwerd - Ameland route. In 1995 renamed the ROTTUM and transferred to the Lauwersoog - Schiermonnikoog route.

WASA LINE

THE COMPANY *Wasa Line* is a joint Finnish/Swedish company, at present owned by *Silja Line*. It will take over the Vaasa (Finland) - Umeå (Sweden) service from *Silja Line* on 1st July 1999. This is to enable subsidies to be paid for this route which will become uneconomic following the ending of duty-free sales on vessel plying between EU countries. The original operator, *Vaasanlaivat* (also trading as *Wasa Line*) was taken over by *Silja Line* in 1990 and operations integrated into *Silja Line* in 1993.

MANAGEMENT Managing Director & Marketing Manager: Taito Rintala.

ADDRESS *Finland:* POB 213, FIN-6501 VAASA, Finland, ***Sweden:*** Umeå Hamn, S-913 32 HOLMSUND, Sweden.

TELEPHONE Administration: *Finland:* +358 (0)6 323 3100, ***Sweden:*** +46 (0)90 24780, **Reservations: *Finland:*** +358 (0)6 323 3630, ***Sweden:*** +46 (0)90 714 400 **Fax: *Finland*:** +358 (0)6 323 3249, ***Sweden:*** +46 (0)90 714 408.

ROUTE OPERATED Vaasa (Finland) - Umeå (Sweden) (4 hrs; *(1)*; 1/2 per day).

CONVENTIONAL FERRY

1	FENNIA	10515t	66	18k	1200P	265C	36T	BA	Landskrona, SW	FI

FENNIA Built for *Rederi AB Silja* of Finland to operate services between Sweden and Finland. In 1970 she was transferred to *Stockholms Rederi AB Svea*, when *Silja Line* became a marketing organisation. In 1983 she was withdrawn and operated for a short period with *B&I Line* of Ireland between Rosslare and Pembroke Dock. In 1984 she was sold to *Jakob Line*. In 1985 she was sold to *Vaasanlaivat*. In 1992 she was returned to *Jakob Line*. During winter 1992/3 she operated for *Baltic Link* between Norrköping (Sweden) and Riga (Latvia), but returned to *Silja Line* in summer 1993 and was used on the Vaasa - Umeå and Pietarsaari - Skellefteå services. The latter service will not operate in 1999 and, on 1st July, she will be transferred to the new *Wasa Line*.

SECTION 7 - OTHER VESSELS

The following vessels are, at the time of going to print, not operating and are owned by companies which do not currently operate services. They are therefore available for possible re-deployment, either in the area covered by this book or elsewhere. Withdrawn vessels not yet disposed of owned by operating companies are shown under the appropriate company and marked '•'.

DIFKO Færge A/S

1	DIFKO FYN	4104t	87	12.7k	253P	170C	48T	BA	Sunderland, GB	DK
2	DIFKO KORSØR	4104t	87	12.7k	253P	170C	48T	BA	Sunderland, GB	DK
3	DIFKO NYBORG	4104t	87	12.7k	253P	170C	48T	BA	Sunderland, GB	DK

DIFKO FYN Built as the SUPERFLEX ECHO for *Vognmandsruten*. She was unused until 1995, when she was renamed the DIFKO FYN and placed on the Nyborg - Korsør service. In 1998, following the opening of the Great Belt fixed link, the service ceased and she was laid up at Helsingborg in the care of *HH-Ferries*. She is available for them to charter at short notice should one of their own vessels be unavailable.

DIFKO KORSØR, DIFKO NYBORG Built as the SUPERFLEX CHARLIE and SUPERFLEX ALPHA respectively for *Vognmandsruten* to establish a new service between Korsør (Fyn) and Nyborg (Sjælland). In 1990 this company was taken over by *DIFKO* and the vessels renamed the DIFKO KORSØR and DIFKO NYBORG. In 1998, following the opening of the Great Belt road fixed link, the service ceased and they were laid up.

Gøkstad AS

1	VESTFOLD	8383t	91	15k	700P	250C	30T	BA	Hommelvik, NO	NO

VESTFOLD Built for *Gøkstad AS* trading as *Bastøfergen* between Moss and Horten (Norway). At the end of 1995, the service was taken over by *Bastø Fosen* and she was withdrawn from service.

Mercandia

1	HEIMDAL	9975t	83	15k	540P	275C	74T	BAQ	Frederikshavn, DK	DK

HEIMDAL Built as the MERCANDIAN ADMIRAL II, a ro-ro freight ferry, for *Mercandia* of Denmark. Used on various freight services. In 1988 she was chartered to *Comanav* of Algeria for service between Algeria and France and renamed the FERRYMAR I. In 1990 chartered by *DSB*, converted into a passenger/vehicle ferry, renamed the HEIMDAL and introduced onto the Knudshoved - Halsskov service. The charter ceased in 1998 when the Great Belt Bridge opened.

Northern Maritime (Stena Group)

1	STENA ROYAL	28833t	91	21k	1350P	710C	145T	BAS	Temse, BE	BD

STENA ROYAL Built as the PRINS FILIP for *Regie voor Maritiem Transport (RMT)* of Belgium the Oostende - Dover service. Although completed in 1991, she did not enter service until May 1992. In 1994 the British port became Ramsgate. Withdrawn in 1997 and laid up for sale. In 1998 she was sold to *Northern Maritime*, part of the *Stena Group* and renamed the STENA ROYAL. In November 1998 she was chartered to *P&O Stena Line* to operate on the Dover - Zeebrugge route. The charter was due to end in March 1998, but has been extended.

Sally Line (UK)

1	EUROTRAVELLER	14458t	76	17.5k	1040P	-	58L	BA2	Bremerhaven, GY	BA

EUROTRAVELLER Built as the GEDSER for *Gedser-Travemünde Ruten* of Denmark for their service between Gedser (Denmark) and Travemünde (Germany). In 1986 she was purchased by *Thorsviks Rederi A/S* of Norway and chartered to *Sally Ferries*, re-registered in the Bahamas, renamed the VIKING 2 and entered service on the Ramsgate - Dunkerque service. In early 1989 she was renamed the SALLY SKY and during winter 1989/90 she was 'stretched' to increase vehicle capacity. At the end of 1996 she was withdrawn from the Dunkerque service. In 1997 she was renamed the EUROTRAVELLER, transferred to *Holyman-Sally Ferries* and, in March, was introduced onto the Ramsgate - Oostende route. In 1998, when *Holyman-Sally Ferries* came to an end, she operated in a freight-only role for *Sally Line* under the *Sally Freight* name. Passenger capacity services were resumed in May, under the name of *Sally Direct*. All *Sally Line* operations ended in November 1998 and she was withdrawn for sale and laid up.

Stena Rederi (Stena Group)

| 1 | STENA INVICTA | 19763t | 85 | 17.5k | 1750P | 320C | 42T | BA2 | Nakskov, DK | GB |

STENA INVICTA Built as the PEDER PAARS for *DSB (Danish State Railways)* for their service between Kalundborg (Sjælland) and Århus (Jylland). In 1990 purchased by *Stena Rederi* of Sweden for delivery in 1991. In 1991 renamed the STENA INVICTA and entered service on the *Sealink Stena Line* Dover - Calais service. She was withdrawn from the route in February 1998, before the formation of *P&O Stena Line*. In summer 1998, she was chartered to *Silja Line* to operate between Vaasa and Umeå under the marketing name 'WASA JUBILEE'. In autumn 1998 she was laid up at Zeebrugge.

LATE NEWS

P&O European Ferries (Irish Sea) The CELTIC STAR (11086t, 1991, 20.8k, 0P, 75T, A, Kawajiri, JA, CY) (ex LOON-PLAGE 1999, ex IOLAOS 1998, ex KOSEI MARU 1998) has been placed on the Liverpool - Dublin service.

P&O Stena Line - P&OSL Canterbury (John Hendy)

INDEX

ABEL MAGWITCH	148	CLEMENTINE	111	EUROPEAN LEADER	131
ADMIRAL OF SCANDINAVIA	64	COLL	89	EUROPEAN NAVIGATOR	131
ALANDIA	157	COLOR FESTIVAL	152	EUROPEAN PATHFINDER	131
ÅLANDSFÄRJAN	186	COMETA	129	EUROPEAN PATHWAY	137
ALLASDALE LASS	96	COMMODORE CLIPPER	114	EUROPEAN PIONEER	131
ALTELAND	142	COMMODORE GOODWILL	114	EUROPEAN SEAFARER	131
AMANDINE	111	CONDOR 9	62	EUROPEAN SEAWAY	137
AMAZON	110	CONDOR 10	62	EUROPEAN TIDEWAY	133
AMORELLA	186	CONDOR EXPRESS	62	EUROPEAN TRADER	131
ANJA 11	156	CONDOR VITESSE	62	EUROTRAVELLER	188
APOLLO	165	CONTENDER	130	EUROVOYAGER	141
ÁRAINN MHÓR	89	COTES DES ISLES	146	EVA ODEN	119
ARAN EXPRESS	148	COURIER	146	EYNHALLOW	99
ARAN FLYER	148	COUTANCES	143	F.B.D. DUNBRODY	90
ARAN SEABIRD	148	CROMARTY ROSE	104	FANTAASIA	182
ARVEPRINS KNUD	173	CROWN OF SCANDINAVIA	155	FELIX	177
ASK	173	CYMBELINE	111	FENCER	146
ATLANTIC II	80	DANA ANGLIA	64	FENJA	173
AURORA AF HELSINGBORG	176	DANA CIMBRIA	118	FENNIA	187
BALMORAL	148	DANA FUTURA	118	FILLA	105
BALTIC EAGLE	124	DANA HAFNIA	119	FINNBIRCH	124
BALTIC EIDER	124	DANA MAXIMA	118	FINNCLIPPER	162
BALTIC JET	169	DANA MINERVA	118	FINNEAGLE	162
BALTIC KRISTINA	159	DANMARK	173	FINNFOREST	124
BALTIC STAR	149	DART 1	116	FINNHANSA	162
BARFLEUR	58	DART 2	116	FINNJET	178
BASTØ I	149	DART 4	116	FINNPARTNER	162
BASTØ II	149	DART 5	116	FINNRIVER	124
BELNAHUA	89	DART 6	116	FINNROSE	124
BEN-MY-CHREE	79	DART 7	116	FINNTRADER	162
BERGEN	163	DART 8	117	FIVLA	105
BERLIN EXPRESS	176	DART 9	117	FREEDOM 90	146
BIGGA	105	DART 10	117	FRIESLAND	155
BIRKA PRINCESS	150	DAWN MERCHANT	68	FRIGG SYDFYEN	173
BOHUS	152	DEGERÖ	142	FRISIA I	168
BOLERO	130	DELPHIN	185	FRISIA II	168
BOOMERANG	170	DEUTSCHLAND	173	FRISIA III	168
BRAKZAND	187	DIAMANT	80	FRISIA V	168
BRAMBLE BUSH BAY	144	DIFKO FYN	188	FRISIA VI	168
BRAVE MERCHANT	68	DIFKO KORSØR	188	FRISIA VIII	168
BRETAGNE	58	DIFKO NYBORG	188	FRISIA IX	168
BRITTA ODEN	119	DONEMARK	146	FRISIA X	168
BRUERNISH	92	DOUBLE O SEVEN	146	FYLGA	105
CAEDMON	108	DRONNING INGRID	173	GABRIELE WEHR	133
CAILIN AN AISEAG	97	DRONNING MARGRETHE II	173	GABRIELLA	186
CALEDONIAN ISLES	92	DUC DE NORMANDIE	58	GEIRA	105
CANNA	92	EARL SIGURD	99	GELTING SYD	161
CAP AFRIQUE	117	EARL THORFINN	99	GEORG OTS	182
CARRIGALOE	96	EBENEZER SCROOGE	148	GITTE 3	156
CATHERINE	114	EDGCOMBE BELLE	146	GLENACHULISH	97
CELANDINE	114	EDMUND D	102	GLENBROOK	96
CELESTINE	111	EGLANTINE	111	GOD MET ONS III	107
CELTIC STAR	131	EIGG	92	GOLDEN MARIANA	99
CENRED	108	EILEAN BHEARNARAIGH	96	GOOD SHEPHERD IV	105
CENWULF	108	EILEAN DHIURA	89	GOSPORT QUEEN	146
CHRISTIAN IV	152	EILEAN NA H-OIGE	96	GÖTALAND	176
CINDERELLA	186	ELK	133	GOTLAND	154
CLANSMAN	92	ERNEST BEVIN	109	GRAEMSAY	99
CLAYMORE	78	ESTRADEN	110	GREAT EXPECTATIONS	148
		EUROPEAN ENDEAVOUR	131	GREIFSWALD	160
		EUROPEAN ENVOY	131	GRIMA	105
		EUROPEAN FREEWAY	133	GRY MARITHA	98
		EUROPEAN HIGHLANDER	131	HAMLET	173
		EUROPEAN HIGHWAY	137	HAPPY HOOKER	146

HARALD JARL	164	LOCHMOR	93	NORDLYS	164		
HAVELET	62	LODBROG	173	NORDNORGE	164		
HEBRIDEAN ISLES	92	LOFOTEN	164	NORDVÆR	129		
HEIMDAL	188	LORD OF THE ISLES	93	NORKING	133		
HENDRA	105	LOVERVAL	111	NORLAND	73		
HERALDEN	142	LOVISA GORTHON	142	NORMANDIE	58		
HIGHER FERRY	145	LYNHER	145	NORMANDY	67		
HINRICH KOPF	158	LYONESSE LADY	98	NORQUEEN	133		
HOLGER DANSKE	173	LYRA	111	NORRÖNA	85		
HOTSPUR IV	148	MADS MOLS	166	NORSE MERSEY	133		
HOVERSPEED GREAT BRITAIN	80	MAERSK ANGLIA	113	NORSEA	73		
HOY HEAD	99	MAERSK EXPORTER	130	NORSKY	136		
HSC NO 1	168	MAERSK FLANDERS	130	NORSTAR	73		
IDUN VIKING	146	MAERSK IMPORTER	130	NORSTREAM	136		
ISABELLA	186	MAI MOLS	166	NORSUN	73		
ISLAND COMMODORE	114	MAID OF GLENCOUL	97	ODIN SYDFYEN	173		
ISLAND DISCOVERY	148	MALLARD	144	OERD	187		
ISLE OF ARRAN	92	MAREN MOLS	166	OILEAN ARANN	146		
ISLE OF CUMBRAE	92	MARIELLA	186	OLDENBURG	148		
ISLE OF INISHMORE	67	MARTHA RUSS	142	OOST-VLIELAND	155		
ISLE OF INNISFREE	67	MARTIN CHUZZELWIT	148	OSTFRIESLAND	159		
ISLE OF LEWIS	92	MAX MOLS	166	OUR LADY PAMELA	108		
ISLE OF MULL	92	MECKLENBURG-VORPOMMERN	173	OUR LADY PATRICIA	108		
JAMES NEWMAN	109	MELOODIA	182	OVERCHURCH	148		
JENS KOFOED	150	MELUSINE	114	P&OSL BURGUNDY	76		
JETLINER	73	MENJA	173	P&OSL CALAIS	76		
JOCHEN STEFFEN	158	MERCANDIA IV	163	P&OSL CANTERBURY	76		
JOHN BURNS	109	MERCANDIA VIII	163	P&OSL DOVER	76		
JONATHAN SWIFT	68	MERCHANT BRAVERY	110	P&OSL KENT	76		
JUNIPER	141	MERCHANT BRILLIANT	110	P&OSL PICARDY	76		
JUNO	92	MERCHANT VENTURE	128	P&OSL PROVENCE	76		
JUPITER	66	MERLE	110	PALANGA	166		
JUPITER	92	MERSEY VIKING	71	PEDER OLSEN	150		
KAHLEBERG	160	METTE MOLS	166	PENTALINA B	102		
KARL CARSTENS	173	MIDNATSOL	164	PETER PAN	184		
KAUNAS	166	MIDSLAND	155	PETER WESSEL	152		
KENILWORTH	146	MIE MOLS	166	PETERSBURG	160		
KING HARRY FERRY	144	MINI STAR	142	PEVERIL	127		
KING OF SCANDINAVIA	64	MISNEACH	90	PHILIP PIRRIP	148		
KINGSWEAR BELLE	146	MOLENGAT	183	PICASSO	123		
KOADA	105	MOONDANCE	138	PIONEER	93		
KOEGELWIECK	156	MORVERN	89	PLYM	145		
KONG HARALD	164	MOUNTWOOD	148	POLARLYS	164		
KONINGIN BEATRIX	170	MÜNSTERLAND	159	POLONIA	185		
KONINGIN BEATRIX	86	NARVIK	164	POMERANIA	169		
KRAKA	173	NEPTUNIA	159	PORTAFERRY FERRY	106		
KRONPRINS FREDERIK	173	NEW ADVANCE	105	PORTSMOUTH QUEEN	146		
KRONPRINS HARALD	152	NIEBOROW	169	POVL ANKER	150		
LADY OF MANN	79	NILS DACKE	184	PRIDE OF BILBAO	75		
LAGAN VIKING	71	NILS HOLGERSSON	184	PRIDE OF CHERBOURG	75		
LEIRNA	105	NO 3	145	PRIDE OF FLANDERS	133		
LINK STAR	142	NO 4	145	PRIDE OF HAMPSHIRE	75		
LITTLE ISLAND FERRY	146	NO 5	144	PRIDE OF LE HAVRE	75		
LIV VIKING	146	NORBANK	133	PRIDE OF PORTSMOUTH	75		
LOCH ALAINN	92	NORBAY	133	PRIDE OF RATHLIN	71		
LOCH BHRUSDA	92	NORCAPE	133	PRIDE OF SUFFOLK	133		
LOCH BUIE	92	NORCOVE	133	PRIDE OF THE TYNE	148		
LOCH DUNVEGAN	92	NORDHAV	129	PRIMROSE	141		
LOCH FYNE	92	NORDIC JET	169	PRINCE OF SCANDINAVIA	64		
LOCH LINNHE	92	NORDJARL	129	PRINCESS OF SCANDINAVIA	64		
LOCH RANZA	92	NORDKAPP	164	PRINS HENRIK	173		
LOCH RIDDON	92	NORDKYN	129	PRINS JOACHIM	173		
LOCH STRIVEN	93	NORDLANDIA	156	PRINS JOHAN FRISO	170		
LOCH TARBERT	93	NORDLICHT	159	PRINS RICHARD	173		

Name	Page	Name	Page	Name	Page
PRINS WILLEM-ALEXANDER	170	SHEARWATER 6	104	TAMAR	145
PRINSES CHRISTINA	170	SHIELDSMAN	148	THE PRINCESS ANNE	80
PRINSES JULIANA	170	SIER	187	THE PRINCESS MARGARET	80
PRINSESSE BENEDIKTE	173	SILESIA	169	THE SECOND SNARK	146
PRINSESSE RAGNHILD	152	SILJA EUROPA	178	THE TOM AVIS	145
PURBECK	123	SILJA FESTIVAL	178	THE TOM CASEY	145
QUEEN OF SCANDINAVIA	155	SILJA SERENADE	178	THJELVAR	154
QUIBERON	58	SILJA SYMPHONY	178	THOMAS WEHR	133
RAASAY	93	SILVIA ANA L	153	THOR SYDFYEN	173
RAGNA GORTHON	142	SKAGEN	152	THORA	105
RAPIDE	80	SKÅNE	176	THORSVOE	99
RED EAGLE	104	SOLENT ENTERPRISE	146	TIDERO STAR	133
RED FALCON	104	SOLIDOR 3	65	TOR ANGLIA	119
RED JET 1	104	SOLIDOR 4	65	TOR BELGIA	119
RED JET 2	104	SOUND OF SANDA	107	TOR BRITANNIA	119
RED JET 3	104	SOUND OF SCALPAY	107	TOR CALEDONIA	119
RED OSPREY	104	SOUND OF SCARBA	107	TOR DANIA	119
REEDHAM FERRY	145	SOUND OF SHUNA	107	TOR FLANDRIA	119
REGINA BALTICA	159	SOUND OF SLEAT	107	TOR GOTHIA	119
REGJA VIKING	146	SPHEROID	110	TOR HOLLANDIA	119
RENFREW ROSE	148	SPODSBJERG	173	TOR HUMBRIA	120
RHUM	89	SPROGØ	173	TOR NORVEGIA	120
RICHARD WITH	164	ST CATHERINE	108	TOR SCANDIA	120
RIVER LUNE	128	ST CECILIA	108	TOR SELANDIA	120
RIVERDANCE	138	ST CLAIR	100	TOR SUECIA	120
ROBIN HOOD	184	ST FAITH	108	TRANEKÆR	173
RODONA	113	ST HELEN	108	TRANQUILITY	146
ROGALIN	169	ST OLA	100	TRANS BOTNIA	142
ROMSØ	173	ST ROGNVALD	137	TRANSBALTICA	124
ROSE OF ARAN	146	ST SUNNIVA	100	TRANSEUROPA	162
ROSEBAY	139	STAR WIND	177	TRANSGARD	142
ROSEHAUGH	97	STENA CALEDONIA	86	TRANSLUBECA	120
ROSELLA	186	STENA CARISMA	182	TRELLEBORG	176
ROSLAGEN	157	STENA CHALLENGER	86	TRIDENT 5	65
ROTTUM	187	STENA DANICA	179	TT-TRAVELLER	184
ROVER	146	STENA DISCOVERY	86	TUNGENES	129
RÜGEN	173	STENA EUROPE	179	TYCHO BRAHE	173
RUSS	162	STENA EXPLORER	87	ULVA	95
SAGA MOON	128	STENA GALLOWAY	86	UNDINE	113
SAGA STAR	184	STENA GERMANICA	179	UNITED CARRIER	142
SANDEFJORD	152	STENA GOTHICA	119	UNITED EXPRESS	142
SAPPHIRE	113	STENA INVICTA	189	UNITED TRADER	142
SASSNITZ	173	STENA JUTLANDICA	179	URD	173
SATURN	93	STENA LYNX III	87	VAL DE LOIRE	58
SCANIA	176	STENA NAUTICA	180	VALENTINE	114
SCHLESWIG-HOLSTEIN	173	STENA PRINCE	180	VANA TALLINN	182
SCHULPENGAT	184	STENA ROYAL	188	VARAGEN	99
SCILLONIAN III	98	STENA SAGA	180	VARANGERFJORD	146
SEA SPRINTER	148	STENA SCANDINAVICA	180	VESTERÅLEN	164
SEA WIND	177	STENA SEARIDER	139	VESTFOLD	188
SEACAT DANMARK	80	STENA SEATRADER	139	VIKINGLAND	171
SEACAT ISLE OF MAN	80	STENA SHIPPER	113	VILNIUS	166
SEACAT SCOTLAND	80	STENA VOYAGER	87	VISBY	154
SEAFRANCE CEZANNE	84	STIG GORTHON	142	WAPPEN VON BORKUM	159
SEAFRANCE MANET	84	STRANGFORD FERRY	106	WASA QUEEN	178
SEAFRANCE MONET	84	SUPERFERRY	88	WAVERLEY	148
SEAFRANCE NORD PAS-DE-CALAIS	137	SUPERSEACAT ONE	177	WESTERLAND	171
		SUPERSEACAT TWO	80	WESTFALEN	159
SEAFRANCE RENOIR	84	SUPERSEACAT THREE	80	WILHELM KAISEN	158
SERENADEN	142	SUPERSEACAT FOUR	80	WILKINS MICAWBER	148
SHANNON DOLPHIN	105	SUPERSTAR EXPRESS	76	WOODCHURCH	148
SHANNON WILLOW	105	SYMPHORINE	113	YOKER SWAN	148
SHAPINSAY	99	TALLINK AUTOEXPRESS	183		
SHEARWATER 5	104	TALLINK EXPRESS I	183		